Café *con* Leche

Brent Garzelli & Cheryl L. Garzelli

Café con Leche
Copyright © 2023 by Brent Garzelli & Cheryl L. Garzelli

All rights reserved. No part of this publication may be reproduced, distributed, or transmitted in any form or by any means, including photocopying, recording, or other electronic or mechanical methods, without the prior written permission of the author, except in the case of brief quotations embodied in critical reviews and certain other non-commercial uses permitted by copyright law.

ISBN
978-1-962611-09-1 (Paperback)
978-1-962611-10-7 (eBook)

DEDICATION

This story, like all my stories, is meant to bring glory to our Lord, Jesus Christ. His Gospel is repeated within, as He commanded all Christians in the Great Commission. The story, itself, is purely fiction loosely based on events in my own life and the lives of those I have known.

I also want to thank my fellow Air Force Chaplains at Maxwell AFB, Alabama and Howard AB, Panama. Chaplains Houseman, Jones, Stewart, Beamon and others each helped me grow as a chaplain and minister.

Finally, I could not have written a single word without the support of my wife of 47 years, Cheryl. I wanted to mention our daughter, Erin, who makes me swell with pride when I think of how she is allowing the Lord to lead her and guide her to do His will. I also want to pay homage to our dog, Chewi, who sat at my feet as I typed every word.

NOTATION

I have used several quotes from Scripture in the body of this book. Unless specifically notated, all Scripture is quoted from the King James Version of the Holy Bible.

IN MEMORY

It was my great pleasure to have known Mrs. Ronnie Bauer who along with her infant son gave their lives in service to our Lord. Along with her husband and another child, they built a house on a river barge and ministered to indigenous peoples along the Amazon River basin. Ronnie's tragic death inspired me to write about the death of one of the characters of this book.

AUTHOR'S NOTE

There are several specific instances of racial prejudice listed in the manuscript. These are not merely works of fiction or my imagination, but most are recollections from my own life. As a former pastor, I have witnessed the evil that can transpire in "Prayer Meetings." I witnessed buses loaded with young Black children being sent to live with North Dakota families for the summer and hundreds of North Dakota residents coming to Valley City, North Dakota to see a Black person. I lived in Syracuse, New York during the Race Riots and watched the destruction of a local Sears store a block from our home. I lived in the heart of the Civil Rights Movement, Montgomery, Alabama for nine years. As a Children's Social Worker for eight years, I witnessed several cases of sexual abuse in all races.

Since I typed the first word of my manuscript, I intended to make two major points-Racial Discrimination is not Geographic. It occurs everywhere and is no more prevalent in the South than the North. Secondly, only God offers Hope. No matter how bad things are or look to become, only God offers us hope for a brighter future with Him.

As you read about the lives of Tyisha and Jeremiah, be blessed by every word.

TABLE OF CONTENTS

Dedication iii
Notation iv
In Memory iv
Author's Note v

Chapter 1 1
Chapter 2 6
Chapter 3 24
Chapter 4 31
Chapter 5 35
Chapter 6 53
Chapter 7 62
Chapter 8 72
Chapter 9 87
Chapter 10 92
Chapter 11 107
Chapter 12 120
Chapter 13 136
Chapter 14 145
Chapter 15 152
Chapter 16 163
Chapter 17 175
Chapter 18 183
Chapter 19 193
Chapter 20 202
Chapter 21 212
Chapter 22 227

Epilogue 235

CHAPTER 1

The view was always the same, yet different every time. Sitting on her favorite rock, of which there were few in southern Alabama, she looked from the back of her grandparents' plantation across the wide Chattahoochee River toward the peanut fields of southern Georgia.

From Ty's perch in southeast Alabama, she could see the panhandle of Florida to the south, less than a mile away. The local folks called the region the "wiregrass area" indicating the predominant flora in southeast Alabama, northwest Florida and southwest Georgia. There was no town nearer than Susie, Alabama several miles away and that was fine with Ty. For the past ten years, she had been forced to attend a segregated public school a long bus ride to the north and go to church with her grandparents in Susie, where she was tolerated but not accepted. The blacks in her school called her "peanut butter" and the whites in her church called her "black" and worse. She had been shunned in both places and could not wait to leave the place she had called "home" for much of the previous decade. Through her life, Ty had come to cherish her solitude, especially the hours she spent apart from her grandparents.

Ty McFarren, whose real name was Tyisha Watt, had never known her father and her mother died with a brain tumor when she was eight years old. Ty's mother, Linda Watt, had wanted to raise her child with no ties to her own family. At birth, Linda had changed Ty's surname to "McFarren" and documented the same on Ty's birth certificate.

Ty was left to be raised by grandparents who would have loved to place her in foster care. Crook and Harrietta Watt had been in a "Catch 22" when their daughter died. Linda, their daughter, was the little "prim and proper" Baptist girl that spent ninety percent of her time in her dorm room in college. She finally gave into social pressure and went to a party off campus in her junior year at Southeast University of Alabama where she consumed excessive amounts of alcohol, with one mixed drink containing copious amounts of Vodka. Ty was the biproduct. Every time she looked in a mirror, Ty was reminded that her father was black, though she had no idea who he was, and her mother was white.

When Linda Watt told her parents that she was pregnant and that the father was a black man, whom she had never met before and had been unable to find later, her parents told her there was only one solution for her dilemma-have an abortion. Linda had been raised in a Baptist church to believe that abortion was the taking of an innocent life, so she refused. Crook and Harrietta had a reputation to preserve. The Watt family's forefathers had owned the land on which they lived since 1821 and attended the church in Susie since it was founded in 1848. There were only whites in their church and the Watts only associated with fellow whites in the area. There was no room in their life plan for a bi-racial child. Since their daughter, Linda, would not listen to reason, they asked her to leave their home.

To avoid unwanted scrutiny and criticism from the loving Christians in her home church and from her parents, Linda left in the middle of the night with her new baby and traveled to Atlanta, Georgia. Not willing to trouble her parents, she had not even left them a forwarding address or phone number. There, by herself, she raised Ty. She never finished her degree, so Linda worked for several years as a waitress in a local restaurant while Ty stayed with Linda's girlfriend and roommate during the afternoon and evening.

Almost a decade after leaving her family's home, Linda's headaches intensified. She was sure she was suffering from migraines, and the pain always seemed confined to the right side of her brain. Nausea almost always followed, and no number of aspirin seemed to reduce the pain. Though she could not afford it, she went to a medical clinic for the poor in downtown Atlanta and was immediately referred to a local hospital for an x-ray. Linda's headaches were quickly diagnosed to be the result of an inoperable brain tumor and she had less than three months to live.

Before her mind became incapable of functioning, she contacted her parents for the first time in years. Linda told them of her predicament, knowing they could care less. Crook and Harrietta had not tried to find her or to contact her. They had even changed their wills to bestow all their family wealth to their son, Linda's younger brother, Tres. His actual name was Crook Watt III. They were quite content to leave things as they were. Crook and Harrietta's friends and fellow churchmen did not know the Watts had a bi-racial grandchild, and the Watts were more than happy to continue the charade.

Linda's imminent death presented a quandary for her parents. They had "buried" her years earlier when Linda had refused to abort Ty. Now, she was coming back to southern Alabama with a bi-racial daughter. They were predisposed to make Ty a ward of the court, but to do so would have brought the wrath of the local people in church and Susie society. Besides, they might get some sympathy from the same people if they took the little mongrel into their home. But they did not have to like her. In public or at church, they would present themselves as the "suffering" grandparents, but they could ostracize Ty at home.

Linda did not survive three months but passed away in the middle of a cloudy afternoon in January after only a month at her parent's home. She was buried in a far corner of the family cemetery with a discrete headstone and only Ty cried at the graveside service. Crook and Harrietta did not shed a tear. Their daughter had been a total disappointment to them and had dumped Ty on them, an embarrassment that just could not be outlived. Now, Crook and Harrietta just wanted to endure eight more years of Ty in their home. Then, she would go to college or the military with their blessing; anywhere as long as she went.

Ty stood up from her perch, overwhelmed by her memories of a loveless life. That is what her life had been. The only one that ever loved her had been a mother that died far too soon.

This was Ty's last trip to her favorite rock. On their way back from church one Sunday night, a drunk driver had hit Crook and Harrietta in a head-on collision. They were both killed instantly as the drunk driver walked away from the wreck.

A week later, Tres and his family moved into the large house where he had grown up in the middle of his parents' 3200-acre plantation. Ty was a student at the Tuskegee Institute seeking to obtain the bachelor's degree her mother never achieved. She had no desire to occupy the house she had tried so hard to leave.

Ty had come back to her hometown for the reading of the "Last Will and Testament" of her grandparents. She was sure it was a waste of time, but she was going to come just in case of a surprise. As the family's attorney read the document, Ty was overjoyed to hear that she was to receive everything her grandparents had possessed of Linda Watt's. Her grandparents certainly had no use of her mother's memorabilia while Linda lived or after she died, and her uncle could have cared less with his total disdain for his sister. Ty's mother had graduated as the valedictorian of her high school class and had left Ty her grade cards back to first grade. There were photos of Linda in her childhood with her parents, friends and even her despicable younger brother. The box from her grandparents' home contained school albums and trophies from her mother's glory days as a winner of numerous swimming contests. The albums had numerous entries on each cover from Linda's classmates, most of whom were total strangers to Ty. Ty's own albums were devoid of entries. After eight years as a student at the Suzie School for Negroes, one of Ty's classmates wrote: "You are a one-of-a-kind! There are forty-two of us graduating and you are the only one with green eyes."

After the hearing, Ty asked her uncle, who barely acknowledged her presence, if she could return to her rock to say "farewell." He said she could return to "his" plantation for three hours, but he never wanted to see her there again. If she returned for any reason, he would ask the sheriff to escort her from "his" property.

Ty walked back to her car, a 1963 Oldsmobile, and drove away from the plantation for the last time and never looked back in her mirrors.

Alabama was a strange place in 1968. It had been "ground zero" for the civil rights movement. Rosa Parks and several Black Alabama clergies had organized the Montgomery bus strike. A local pastor, Rev. Martin Luther King, Jr. had pushed for a march from Selma to Montgomery, Alabama to bring attention to the restrictions to voting for blacks in Alabama. One attempt led to "Bloody Sunday" as marchers were gassed by teargas and beaten by clubs wielded by Alabama State Troopers and local police. Over fifty marchers were hospitalized.

Governor George Wallace was perhaps the most controversial governor in the nation, and he served in a state that was constantly on the verge of racial chaos. In his 1963 inaugural address, Governor Wallace put a face to the scourge of the southern culture when he said he was for "segregation now, segregation tomorrow, segregation forever." Apparently, he had never heard the quote, "Better to remain silent and be thought a fool than to speak and remove all doubt." But Governor Wallace was not content to merely sound like a man from before the Civil War, so he demonstrated the depths of his ignorance by standing on the steps of the entrance to the University of Alabama to prevent black students from enrolling.

This was Ty's world. She lived in a state trying desperately to find a way for whites and blacks to relate. Ty represented both races and yet was accepted by neither. Her mother, the only person that had ever loved her, was long since dead and her loveless grandparents had recently passed from this world. Her only known family member, Uncle Tres, had threatened to have her arrested should she ever return to "his" plantation.

Ty was in her last year at Tuskegee Institute and about to start her student teaching at the George Washington Carver Elementary School. It was a segregated local school for black children named after the man who single-handedly changed agriculture in the Deep South.

Since her earliest recollections at her grandparents' home, Ty had never experienced love and received no guidance from them. She knew if she was to have any life and achieve something of value, it had to be somewhere else. She had spent most of her life in Alabama and was tired of being the "half-breed," shunned and despised by the few who acknowledged her existence.

But during her student teaching, she had an epiphany-she loved teaching, she loved the children, and she was good at it. For the first time in her life, she knew what she should do with her life, and she finally had purpose. In a school with hand-me-down desks and books that were so worn out that half were falling out of the binding, Ty taught and loved the interaction between her and her students.

CHAPTER 2

It was a tumultuous time to be a black woman in Alabama and Jorgina Boudoir was a black woman. She loved to wear the brightly colored gélés of her forefathers, the Yoruba people. She was already a tall lady but wore a gelée at least a foot taller than her lithe frame. Her students loved to guess which flamboyant headdress their teacher would wear each day.

Jorgina was a professional teacher who was married to her career. She had no husband and wanted none. She had one vice in life-she loved to travel throughout the south. She had stood at the bottom of Little River falls and looked toward the top and rested on a precipice above DeSoto falls and wondered how the Lord had made such wonders in proximity. She had visited her brother and his family, who lived on an island in Okefenokee Swamp and their water source always baffled her. Her niece would take a five-gallon-bucket and dip it in the swamp in front of their log cabin each morning, trying to avoid the thousands of alligators. The water obtained was for the family's drinking and cooking water for the day. When she asked her brother why he and his family did not suffer from the many illnesses wrought by consuming still warm water, her brother simply pointed to a stand of cypress trees hanging over the brown stagnant water.

"Sis, them trees drop their needles in the water every fall. They is acidic and the acid kills all of the germs and bacteria in the water. You can drink right out of the boat when you is giggin' without any fear."

***

The students changed in name each year, but Jorgina's love for them did not. She taught them the three "R's" (readin,' ritin' and 'rithmatic). At the end of every school day, she stood at her classroom door and hugged and kissed her charges as they went home. Many went to homes with no food. Jorgina asked each student's parents for permission to take each student home with her on an alternating basis, three students at a time. The parents had all agreed since Jorgina had portrayed this act of kindness to give each student a goal for their future after seeing the personal side of their teacher's life. Jorgina cooked barbequed pork, using her father's secret recipe for the sauce or pickled suckers with yams or potato cakes. No matter what she prepared, her hungriest students gobbled it like it had been prepared by a chef at Tavern on the Green.

Since becoming a Christian in college, Jorgina had sensed that she had two missions in life-witness to others of her Lord and find and train her own replacement in the classroom. Now in her 50's, she had led dozens to know the Lord and now she sensed her new student teacher, Tyisha McFarren, had been placed in her charge by God Almighty. Ty clearly had a deep-seated pain and anger in her, but what person of color didn't in the 1960's in Alabama? Jorgina had grown up through the years of hangings of blacks and legal segregation. Segregation was supposedly diminishing, but she still only traveled in the daytime and her students never received the financial support of the local school board that the white children received.

Jorgina always referred to Tyisha by her full name and not "Ty," though Ty was not offended by her shortened nickname. Secretly, Ty enjoyed being referred to as "Tyisha." It was the first time in her life that she had been shown respect and by her superior, no less. Ty had never been shown love, so she was somewhat taken aback by the special way she was treated by Miss Jorgina. This tall woman in her gélé and matching ìró, was free with her hugs and forehead kisses. Ty was unsure of what these actions indicated, but she knew she liked it.

"Miss Tyisha, how you be this fine Lord's Day? She was at least three inches taller than her younger protégé, but there was absolutely no intimidation. Their relationship was more like peers rather than mentor and apprentice.

"Every day is a great day when we can bring a blessin' to those in our classroom." From anyone but Tyisha, Jorgina would assume most people were just trying to impress her. Tyisha loved the children almost as much as she did, and she was certain Tyisha was destined to be a great teacher. Jorgina recognized that her job was not to make Tyisha a good teacher, but the best teacher the Lord had prepared her to be.

Tyisha had learned to play the game. She knew the vocabulary of the Christians like "atonement, salvation, and forgiveness." She had learned well during her years in the Suzie Baptist Church; anything just to survive being with those that hated her due to her skin color. In the presence of blacks, she had learned to adapt to their unique Alabama Ebonics. Blacks had called her "half n' half, not black enough, skunk, etc." One of her first black boyfriends had referred to her as his "mixed mama" and then wondered why the relationship died at that point.

She had not been accepted anymore by the whites. They had called her a "half-breed, Oreo," and a host of other more derogatory slurs. Tyisha had simply smiled her disarming smile and pretended their words did not hurt her; but "words can break your bones" and sometimes worse. Tyisha came to believe she really had no people and she had accepted her loneliness. That is, until she met Miss Jorgina Boudoir. There was something different about her "God-talk." She seemed to believe in a God who loved us even when we did not love one another. Her love was infectious, and she never indicated any less affection for Tyisha because of her bi-racial status. For one of the first times in her life, Tyisha was beginning to respect an elder, and respect was quickly becoming a love for Miss Jorgina.

They stood on the edge of a red dirt playground and watched their children play on the homemade gym equipment. The men of the community had made a set of swings, a wood-framed "monkey bars," and a slide with a bottom made of ridged sheet metal flattened with wooden hammers. The children could have cared less if their playground equipment was made by the community or "store bought." They screamed and played the games they had invented and enjoyed each other's company.

Café con Leche

"Tyisha, you got a powerful lot of hurt in you girl," Miss Jorgina verbalized her opinion quite unsolicited. "I know some of it is the color of your skin. I know where that pain comes from. I got plenty of my own. I watched my daddy die when he was forty-eight years old from slaving as much as our forefathers in that cotton field. I watched my momma die early from grief and I watched two of my older brothers go to prison from the anger in their souls.

Young lady, I had just as much anger and hurt in me as my brothers, but the Lord made Himself known to me and He changed me. I'll remember that night forever.

I had a boyfriend who invited me to go to a "Spring Revival" in a church in our little hometown and "fill a pew." I didn't care anything about church, but I cared about the boy, so I agreed to go. They had a guest speaker that night who was an ex-professional wrestler. He pounded the pulpit so hard that he nearly broke it. At the conclusion of his sermon, he extended an invitation to all of us who were not Christians to come forward and give our lives to our Savior. I turned to the boy that brought me and told him I had to go right then.

A storm was raging outside and when we reached the front porch, he told me he would go ahead, open the car, and pick me up under the front portico. He ran out into the pouring rain to the car, but try as he could, the keys would not open the door. Just then, lightning struck the transformer on the pole above him and sparks rained down over him and the car. I ran out to him nearly hysterical, and he said, "Jorgina, you is under conviction of the Holy Spirit." He picked me up and literally carried me back into the church up to the altar. I was a bit smaller then than I am now. All the lights were out all over that little town and the deacons of the church had lit candles in the auditorium. The preacher and the pastor of the church came down to the sanctuary floor and told me that the Lord was dealing with my soul. They told me that Jesus is the "only way to heaven" and He alone could give me peace and provide salvation through His death on the Cross and resurrection from the dead. Through my tears, I told them that I was so tired of hating and anger and I just wanted some relief.

Tyisha, anger and hate will kill a person. It will sap every bit of strength out of a person and leave you empty inside. I was only fourteen years old, but I was whooped. My brothers and I were moved from one home to another, and I was tired of hating the plantation owners, the people who hired my mama to iron their clothes, and the white folks that made me drink out of a different water fountain.

The pastor told me how the Lord Jesus Christ would forgive my sins, help me to forgive those who had wronged me and give me hope of true freedom. Through my tears, I told the pastor that I wanted this "salvation by grace." At his urging, I knelt with him and prayed for the Lord to save me. I knew the minute I prayed that prayer the Lord Jesus Christ had adopted me into His kingdom, and I have tried to serve Him every day since. I was baptized a week later in the creek down under the bridge with all the church members as onlookers.

Little sister, it is time for you to give up your anger and hate and accept the love of our Lord. He wants to do great things with you, but you have to get rid of all the hate before He can use you. Don't you want the salvation provided freely to us by Jesus Christ?"

Tyisha looked down at the red soil with a tear in her eye and said to one of the few people, other than her mother, whom she had ever loved, "Miss Jorgina, you know I love you, but you're asking me to change my whole life, such as it is. I have to think about everything. I was taken to church every Sunday, most Sunday nights, and most Wednesday nights, by some of the meanest people I have ever known. I would be a Christian today if it were not for Christians."

"Listen, Tyisha, you cannot place your eternal fate in the hands of those people that made you go to church. There is no salvation in church attendance or church membership, though many seem to think so; only the Lord saves. As I told you, Jesus Christ is right here with us on this playground, and He wants to heal you from all the hate and fill you with love. Won't you be saved?"

"Miss Jorgina, you have given me a lot to think on. I promise to consider what you have told me and make a decision. If I choose the salvation the Lord offers, you will be the first person to know."

Tyisha was much more logical than emotional. As the bell rang signifying the end of the recess, Miss Jorgina led the children in, and Tyisha walked behind the class with a tear in her eye. Ty knew what she needed to do.

One afternoon, after the children had left for the day, Tyisha walked up to her mentor and began to cry unable to tell Miss Jorgina why. But

Café con Leche

Miss Jorgina knew. She hugged up her young protégé and said, "You're making the right choice, child."

Miss Jorgina took Tyisha's hands and both ladies closed their eyes as Miss Jorgina prayed.

"Lord, Miss Tyisha seeks the salvation that only You can give. Give her pardon from her own sins and the pain, sorrow, hate, and anger she has felt in her life. Show her joy like she has never dreamed. I pray it all in your holy name, Jesus. Amen."

Miss Jorgina squeezed Tyisha's hands and said, "Honey, now you pray with all of your heart that the Lord will forgive your sins, and give you His salvation, and He will."

"Lord, I have lived my life with anger. I have wished others would die or suffer mightily. I was happy when my grandparents were killed. I know it was wrong and I don't want to go on hating others. Please, Lord, save me from my sins and make me whole. Take me, Father, and use me for your glory! Amen.

Miss Jorgina, I want to tell the whole world about my salvation. Would your pastor baptize me?"

"I am sure he would, but you let me ask him and make all the arrangements. As a new Christian, you will need to grow in Christ and there are many of us in the Church that want to help you. I hope you can go to worship service on Sunday. I'll be in touch with my pastor and get back with you as soon as I make the arrangements for your baptism."

"Miss Jorgina, I cannot thank you enough for all your care and love. I know you will be blessed by our Lord."

"Tyisha, you have been a blessing to me already and now that we are sisters in the faith, I will be blessed each time you lead others to Christ."

***

Jorgina and Tyisha had a student named Monique. She was ten years old and still in their second-grade class. She had been an above average student until the end of her first-grade year when her grades plummeted precipitously, and she was held back two years in a row. She was perpetually depressed, physically advanced over the other students, and declined to stay overnight at Miss Jorgina's home. She stayed to herself and had no close relationships with any of her classmates or her teachers. Each day, she was the last one out of the classroom and walked toward her home in the worst part of Tuskegee. Because of her size, she had often been caught by her teachers threatening other students or stealing their lunch money. Her anger, though repressed, was palpable.

Tyisha was particularly aware of Monique's anger and resultant depression, since these emotions had encapsulated Tyisha's teen years prior to the death of her grandparents. And Tyisha was fairly sure as to the cause of Monique's anger.

One morning, after Monique had one of her famous "meltdowns," Tyisha volunteered to take her out in the hall and speak with her hoping to calm Monique. So often had Monique needed to exit the room that there were two desks that remained in the hall. Teacher and student sat in the desks, but Monique winced in pain as she lowered herself gently into the seat.

"Monique, why are you cryin'? Did someone do somethin' to you?"

"No, Miss Tyisha. Can I stand up? It hurts a powerful lot to sit down."

Tyisha instantly empathized with this wounded little girl and instinctively recognized Monique's actions were those of a victim and not a protagonist, as so many believed.

In pain, Monique slowly rose to her feet and turned toward her teacher.

"Miss Tyisha, I can't talk about it no more. He told me he would hurt me worse if I was to tell anyone."

"Was 'he' someone in your family, Monique?"

Tyisha knew that there was no man in Monique's family, but she wanted to give Monique an open-ended question to encourage further discussion.

"No, Miss Tyisha. I ain't got no men in my family. Me and my little brother got a daddy, but he left us when I was just five and my brother couldn't even walk. Our mammy loves us, but she is gone more than she is at home. She keeps the kids of a white family over on Montgomery Highway and I have to cook our supper and watch my little brother. Our mammy's boyfriend comes over and watches my little brother before he goes to school at lunchtime. Sometimes Johnny Raye, that's my mammy's boyfriend, stays around till our mammy comes home at night."

Tyisha knew the rest of the story. She still remembered those days when her grandmother went to her Bible study and her grandfather was always waiting to abuse her. She remembered hiding from the lecherous old man in the barn between some bales of cotton. But many times, her grandfather had found her and raped her and left her in such pain that she had to make up a story for her grandmother, friends, and teachers at school. The sexual abuse, usually only attempted, had continued unabated until she went to college and her grandparents had been killed in an auto crash.

"Monique, you don't have to tell me if Johnny Raye hurt you, just nod your head. If he did hurt you, I will make sure he never knows how we found out. Did Johnny Raye do this to you?"

Slowly at first, Monique nodded her head affirmatively. As she gained confidence, her head moved faster and faster.

"Monique, I don't want you to think for a moment that you are in trouble, but I want you to tell Miss Jorgina exactly what you just told me. Is that okay?"

Monique was hesitant, but eventually said, "but you can't use his name."

Tyisha agreed she would not and asked to change places with Miss Jorgina in the classroom. Quickly, Tyisha briefed Jorgina about the obvious sexual abuse that had been perpetrated on Monique and asked Jorgina to take the next step. Meanwhile, Tyisha returned to the front of the class and gave the students the words for the week's spelling bee.

After Jorgina was convinced that Monique was the victim of sexual abuse, she took Monique to the nurse's office and allowed her to lie down on a small bed. After Monique was comfortable, Jorgina excused herself and went to the principal of the school, a man, and told him exactly what Monique both had said and demonstrated to her. The principal knew a deputy at the Macon County Sheriff's Office, called him and explained the situation. The deputy promised to interview Monique as soon as possible. After a half an hour, the deputy arrived and was taken to the nurse's office where he and a female teacher interviewed Monique. After the interview, Monique was transported to the local hospital for a complete physical examination by a doctor to determine the amount of damage to her body and the presence of any sexually transmitted diseases. Fortunately, the doctor predicted that Monique's sexual organs had not been permanently damaged. He felt the chance of an STD was low, but he could not confirm the presence or absence until the following day. True to his word, the doctor called the deputy a few days later and confirmed that Monique had no STD.

Monique still suffered from one irrefutable fact-she was black. If a white child had been victimized to the same extent, he/she would have been immediately made a ward of the court and the perpetrator would have been jailed with prosecution likely to follow.

However, Monique and her race did not merit the same protections in Alabama. The deputy was a Christian man who lived his faith and decided to do for Monique what the law would not. The deputy went to the home of Johnny Raye and knocked on the door.

When Johnny Raye appeared at the door, the deputy shoved the door open and hit the shocked perpetrator with his night stick. Johnny Raye fell to the floor and before he could come back to his feet, the deputy struck him again across the back of his thighs.

Writhing in pain, Johnny Raye said, "Man, what I ever do to you?"

"You never did anything to me, boy, but you hurt a little girl and I am here to be judge and jury."

With that proclamation, the deputy hit Johnny Raye across the back. The pain was so intense that Johnny rolled over to try to hide his back without considering that he had left his stomach and chest exposed. Without letting out a howl from the first blow, the next blow hit Johnny Raye across his chest and broke at least two ribs. Johnny Raye could not scream in pain as he wanted to do since every breath was now a challenge.

The last blow was squarely below the belt as the deputy grabbed the semiconscious Johnny Raye up and looked him straight in the eyes:

"Son, if you ever get close to that little girl again or her mother, I'll be back with some of my friends and we will have guns, not clubs. This is your only warning. And if I hear you have even talked to her or her mother, I will be telling some of the men in your part of town about your preference for little girls and let them deal with you. Do You Understand?"

Johnny Raye shook his head since he was unable to talk. The deputy let Johnny Raye's head fall back to the floor and walked out, leaving a bruised and battered Johnny Raye to get up and take himself to the hospital.

Miss Jorgina Boudoir took Monique home following her release from the hospital and told Monique's mother what had transpired. She confirmed that Monique had never verbalized the name of her perpetrator, but that a Macon County deputy believed Monique had been molested by a Mr. Johnny Raye.

Café con Leche

***

Jorgina Boudoir loved her weekends and her freedom to travel in the natural beauty that the State of Alabama provided. She enjoyed getting in her small Triumph and driving. Her headdress would not fit under the ceiling of her sports car, so she would remove it while driving. She had driven to Huntsville where the rockets were assembled and on northeast to the foothills of the Smoky Mountains. She had traveled to Jasper and floated a stretch of the beautiful Warrior River with a friend.

One Saturday morning, she awakened intent on going north to Lake Martin and eventually driving through the DeSoto State Park near Ft. Payne. It was a beautiful spring morning and azaleas were blooming all over Tuskegee. She drove up Highway 199 crossing what was to become Interstate 85 until she reached the junction of Highway 14. Turning west in the lovely rolling hills of central Alabama, Jorgina crossed over the bridge on the Tallapoosa River at Tallassee. The river rushed over the rocks tumbling downward toward its confluence with the Coosa River forming the Alabama River that flowed all the way to Mobile Bay on the Gulf of Mexico.

As she drove on to the east, she thought about the city of Montgomery thirty miles to the southwest. It had been the original capital of the Confederate States of America and Jorgina's own forefathers had been offloaded from a river boat on the Alabama River, marched with shackles both on their feet and hands, to a circular raised platform and sold as slaves to local plantation owners. Now more than a century later, white Alabamians still hated her and her people. The whites were in church every Sunday and Wednesday evening, but reserved the rest of the week for hating those who were "not their kind of people." Jorgina had acquired more education and experience than ninety percent of her fellow Alabamians but had still been relegated to drinking from separate water faucets and had to sit in the balcony at the local movie theatre.

Jorgina came to Highway 229 and turned to the north. She determined to not think about the pain of the past and even her present. Rather, she thought about the incredible changes coming for her and her people due to the efforts of Rev. Martin Luther King, Jr. and so many others who had decided to seek equal rights for the blacks despite the personal repercussions. She was proud of her visits to the Dexter Avenue Baptist Church in front of the Alabama State Capitol and being personally involved in the civil rights movement. A smile came across her face as she drove along the island-filled Lake Martin. Since there was nearly no traffic, she literally stopped on the bridge that crosses the width of the lake and consumed the smells and sights of the lake. Although a manmade lake, Jorgina was sure that the Lord had to have made something so beautiful.

She continued northward parallel to the shore of Lake Martin until she reached Alexander City and turned northeastward on Highway 22. Just out of the city limits, Jorgina passed a general store with a couple of fuel pumps out front. She pulled in and saw four older white men playing checkers on the front porch. To the last man they looked at her with disgust. "Who was this blackie in the 'ferin' sports car in the white man's world?" Barely slowing down, Jorgina hit the accelerator and drove back onto the highway. As she left the racists in their decaying world, she visualized them in white sheets with archaic head dresses, not like her colorful gélée full of life, but the white of dry bones worn by those full of hate and lovers of death.

Jorgina had promised to put the painful memories of the civil rights movement out of her head and enjoy the warm air of spring, but she could not forget the death of Viola Liuzzo. Jorgina had been in Selma, Alabama on "Bloody Sunday." While there, she had met the most impressive white woman she had ever known. Viola Liuzzo had been the mother of five children and had a good marriage, but she could not forget her childhood. She had grown up in Chattanooga, Tennessee and remembered how she and her sister were discriminated against for their poverty. But the blacks were treated even worse.

When Rev. Martin Luther King, Jr. invited anyone to come help his people obtain their civil rights, several northern whites, including Viola Liuzzo, responded. She left her five children and husband in Detroit, Michigan and drove to Montgomery, Alabama. After introducing herself to the leadership of the movement, she started making trips to Selma, Alabama and transporting participants for the march back to Montgomery. On one trip, she was transporting a young nineteen-year-old black man named Leroy Moton. A carload of Ku Klux Klan drove up next to them and shot Mrs. Liuzzo twice in the head. The blood blew all over Mr. Moton and he pretended to be dead, the only thing that saved his life. Mrs.

Liuzzo became the only white woman to die in the civil rights movement. Viola Liuzzo's assassination had not been in vain. Her death had inspired a young girl named Jorgina Boudoir to take up the banner and lead her fellow blacks to seek nothing less than "equal rights." Jorgina knew that, like Viola Liuzzo, doing what was right could cost her everything. With this sobering memory, she drove on north on Highway 63 from Alexander City to where it intersected with Highway 9 and took Highway 9 all the way to DeSoto State Park.

Few people, including Alabamians, knew that the DeSoto canyon was the deepest canyon east of the Rocky Mountains and it had several scenic overlooks as well as waterfalls. Every spring, Jorgina planned to drive through its deep canyons and pine-covered ridges and feel that her God was near her. She had seen the worst of mankind, but she had also seen the best. She had watched the police and their snarling dogs in Selma, and she had seen Viola Liuzzo willing to give her life for others. "No greater love than this."

Jorgina stopped at a scenic overlook at the DeSoto River falls and took out her road map she always kept with her. She started planning her return trip home so she could see a different part of her native Alabama. After taking a few photos of the falls, she drove her car back down the canyon, barely noticing the pickup truck behind her.

The 1956 Ford pickup was huge compared to Jorgina's little Triumph sports car. As she started to slow down on a sharp curve, the pickup sped up on her right side and struck the left side of her car. She screamed and instinctively looked at the demonic face of the driver of the vehicle. The driver and his passenger were two white crackers. They looked at her like they didn't think a black woman should be in their part of Alabama.

The Ford pickup struck Jorgina one last time as her car careened over the edge of the highway and down a five-hundred-foot drop to the river below. Jorgina's car exploded on impact, but she was already dead. Her brightly colored headdress was thrown clear of the car and floated down the river in memory of the wonderful Christian woman who had once worn it.

The two thugs looked in all directions and thought their evil had gone undetected, but God knew. Their judgment was still ahead.

A local man on his way home to Ft. Payne, Alabama spotted the burning wreck and called the Sheriff's office. When the deputies arrived and discovered the victim was a black female, they quickly concluded she had died in an accident. They saw the shattered glass from a headlight on the highway before there was any collision with the guard rail, but to acknowledge its existence would mean they had to investigate further, and a black female just wasn't worth the effort.

***

Tyisha cried every moment of Jorgina's funeral in the school gym. Every student was allowed to forego class and attend the service of their teacher and the most-beloved teacher in the school.

Jorgina's pastor and brother-in-Christ led the service. After the congregation joined in singing "Children We All Shall Be Free," there was not a dry eye in the gym. Even the overflow crowd in the halls surrounding the gym cried as all remembered a woman of grace, conviction and love for all of those the Lord had placed in her life.

For the first time since losing her mother, Tyisha had met one of the few persons who had truly loved her. But not just Tyisha, Jorgina never missed a day hugging each of her students as they left at the end of the school day. Jorgina had patiently told Tyisha to forgive those who had treated her wrongly since Tyisha's anger only did harm to herself. Jorgina had not only taught Tyisha how to be a teacher, but how to be a loving child of God.

For the first time in her life, Tyisha really wanted to know the God that Jorgina professed and lived for and be more like the woman who had loved her.

"Brothers and Sisters, there's not one gathered here who wasn't touched by Sister Jorgina Boudoir. She was willing to give all that she had to give for all of us or any one of us. She still had dog bite scars from "Bloody Sunday" and she knew Dr. Martin Luther King, Jr., Mrs. Viola Liuzzo, Miss Rosa Parks, and Rev. Ralph David Abernathy, Jr. But most importantly, she knew our Lord Jesus Christ.

Everyone who knew Miss Jorgina knew her Lord 'cuz' she showed her love to all she met. She told me once that she "didn't care if you 'wuz' black or white cause the Lord made us all." It's too bad them fellas with the dogs on the Edmund Pettus Bridge didn't think that way. The bridge was named after a former "Grand Dragon" of the Alabama Ku Klux Klan and the hatred that was shown to our brothers and sisters there would have made most people bitter. But Miss Jorgina wasn't most people. Her scars

Café con Leche

only made her more thankful for the gifts the Lord has given our people. We have received so many rights that weren't afforded our forefathers and there is still much to be done…"

The preacher continued giving accolades to Miss Jorgina, but unlike so many funerals, all the compliments were true. Miss Jorgina had made a huge difference in the lives of all who knew her.

Tyisha made a promise to her deceased friend and mentor to continue the pilgrimage Miss Jorgina had started. There was only a month left in the school year and the school principal had asked Tyisha to complete it in the place of Miss Jorgina. Tyisha had promised to do so, but knew she had to go wherever the Lord opened a door to her. The principal further offered her a position as a full-time teacher in the school after she obtained her teacher's certificate. Though the offer was tempting, Tyisha had decided she needed to leave the South. She had lived there her entire life and it had become painfully obvious that the blacks did not care for her because she was too white, and the whites hated her because she was too black. Tyisha had learned from Jorgina much more than teaching techniques. Tyisha had learned to pray. One afternoon following the end of the school day, she went into the classroom of fellow teacher, Mrs. Rosetta Heights. Mrs. Heights was an outspoken Christian who believed and practiced her faith. She was widely known by the staff as a "prayer warrior."

Tyisha explained her dilemma to Mrs. Heights and asked Mrs. Heights to pray for her and tell Tyisha just how Ty should try to serve the Lord.

"Ty, you got to forget about being white and black. You are the way the Lord made you and you got to find His will for your life. I know you don't want to hear it, but the Lord may have a ministry for you right here in Alabama. Then again, He may want you in another part of this country or even another part of the world. Wherever He wants you, He will open a door to show you the way. Your job is to walk through it.

Now, young sister, whatever the Lord calls you to do will require talents and abilities. The talents you already got and you was born with 'em.' The abilities need training and experience. Some of 'em you already got, but some the Lord will hone in you.

I seen you with the children and you is definitely good with 'em. But what if the Lord takes you to some ferin' country like Panama? Well, you gots to learn Spanish to teach those children there. That there is an ability.

If there is one thing I know for shore, it is that the Lord never calls us to serve Him unless He has given us the talent and gives us a chance to develop abilities to do the ministry.

Sister, I be going to pray for the Lord to reveal His will to you and I's going to ask some fellow Christians to do the same, but you'se gots to do the same. You pray until the Lord shows you His will and walk through door. Now, that place may be here or somewhere else, but you'se gots to do His will if you is ever to be at peace."

Tyisha left and verbalized her appreciation to Mrs. Heights, though she wanted a definitive answer from the senior Christian. She wanted to know just where she should go and what she should do when she got there. But God seldom works in that way. Tyisha did not want to remain in Alabama and was hoping the Lord would take her to some place where she would finally be accepted and even loved by other people. Mrs. Heights had made it clear-the Lord might want Tyisha to minister for Him right here in Alabama. The very thought was depressing since Tyisha had already made up her mind to leave at the end of the school year.

***

The morning after the funeral of Miss Jorgina, Tyisha received a phone call from Miss Jorgina's pastor.

"Miss Tyisha, on the morning prior to Miss Jorgina's death, she came by my office at the church and said you had decided to follow Christ. She said you wanted to announce that decision to the world and be baptized as the Lord ordered us. Is that right?"

Tyisha didn't need to think about the answer. She didn't know what Miss Jorgina had told her pastor, but she knew her friend would make every attempt to help her follow the Lord's commandments.

"Yes, pastor, Miss Jorgina promised me she would discuss my salvation and pending baptism with you. I am so happy she did so before going to rest with our Lord. Are you willing to baptize me?"

"Dear sister, if Miss Jorgina was convinced of your salvation, so am I. Can you be with us next Sunday? We can have our service, weather permitting, on Chewacla Creek and at the end of the worship time I will call you into the creek and baptize you."

Café con Leche

"Yes, pastor, I am so anxious to start my new life in Christ. I feel like Miss Jorgina gave her life for the faith and I want to carry on where she left off. You pick the place, and I will be there."

"Okay, we'll meet for worship on the Notasulga Road where it crosses the Chewacla Creek. I have enough time to call most of the members before next Sunday and many of the members will call others in the congregation. We'll meet there at 9:30 a.m. and I look forward to singing and praising our Lord and baptizing you into the faith. God bless you and I will see you then."

***

As agreed, Tyisha came to the side of the Chewacla Creek about 9:00 a.m. and waited for the congregation and pastor to arrive. She looked at the shallow creek slowly flowing by and wondered just how the whole event would change her life. Already she had noted a pleasing change in her attitude. Slowly, her anger, hatred and depression were waning. They had been her constant companions for most of her young life and had never allowed her to be close to most people, black or white. Since making her commitment to the Lord Jesus Christ, Tyisha had noted a slow change. She was witnessing a sincere love in her heart for others; her students, fellow Christians, and those that the Lord placed in her life. Tyisha enjoyed this new person she was becoming and could not continue to harbor hate for her uncle, grandparents and most of the people of Suzie, Alabama.

Early in her Christian life, Miss Jorgina had told her that Tyisha had to let go of her anger and hate if she was to ever find peace in Christ Jesus. There on the banks of the creek by herself, Tyisha remembered the words of her Christ in Matthew 6:15, "But if ye forgive not men their trespasses, neither will your Father forgive your trespass."

"Father," Tyisha cried out, "Forgive my hatred and anger and the hurt that others have caused in me. Forgive my uncle, my grandparents that have passed, the members of my home church and all those that have shunned me when I was so lonely. Father, make me whole so I might serve You!" With this simple prayer, she felt the indwelling of the Holy Spirit and her upcoming baptism took on a whole new meaning.

The pastor and the rest of the congregation arrived, and the choir opened the worship time by singing *I Heard the Voice of Jesus Say.* They could not have picked a more appropriate song. The line "I found in Him a resting-place" brought tears to Tyisha's eyes.

Following the sermon, the pastor walked into the side of the creek and beckoned for Tyisha to join him as the choir sang *Been in the Storm So Long.* Tyisha wanted to scream to the world just how much Jesus had done for her. By being baptized she was telling the world that she had committed all that she was to the cause of Christ. Her short life had been a "storm" for so long and she felt the minute that she came up out of the water that her storm finally had purpose. Maybe the Lord could use the pain of her past to do His will through her.

***

Tyisha set an appointment with Mrs. Juanita Blanchard at Tuskegee College. Mrs. Blanchard oversaw referring students to potential employers. Tyisha was graduating with a 3.8 GPA and had a glowing referral from both Miss Jorgina and their principal. She knew she would receive multiple offers to interview for teaching positions, even though she was bi-racial. She had asked Mrs. Blanchard to consider her available for positions anywhere in the continental United States, but preferably not the traditional south. Mrs. Blanchard had just looked up from her desk into the face of Tyisha and said, "We could sure use you here. Mrs. Boudoir's death did not end the movement."

"Thank you, Mrs. Blanchard, but I have lived in Georgia or Alabama all my life and I have no people, black or white. I want to see equal rights for all people, mutual respect, but most of all I want people to know the love that Miss Jorgina showed me. Beside my mother, she was one of the few people who ever loved me like God loves me.

I know the Lord is here and that He loves me, but I know He will be with me wherever He opens a door for me. If no offers come my way, then I guess the Lord wants me to stay here. But, if positions open to me in other places, then I believe the Lord is opening a door for me elsewhere and I must walk through it. Mrs. Blanchard, I am on a journey to find the Lord's will for my life. I hope you can help me."

Mrs. Blanchard was a black lady of immense proportions. She sat behind her desk, consuming most of the area with hips that hung off both

Café con Leche

sides of her desk chair. Her smile was contagious, freely given to all who entered her little office.

"Miss Tyisha, I know the Lord, and nothing would give me more pleasure than to help you do His will. You is my sister and I don't care who yo' daddy and mommy was. We both know our Lord an' that's all that matters.

You give me a couple of weeks and just as soon as I hear somethin', I'll let you know. Now, you go take care of Sister Jorgina's childens and teach them how to read, write and love."

Tyisha stood and walked behind the desk to give Mrs. Blanchard a humongous hug. She could not fully encompass the rotund frame, but Mrs. Blanchard knew the sincerity and depth of Tyisha's appreciation.

Tyisha walked the short distance to her elementary school and looked through the window on the door at her class. The children were reading aloud from their "Tom and Jane" readers coming apart at the binding from previous overuse at a local white school. A substitute teacher sitting at the desk was giving direction. Tyisha had no idea where, but she knew whatever the Lord had planned for her, it involved teaching. She loved it and Miss Jorgina was right-Tyisha was good at it. She looked away from the door for a moment and sensed that she and God were on a journey together. The journey had begun and for the first time in her life, she had real hope.

CHAPTER 3

"Girl, you mus' be livin' right." As was her straight-talking way, Mrs. Blanchard explained that she had been looking for teaching positions all over the lower 48 states and she had found six that were a perfect match for Miss Tyisha.

"You come by my office after your school day, and I will let you take all six offers home so you can pray about them. There's a couple that are temptin' me to leave my job here."

"Mrs. Blanchard, I know you go home around 5:00 p.m. I will try to be there by 4:00 p.m. Thank you so much for all your work on my behalf."

Tyisha literally felt herself shaking, she was so excited. She knew that one of the offers found by Mrs. Blanchard was right for her. She was going to be right where God wanted her when He wanted her to be there. Most Christians live their entire life of faith without knowing that sense of completeness, of "oneness" with their Creator; yet Tyisha was a young Christian and knew she was right in the middle of the will of God for her life. All through the school day, she tried valiantly to keep her mind on the academics she was to teach but found her mind wandering to all the experiences ahead, and all north of the Mason-Dixon Line. She knew that Missouri, Kentucky and Maryland had all been "border-states" in the Civil

War, but she would even entertain offers from these states if she sensed the Lord had a place for her there.

As the last bell rang for the school day, she ushered out her students. Her kisses and hugs were more rapid than normal. As the last student left the classroom, she was already closing her textbook and locking up the door. She walked quickly, almost breaking into a trot, down the walk toward the office of Mrs. Blanchard. Tyisha, true to her word, arrived at the office of Mrs. Blanchard at 3:50 p.m.

Out of breath, Tyisha entered Mrs. Blanchard's office and said nearly simultaneously, "Good evening, Mrs. Blanchard. I am so excited to see the offers we talked about. Is there a chance I can bring them with me tonight?"

"Sis, you get your breath while I get them out. I kept them all in a folder which is yours and you can take it with you and read each of them if you like. Here it is." Mrs. Blanchard lovingly handed the folder to Tyisha and sat back behind her desk. "Now sister, you take these and pray that the Lord will help you find the one that is in His will for you."

"Don't worry, Mrs. Blanchard. I have been praying for the Lord to show me His will for weeks now. I can't wait to get started. Thank you so much for all you have done for me. I better get started looking through my future. God bless you." With this, Tyisha stood up and placed the file folder under her arm as if it were some precious jewel. She duplicated her quick steps and hurried to her dorm room to look at the job offers.

The first job offer was tempting. It started at over $7500 dollars per year, nearly twice what she would make in Alabama. But the position was in St. Louis, Missouri and Tyisha hated cities. She did not sense the Lord was in the job offer and she moved on to the second position.

California, always wanting to prove it was a leader in all social issues had actually advertised a teaching position for a black student at Tuskegee Institute. They were willing to pay $8500 per year just to show the world how much they wanted to help a young black succeed. Of course, the powers that be had never considered hiring a young black teacher from Compton or the Watts community near Los Angeles. It was more prestigious to hire a teacher from the home school of Booker T. Washington or George Washington Carver. Tyisha laid the offer aside and thought about throwing it in a nearby trash can.

But there was something special about the third offer. It was from a private school in North Dakota, definitely above the Mason-Dixon Line. She had no words, but simply a feeling that this was the will of God for her. It really made no sense from the perspective of logic-it was the lowest remuneration of any of the six positions and held no chance of being recognized for her obvious skills as a teacher. Yet, for some reason, she knew in the depths of her soul that this was the position for her. Still, Tyisha wanted the confirmation of other Christians. She remembered Miss Jorgina and her wise words, "If God speaks to you, Sister, He speaks to others about you."

Tyisha threw all the offers aside, even the three she had yet to review. She kept the one from North Dakota in her hands and began to pray that the Lord would show her His will. She had no vision, heard no voices, and yet she knew that she should pursue this opportunity. She looked again at the offer.

Mrs. Blanchard had written a very complete job offer, almost as if she had seen something different about this job offer. It was from the Redeemer's Salvation School of Williston, North Dakota. They offered Tyisha $5800 dollars per academic year. The student ratio to teacher was 14:1, unbelievable to Tyisha who had been teaching 38 children in her substandard school in Tuskegee. She read the school's mission statement and re-read the phrase "to share the Gospel with our young students so they can share the Gospel with the world." Tyisha suddenly wondered if she belonged in Williston, North Dakota. She had given her life to the Lord, and she wanted nothing more than to do His will. Suddenly it became less important where she was to go, but what she was being called to do when she went there.

It was too late to call the school on that Thursday night, so she hurriedly went to the Tuskegee library. She checked out every book she could find with the vaguest reference to North Dakota, especially Williston, North Dakota. She inhaled the information and went to church the following Sunday and asked her pastor and some of her most revered brothers and sisters to pray for the Lord to confirm His will to her.

During her free hour on the following day while the Art teacher came into her room, she went to the teacher's lounge and called the Redeemer's Salvation School. She asked to speak with the headmaster of the school and

Café con Leche

when he answered, she identified herself. She told Mr. Christian Christensen she was very interested in the position and felt the Lord was leading her in his direction. She asked him to send her any relevant information, a job application, and promised to send him a resume as soon as possible.

"Thank you, Mr. Christensen I look forward to hearing from you soon."

"And thank you Miss McFarren. We have been praying as a staff that the Lord would send us the right person to do his will here in rural North Dakota. We hope you are that person. I will be sending you the information you requested later this same day. God bless you until we speak again."

With that word of encouragement, Tyisha hung up the phone and wondered how anyone named "Christian Christensen" could avoid being the headmaster of a Christian school. Before the end of the conversation, she had already sensed this was the position the Lord had prepared for her. She was ecstatic and could not wait to begin the process of moving.

***

Tyisha knew early in her life that her grandparents, who had been blessed with excess money and land, would never financially help her. Just north of her grandfather's farm was an eight-hundred-acre farm owned by a widow named "Lizzie Mitchell." Tyisha's grandfather had repeatedly asked to buy the land from Mrs. Mitchell, but she would not entertain any offer. She told Mr. Watts that she and her husband had "cleared the brush in every fence row and gully with an axe and corn knife" and she would not leave the land until the Lord took her home.

"Aunt Lizzie" as Tyisha and other local children called Mrs. Mitchell, had a heart made of gold. She oozed love and concern for all of those who were placed in her life by the Lord and her love was not reserved for only white children.

Tyisha would take her checkerboard set the mile and a half to the home of Aunt Lizzie throughout the year when the weather allowed and sit at a favorite stump in the front yard and play checkers for hours with her favorite person in the whole world. Amazingly enough, Tyisha became an expert at checkers and won almost every match with her elder adversary. Of course, Tyisha's prowess at the game was aided by Aunt Lizzie's propensity for losing.

Aunt Lizzie was a native of southern Alabama and an expert on all things "Creek or Muscogee Indians." One warm afternoon in June, Aunt Lizzie said, "Let's go down by the river and find some arrowheads."

Aunt Lizzie had an old mule that she kept for company more than for working the land. She quickly hitched the old mule up to a bridle and harness and led her down the hill to the side of the Chattahoochee River where she kept an old single-bottom plow. Tyisha watched as the old lady adeptly backed the mule up to the plow and hitched up the harness.

She had not plowed over one hundred feet when she turned up a near perfect arrowhead. Aunt Lizzie and Tyisha marveled at the workmanship. "The Creek hunted deer, turkey, and other animals near the river. They also raised crops of corn, melons, beans, squash, and sweet potatoes right here on this good soil. This river and many others here in the southeast provided a good life to the people who lived here for hundreds of years before the white man showed up."

Aunt Lizzie had other unique qualities. She had a bricklayer's hammer lying on her porch, and she would often tell Tyisha, "Let's go find us some fossils." With her hammer in hand, the two would walk down a small stream near the house and she would stop, pick up a rock, strike it with her hammer and inside would almost always be the outline of a leaf, a mussel, or some ancient sea creature fossil. Tyisha never discovered Aunt Lizzie's secret but was awed by her unique gift.

One warm afternoon, as they sat on Aunt Lizzie's front porch drinking lemonade, Aunt Lizzie looked at Tyisha and said, "Girl, it is obvious that you are going to need money someday and your grandparents are never going to help you. I want to start a bank account in your name and only yours. I have some jobs around here and I want you to do them. I'll pay you a few dollars and put the rest of your earnings in the bank for you. They will come in handy one day." Tyisha spent days after school raking leaves, feeding Aunt Lizzie's chickens and mule, and cleaning out the barn. Aunt Lizzie paid her $1.65 per hour and deposited $1.00 of the total in a bank account for Tyisha.

Tyisha rose from her "walk down memory lane" and walked to the window in the teacher's lounge. She nearly cried as she thought of Aunt Lizzie's passing while she was attending college in Tuskegee Institute. Aunt Lizzie was one of the persons that had truly loved her in her teen years, despite her skin color, wavy brown hair, and high cheek bones.

Tyisha had never touched the bank account started by Aunt Lizzie and the bank had informed her that it now contained over $3800. It was more than Tyisha would need to move to North Dakota and pay for her first month's rent and utilities and she would still have some money for extras like food and travel expenses.

She had bought a 1963 Oldsmobile in her freshman year of college from a professor whose daughter had left it behind when she entered the Air Force at nearby Maxwell AFB, Alabama. Tyisha wasn't sure it would make the long trip to western North Dakota, but she had faith that the Lord would take her safely on if the teaching position was truly His will for her life.

Tyisha read about North Dakota, graded her class's papers, and prepared lesson plans for the coming week. On Sunday, she arose early to pray and read her Bible. She went to her new church, the Byler Chapel African Methodist Episcopal Zion Church. She had only been a member for a couple of months, but she already loved the congregation. They were more concerned with the condition of her soul than the color of her skin.

During the beginning of the worship service, several congregants stood and announced various ministries that needed help or an upcoming church dinner. Finally, Tyisha stood and told the congregation about the job opportunity in North Dakota and asked that they pray for her to be wise and see where the Lord wanted to lead her.

At the conclusion of the worship service, the pastor met each congregant at the front door of the sanctuary and shook their hands. Each tickled his ears like, "Pastor, that was the best sermon I ever heard," or "You is a natural-born speaker." Tyisha was becoming a "Churchian", and she walked out of the church shaking the hand of the pastor and said, "You must be a bishop of God. Them was just the words I needed to hear today." As a teacher, she had perfect diction and grammar, but she wanted to use Ebonics to more easily fit in with her black brethren. The pastor was completely aware that all his congregants' complements were "shallow, at best" even if well-intentioned.

Tyisha had no more than completed her obvious flattery when she walked down the steps of the church. An older gentleman named Elmore Johnson was waiting for her at the foot of the stairs. He was one of the few black cattle producers in southern Alabama, but he was a stalwart

Christian and highly respected member of the congregation. He had a son named "Elijah." Elijah was thirty years old and had never been married.

"You gots just a minute, Miss Tyisha? I gots this big ol' cattle truck and with a little cleanin,' it'd be perfect to haul your stuff up to North Dakota. My son, Elijah, could drive you two up there and he could hook your car to the truck and pull it behind. He ain't real tall, but he be strong as an ox."

Tyisha wanted to thank him profusely, but knew Mr. Johnson was more intent on helping his son find a wife than helping Tyisha fulfill the will of God.

"Thank you for your offer, but I am not sure I am taking the teaching position in North Dakota. Besides, I only have a dorm room of belongings and I could fit what I have in a rental trailer. If I need to use your truck, I will contact you later. You are awfully sweet to offer."

This was not the answer the old man wanted to hear. He had already started a list of names for his grandchildren he was sure Tyisha would give him. Tyisha walked away to meet some friends at lunch at a new restaurant entitled "Match 65 Restaurant." She knew that eating there would mean she had less money to spend on meals for the rest of the week.

Nevertheless, the fellowship with the few who had befriended her was worth it. In fact, this was the reason she decided to go to Williston, North Dakota. She was not naïve; she would be exclusively with whites. Tyisha had been despised by both blacks and whites for most of her life, so what was the downside of going to one of the "whitest" states in the United States? At least, she would be removing the discrimination of the blacks toward her. Maybe the Lord could use her in the upper Midwest. All she knew for sure was she needed to leave the South, at least for the foreseeable future.

CHAPTER 4

Tyisha went to teach on Monday with a newfound excitement. She was anticipating the arrival of the application from the Redeemer's Salvation School. Her few friends had reluctantly told her that they believed the Lord wanted her to take the position as had Mrs. Blanchard and Tyisha's pastor.

Each day, she counted the minutes until the end of the school day. She nearly ran to her mailbox outside her dorm in hopes the application had arrived. Finally, on Wednesday, she had a note in the box that said she had a large packet in the main post office. She jumped in her car and drove downtown. The clerk at the window retrieved the package sent from "Williston, North Dakota." Tyisha could hardly control her emotion and profusely thanked the clerk. He wondered if the contents of the package were legal.

At home, Tyisha barely made it through her dorm room door before she ripped open the package and extracted the application. She stayed awake until 1:00 a.m., but she completed the application. The next morning on her way to school, she rushed so she could walk to the next street to the south where there was a mailbox on the corner. She gingerly dropped the application into the mailbox after holding it several seconds. Tyisha knew her life was about to go in a whole new direction. Her life had been miserable, full of hate and anger, yet she was scared by the certain change that was coming.

That same morning at her free hour, Tyisha telephoned Mr. Christensen and told him she had just mailed her application. He sounded almost joyful and told her he and his staff would eagerly await its arrival.

Enough of waiting for God to show her His will. Enough of hoping others could tell her just what God wanted her to do. It was time for her to decide. Miss Jorgina was right; we usually know the will of God looking back, not forward. If God wanted her in North Dakota, He would open the door for her to receive the position. If not, she would move onto other possibilities.

***

Each day, Tyisha awoke to a ritual she had established. First, she would read a chapter of one of the books of either the New or Old Testament. Then she would pray for strength to be the best teacher she could be that day and a blessing to all her students. Finally, she quoted one of her favorite scriptures from memory, Psalms 118:24.

> "This is the day which the Lord hath made; we will rejoice and be glad in it."

She meant those words. With the completion of her ritual, Tyisha dressed and headed to her school. She felt a release, almost a peace now that she had "let go and let God." She was nearing the end of her year as a student teacher, and it had been a year that changed her life forever. Oh, she still had frequent visits from the principal of the school and some of the senior teachers, but she was substantially in charge of her classroom and students.

She had begun the year with a mentor who had become so much more. Miss Jorgina had brought her a love for teaching, but more importantly she had introduced her to the Lord. For that, Tyisha would be eternally grateful (pun intended).

***

Café con Leche

It was May and that month seemed to drag on forever. Each day seemed like there was too much to do and not enough time to do it. But at the end of the day, there seemed as many days ahead as behind. Then one day, she went to get her mail and there was a letter from Mr. Christian Christensen. She had been selected to fill the position and they were looking forward to her arrival. God had opened the door and she was determined to walk, no run, through it. She telephoned her positive response to the offer.

Mr. Christensen had seemed genuinely excited that he and his Board of Trustees had found Tyisha's application worthy of a teaching contract the following year. Tyisha was ecstatic.

She inquired at the local trailer rental, and they had an outlet in Williston, North Dakota. She would be able to place all of her earthly possessions in a medium-sized trailer and return the trailer at the end of her trip.

After grading her class's papers each night, she would put them aside and pull out her highway maps and plan her trip. Tyisha had never been out of the south, and she was looking forward to seeing places she had only read about. She planned to drive toward Montgomery on the nearly completed Interstate 85 and then drive north on the Eastern Bypass to Highway 231. She would take Highway 231 north to Wetumpka, Alabama and then turn on Highway 111 up the west side of Lake Jordan for 15 miles and turn west until the highway intersected with Interstate 65.

Tyisha had been writing down a long list of each highway she would travel and where to turn. She looked again at the list, wadded up the page and threw it in the trash. She had over $800 she had budgeted for her trip and with gas at an average of $.32 per gallon she could take the "scenic route." Tyisha vowed she would put forth all of her energies toward teaching her class the last few days of the academic year and only open her highway maps when she was actually in route to her new home.

Each day, Tyisha vowed to teach her students right up to the last day of the school year. At the end of each day, she hugged the children longer, kissed more of them on the forehead and knew she would miss every one of them, especially a young girl named Monique, who was finally promoted to third grade.

It was May 24, the last day of the academic year. Tyisha said "good-bye" to each student as they left the classroom with their personal belongings in hand. It had been a hard year with one surprising death after another.

Sister Jorgina had been taken from her, leaving her feeling alone once again. The leader of the civil rights movement, Martin Luther King, Jr., had been shot and killed in Memphis only weeks earlier. Tyisha sensed his death was not for ought. Her own father, whoever he was, and all her students had benefited by the work of Dr. King on their behalf.

"Miss Tyisha, you got a minute?"

Tyisha whirled around to find a fellow teacher standing inside the doorway.

"Miss Jewel, I always have time for you."

"Miss Tyisha, we lost a wonderful sister when we lost Miss Jorgina. She taught side by side with me for almost thirty years and in all those years, she accumulated dozens of charts, written exercises and tests.

She would have wanted you to have them and use them to teach children for the glory of God. I have some at my house which I picked up after Sister Jorgina passed and there's many more right here in my room. I'll bring 'em to you. They are in a couple of boxes."

"Thank you, Miss Jewel. I would love to fulfill Miss Jorgina's dream of teaching the children. I have hours of work ahead before I can turn in my class key to the principal. I'll be here waiting."

With this, Miss Jewel turned toward the hall with a tear in her eye and said over her shoulder, "I'll be back with Miss Jorgina's belongin's."

Tyisha continued packing up her personal items and those of Miss Jorgina with a confused heart. She felt such a loss to leave this room that had been her home away from home for the past year. She missed the warmth and love of a woman who had been taken from her far too soon, especially since Tyisha had known so little love since the passing of her mother.

But Tyisha also felt an excitement about her pending new job and new setting. She couldn't wait to leave the south and begin the rest of her life, a life full of hope and opportunity. Monday was coming and with it, a trip to not only a new place, but a new life. Tyisha could not wait.

CHAPTER 5

It was May 27, moving day, finally! She had walked the aisle and graduated with her fellow survivors at Tuskegee Institute the previous Saturday, but now it was time to go. Her car and trailer were parked out on the nearest curb to her dorm, which was nearly empty since most of the college students had left the previous Friday. A friend, whom she had known since their freshman year, had volunteered to help Tyisha move her few belongings to the trailer attached to her car. Gratefully, Tyisha had only a few items to move in her four-feet by six-feet trailer.

She had accumulated several textbooks from her college courses, a couple of lamps, and a small loveseat since her room had been so small. Her wardrobe consisted of two dresses for school, one which she washed each night in the bathroom down the hall, while she wore the other to school the next day, a complete "church suit" with a long dress and matching shoes and hat all in a bright purple that complemented her complexion, and a pair of blue jeans with a matching sweatshirt for everyday wear. Along with her three pair of shoes, box of knickknacks and Miss Jorgina's teaching aids, she had plenty of space remaining. She and her friend had the trailer packed, said their "good-byes" and hugged each other multiple times by 7:00 a.m.

Tyisha drove away from the curb and the college she had called home for the past four years. She could still see her friend standing on the side of the street and waving. Tyisha waved back with her left arm over the roof of the car. She had mixed feelings as she drove northward. She knew she was going further from Suzie, Alabama and she felt a sense of relief, but she knew she would not feel free of her painful past until she crossed over the Mason-Dixon Line. In a sense, she suspected she was feeling many of the same emotions of those black slaves on the "underground railroad" in route to St. Louis, Missouri and other destinations northward. She was leaving the only place she had ever known with no intent of ever returning.

***

Lake Jordan was beautiful as she drove up the west side of the impoundment. She continued north on Alabama Highway 3 until it intersected with the new Interstate 65 and continued toward Birmingham to near Alabaster, Alabama where she had to leave the incomplete roadway back to Highway 3. After entering Birmingham, Alabama, Tyisha drove northwestward past the Birmingham-Southern College to Highway 78 and continued toward Jasper, Alabama and the beautiful Warrior River. Now, she was driving more to the west and the midday sun more than to the north. She entered the shallow valley containing Carbon Hill, Alabama and on through Winfield toward northern Mississippi and Memphis, Tennessee.

Her stomach was growling and seemed to be speaking a language of its own, but Tyisha decided she would drive as far as she could safely drive. If possible, she would continue onto the northwest until she crossed the traditional Mason-Dixon Line to spend the night in hopes her skin color would not be a reason for "no vacancy" at a motel.

No matter how much she desired to go on, one fact prevented her forward motion; her car had less than a quarter of a tank of gasoline. She pulled into a gasoline station in downtown Holly Springs, Mississippi and waited for the gas attendant who was talking to a man inside the station. He was a black man, but not in a hurry to get gas for some half-breed.

"Fill 'er up, Lady?"

"Yes sir, fill it with regular, please."

The station was owned by a white man who would not be pleased with any mistreatment of a customer, despite her or his race. Hence, the attendant pretended to be unaffected by Tyisha's race and was as professional as he could possibly be. He walked around the car, wiping the

Café con Leche

windows off, the front and the rear windshields last, smearing the dirt and bug debris that had accumulated over the past 300 miles. Never once did he use a wet squeegee, leaving streaks all across the driver's view.

The old man walked around to the driver's window and said, "That'll be $4.62 for the gas."

Tyisha took a five-dollar bill out of her purse and handed it to the man.

"Keep the change, sir." The old man's frown turned to an instant smile. Maybe this little biracial gal wasn't so bad after all.

"Sir, I noticed all through your city that there were brightly colored circles denoting the highway routes. That is a great idea and I wish we had them in Tuskegee."

"We ain't got 'em signs cause they is pretty. We gots lots of folks, black and white, in these parts that don't know their numbers and can't read nor write. But they can follow the colored signs to get on the right highway."

Tyisha retorted as she prepared to drive away, "Well, whatever the reason, the signs are still pretty, and I still wish we had them at home."

It was still light at 6:30 p.m., but Tyisha had another three hours of travel to get to Thayer, Missouri just across the traditional Mason-Dixon Line; the border between Missouri and Arkansas. She crossed the Mississippi River bridge at Memphis nearly stopping in the middle in disbelief. She had never seen a river larger than the Chattahoochee River or Alabama River, but the Mississippi River made them look like puddles.

A tugboat pushing a host of empty barges northward lulled her into a daydream. No doubt they were going to Kansas City, Missouri or Omaha, Nebraska where they would be loaded with corn and sent back to New Orleans where the load would be transferred to a sea-going vessel. The load would be sent to Shanghai or some other exotic port of call. The driver behind her honked his horn loudly and persistently, waking Tyisha from her stupor. She gave her car the gas and drove into West Memphis, Arkansas.

She continued northwestward through the old Mississippi Delta of Arkansas on Interstate 55 and exited on Highway 63 toward Jonesboro, Arkansas. In prehistoric times, this was the site where the Mississippi River entered the Gulf of Mexico. The land was fertile and amazingly flat. At its greatest width, it encompassed all of the "boot-heel of Missouri," northeast Arkansas and northern Mississippi. It was the place where clear, fast flowing rivers from the Ozarks in Missouri and Arkansas flowed to the plains to die, before entering the mighty river.

Tyisha was tired and incredibly hungry, but she pressed on since she was only seventy miles from the border of Missouri. Pulling over to the side of Highway 63, Tyisha consulted her highway map and saw towns entitled, "Cotton Plant, Dixie, and Little Dixie." There were just too many reminders of a time when blacks were slaves and treated as chattel. She wanted out of the south, if she had to drive until the morning.

She entered the Ozarks just a few miles northwest of Jonesboro near the town of Black Rock, Arkansas. She had never seen such curves in the highways near Tuskegee or Suzie, Alabama. She could see the forests all around her, full of oaks and hickories. She had never seen anything like the millions of hardwoods that covered every hill and curve she drove around.

It was dark now and she was scared to go very fast since there were little eyes glowing near the highway and even in the roadway. The deer seemed everywhere, and she knew that she must be as aware as possible and get north of the Missouri state line.

She entered Hardy, Arkansas from the south next to the beautiful Spring River. Hardy had been the starting point of one of the last wagon trains in the United States in the 1890's that went over the front range of the Rocky Mountains and ended in the San Luis valley of Colorado.

Finally, she came to Mammoth Springs, Arkansas and Thayer, Missouri on the Missouri/Arkansas state line. They rolled up the streets by 6:00 p.m. and there was no place to eat or sleep. She continued driving the seemingly endless miles north to West Plains, Missouri and there was a motel right on Highway 63 with a sign flashing "vacancy." She pulled in without hesitation and went into the office to obtain a room. After providing information about her car license to the clerk with the strange accent, she took her key to the room and took in a suitcase of the only clothes she owned with her. Tyisha marveled at the clerk's nonchalant attitude. She had seemed totally unconcerned about Tyisha's race. Maybe Tyisha had been right and racial prejudice ended only 20 miles north of the Mason-Dixon Line. She could only wish.

She had not eaten since early that morning, but Tyisha needed sleep more than food. She barely placed her suitcase on a stand in the corner of

Café con Leche

the room before she lay across her bed and at once fell asleep. She was so exhausted; she could not remember any of her dreams and awoke when the sun came through her east window and hit her in the face.

It was already 6:30 a.m., but her exhaustion and hunger were being replaced by an "adrenaline rush." She nearly jumped up, showered, clothed and quickly went to the motel office to check out, with her bag in hand. She asked the clerk on duty where the nearest restaurant was located and once the lady behind the counter gave her directions, she drove her car in the general direction of the restaurant. Nobody had treated her badly, but she just wanted to continue toward the north. Perhaps racism lessened with every mile northward.

Tyisha asked for an order of eggs with bacon, a large cup of orange juice, and some grits. The waitress looked at her and said, "We ain't got no grits, Sis." Tyisha had never witnessed a restaurant anywhere in Alabama that did not serve grits. "Well, doing without grits is just one more thing I'm going to have to learn if I'm going to live up north," she thought. She took the order "to go" and drove northward again on Highway 63 through the prairies surrounding West Plains. She pulled off the highway on a logging road and nearly gobbled her breakfast, so she could continue her trip.

She had originally thought about going west across the state of Missouri, and going north on Highway 71 to Kansas City, she changed her mind and decided to go north on Highway 63 all the way to Rochester, Minnesota. The little towns seemed to fly by, Willow Springs, Cabool, Houston, Licking, Edgar Springs. She finally stopped in Rolla, Missouri for gas and went inside to eat at Cryer's Pizza, locally known for its thin-crust pizzas.

There were only three small tables on the south side of the counter. Tyisha took her medium size pizza and sweet tea to drink and sat at the table nearest the front window looking toward Highway 63.

The adrenaline discharged in abundant quantities, was wearing down and the miles and lack of sleep was taking a toll on Tyisha. She wondered if the clerk behind the counter would be offended if she pushed a couple of tables together and took a nap on the top. She thought he might be opposed, so she finished her pizza and ordered another medium Canadian Bacon/provolone pizza "to go." When it was ready, she took the pizza to her car and drove north toward the Missouri River.

A few miles north of Rolla, she saw the Rolla National Airport just past Vichy, Missouri. She pulled her car to the side of the terminal and parked it out of the way of other vehicles. She laid back and took a nap.

She awoke startled from her own snoring. The sun had begun to shine into the car and the inside had heated to the point sleeping was out of the question. She sat upright again and drove her car northward on Highway 63.

Within twenty miles, Tyisha noticed the names on the mailboxes were different. Names like "Schwartz," "Koch," and others were on store fronts, funeral homes, etc. She had entered the old German Catholic area known for wines and the best theologians the United States has ever produced-the Niebuhr brothers. She drove through little towns like "Freeburg," "Vienna," and "Westphalia."

She came up to the wide Osage River near where it emptied into the Missouri River, and turned westward toward Jefferson City, Missouri. Climbing out of the river valley, she could see the towers of Lincoln University to the left and a large granite-domed capitol to the right. The state capitol of Missouri was an exact replica of the one in Washington, D.C., only one-third the size. Tyisha was duly impressed.

Just west of the capitol, Highway 63 turned to the north across a bridge over the Missouri River. She looked down at the barges tied to mooring on the north side of the river as she crossed the "Big Muddy." Tyisha thought about how much of that sediment came from Yellowstone National Park or the Little Bighorn and the site of Custer's Last Stand. After crossing the fertile valley, Tyisha began the slow climb up to the Great Plains and Columbia, Missouri. South of the city, she pulled into a small town entitled "Ashland" to get some gasoline.

Northward a few miles, Highway 63 meandered through the small city of Columbia near the main campus of the University of Missouri and its famous School of Journalism, perhaps the oldest in the world. There were still a couple of hours of daylight left, but Tyisha was becoming tired, despite the good night's sleep she had received in West Plains.

In quick succession, she passed through Moberly, Macon, and Kirksville. From her maps, she concluded the Iowa line was only a few minutes ahead, so she stopped at a motel near the highway and rented a room. After getting her bag inside the room, she asked the clerk for some

Café con Leche

directions to the nearest restaurant. Tyisha drove to the eating establishment in hopes of getting a good supper before sleeping for the night. When she returned to her room, with a full stomach, she lay across her bed looking at her highway map and fell asleep with it still in her hands.

To this point in her trip, Tyisha had experienced wonderful weather, but Monday was not to be so. She awoke to the light of lightening and the crash of resulting thunder. After dressing, she drove to the motel office and ran inside as the rain began to fall in sheets. The young boy behind the desk said, "Ma'am, did you know we are under a tornado watch? You may want to think again if you are going north. The tornado watch is for a whole bunch of counties in Iowa."

"Well, thank you, but I suspect I can outrun any tornado." With this, Tyisha ran out between the sheets of rain and, with her windshield wipers on full, she continued north on Highway 63 to the first gasoline station. She almost felt guilty asking the young attendant to come out in the rain to fill her tank.

Less than a half-of-an-hour later, she could barely make out the sign on the side of the highway: "The People of Iowa Welcome You." Whether one thought the Mason-Dixon Line was the northern or southern border of Missouri, it didn't matter now. She was clearly north of any slave-holding states and Iowa had fought on the side of the Yankees. Though the blinding rain obscured some of the surroundings, Tyisha had never seen so much corn. It was everywhere in every direction.

South of Ottumwa, Iowa, the sky became so dark Tyisha wondered if the Lord would protect her. She began to believe she should have heeded the young motel clerk's warning and stayed in Kirksville for a while longer. She looked outside toward the west and knew she could never see a tornado's approach if it was a "rain-wrapped tornado."

"Lord, you know I have put myself in a mess I can't fix on my own. Keep me safe and save me from my own stupidity. Thank you, Father, for your unending love." Tyisha had seen or seen the results of several tornadoes in Alabama, but they were little more than whirlwinds compared to the mega-tornadoes of "Tornado Alley."

No more than Tyisha finished her prayer, the rain nearly stopped, but she could see at least a couple of miles to the west. There it was hanging down like the finger of death-a tornado heading due northeast and destined to intersect her path. To the east of Highway 63 was a large corn field with an old three-story farmhouse half of a mile east on a dirt road. Tyisha barely slowed down while her trailer made the turn onto the dirt road on the right wheel. Ahead, Tyisha saw a man, woman, and two little children running toward a storm cellar in the front yard. She threw her car into park and ran toward the cellar. As she got to the sliding door on the front, it opened and the man said, "Come in here, Sis, the Lord has brought you, His safety." With these words of comfort, Tyisha and the family sat on benches built into the walls of the cellar. The man of the house pulled the door and locked it in place. Tyisha felt like one of Noah's family on the Ark.

The noise was deafening, like nothing Tyisha had ever heard before. She had heard previous survivors of tornadoes liken the noise to a freight train, but the overwhelming noise was closer akin to that of a huge vacuum cleaner hose. The candles, their only source of light, blew out as the tornado passed overhead, though the door was closed and secured. Tyisha could feel the air being forcefully pulled from her lungs and breathing was difficult. She watched the two farm children being hugged by their parents as their eyes revealed their horror. Though the entire experience was new to her and extremely frightful, she felt a comforting arm around her that could only be described as "the hand of God."

As quickly as the deafening roar had come, it went until there was no sound at all, only complete silence. The cows and the horses in the barn didn't make a sound. Not even the wind was blowing. The farmer slowly unlocked the sliding steel door and peeked outside. Tyisha wondered if Jesus had peered outside of the tomb of Joseph of Arimathea after awakening from death and the stone was rolled away. The man slowly returned to the side of his wife and children and held them to him.

"The house is gone, the barn and all the animals. We'll rebuild and make them better than ever. Remember, honey, how you wanted a dishwasher. I promise you your new house will have a great new kitchen. We'll get more cows and horses, and I will rebuild the barn and lot. The Lord has been good to us. We are all alive and well and let us give praise to the Giver and Sustainer of Life."

The farmer held his family tight and called Tyisha to join them. They all held hands in the dark as he prayed.

Café con Leche

"Father, You who bring forth life and sustain it, have saved us from death. You have kept your promise to be 'Immanuel, God with us.' We have sensed your presence with us as the tornado spared us. Now, we must begin to correct what has gone wrong, but we know You will be with us no matter where life takes us. Lord, may we be a blessing to others as You have been a blessing to us. In the name of our Savior, and your Son Jesus Christ we pray it. Amen."

With the end of the prayer, all five of the survivors exited the cellar. The farmhouse and barn, which had stood behind it, were gone as were the livestock. One cow lay in the fork of a tree which was lacking any limbs. It had a board piercing its side and had doubtlessly had its neck broken when the funnel threw it into the tree.

To the amazement of all five, Tyisha's car and trailer sat seventy-five feet south of the storm cellar and was unfazed. All the windows had been down and not one was broken.

"Miss, in all of the commotion, we didn't even get your name."

"My name is Tyisha McFarren, but you can just call me Ty. I was on my way to my first teaching position in Williston, North Dakota when I saw the tornado coming."

"Well, we are glad you shared our storm cellar with us. I'm Jed Losch. This is my wife, Betty, and these are our children, Jake and Jennifer." All the Losch family shook her hand, one at a time, and welcomed Ty to what had been their home. They looked down the lane toward Highway 63 and a line of trucks was coming their way.

Neighbors were beginning to arrive and see if the family had survived. Some of the men looked at the site where the barn had stood and planned to rebuild it. Others were talking to one another about how they could alternate weeding their corn crops and building the house. Tyisha did not sense she was being excluded, but only that she was in the way. Walking up first to the husband and then to his wife and the children, Tyisha said her "Good-byes" to each one and thanked them for sharing their fortress. The wife returned to picking up photos and small knickknacks scattered in the path of the tornado, with tears in her eyes. Tyisha sensed it was time to go on.

Back on Highway 63, she continued northward, but the shaking in her hands would not abate. The experience with the tornado had affected her much more than she had thought. She stopped at the first motel in Ottumwa, Iowa and rented a room for the night. After buying supper at a local restaurant, she returned to her room. Tyisha needed someone to share her day's experiences, but she was alone or so she thought. She lay on her bed and after an hour of fitful tossing and turning, she finally fell asleep.

"Tyisha awaken! I am the Lord your God."

She jumped from the bed thinking the motel clerk was warning her of another impending tornado. Slowly, she began to awaken and realized who was speaking her name. The whole room became as bright as day and not one light was on. Tyisha fell to her knees and responded in a quaking voice, "Here am I Lord."

"I have seen your tears, heard your prayers and known the suffering of your heart. They have not been in vain. They have helped prepare you for the mission I have for you. There is still suffering and pain ahead for you, but I will be with you through it all. Remember, I am in everything and everything is in Me. I control the tornados and every river flows the way I want it to. Listen to my voice and feel my presence. You can hear me in the wind and feel Me in every touch of the wavering wheat.

I have sustained your life and given you new life this day. Remember me each day, for I have much for you to do. Joy is coming, but not yet. Have faith in Me, little one, and I shall help you persevere through every attack of the evil one."

Tyisha had known she was in the immediate presence of the Almighty and she had lowered her head to the carpet and closed her eyes in reverence. Slowly, the bright light dimmed, and she waited several minutes before she dared to raise her head up.

When she was sure she was alone, she arose and sat on the edge of the bed. What had the Lord meant when He had said, "I have much for you to do?" How had her tragic past prepared her to do the ministry of the Lord? Tyisha had been so excited about the possibility of teaching in North Dakota, but now she realized this was a time for further preparation and was not her final ministry.

Tyisha was exhausted from the events of the day, but too excited to sleep. She finally dozed off around 3:00 a.m. Three and half hours later came far too quickly and determination mixed with adrenaline got her out of bed and dressing for the travel ahead.

Café con Leche

By 7:30 a.m., Ty was sitting at a local restaurant eating her biscuits and gravy with a side order of sausage. Iowa was known for its hog farms and the sausage tasted exceptionally fresh. After her meal, she stopped at a gas station and topped off her gasoline tank. Ty's experience with the tornado and revelation from the Lord Almighty had renewed her vigor and appreciation for life. She had begun the day with a new commitment and understanding of the meaning of Psalms 118:24. Since becoming a Christian, she had recited those words each morning, "This is the day which the Lord hath made; we will rejoice and be glad in it."

Ty pulled onto a farm road to the east of Highway 63. The storm clouds were parting toward the horizon and the sun's rays broke through. The warmth on her face made her remember those days sitting on her rock and looking across the Chattahoochee River, with a dream of finding a better life and running from the one she had.

There in the car alone, she prayed to her God. "Oh, Lord, You have chosen to give me life when I had no life. You have chosen me to serve You. You know me Oh, Lord and my heart. Send me, Oh Lord, Send me. Thank You for each day. It is for You that I live, and it is for You that I am willing to die. May your will be done in everything I do and everything I say. In the name of my Savior and Lord Jesus Christ, I pray it all. Amen."

She sat quietly a few more minutes trying to make sense of the tornado and an encounter with the Holy One. She had no idea where the Lord was taking her, but she was a twenty-two-year-old woman who was willing to make the journey. She started north again on Highway 63 with a bit of "wind at her back." She had seen enough of tree-covered hills and cornfields. It was time to get to Williston, North Dakota and begin her new life. A chill ran from her neck to the small of her back as she sensed life was about to make a radical change.

Tyisha was on her way. She drove as if her life depended on it, which in fact it did. She drove through Oskaloosa, drove underneath Interstate 80, and onto Cedar Falls and Waterloo, where she stopped to get gasoline and eat a late lunch or early supper. Ty was anxious to get started again, so she took her tea to go and continued northward.

She was determined to go as many miles as possible before quitting for the day and the farms and cornfields of northern Iowa passed almost as a blur. The sun was beginning to set as she crossed the state line into

Minnesota. The adrenaline and her mind-over-matter mindset had begun to wane, so Tyisha decided to pull into a motel in Rochester, the home of the famous Mayo Brothers Clinic. Tyisha's little cousin developed leukemia when she was only three years old, and Ty's uncle had taken her to the Mayo Clinic in hope of saving her life. It was too late, and Ty's cousin had tragically died. Ty had often wondered if her uncle had become so hard and cruel after the loss of his daughter. She didn't know and at risk of arrest, she wasn't ever going back to Suzie, Alabama to ask him.

Exhausted, she pulled into a roadside motel, rented a room and went straight to her room. She decided to forego supper, since sleep was sorely needed. Ty didn't even take her shoes off, before falling across the bed. She was asleep and snoring before she pulled the cover over her.

***

To say Tyisha was anxious to get going is an understatement. She was already checked out of her room and on the road by 5:00 a.m. and enjoyed the rising sun to the east. She found Highway 52 on the north side of Rochester and drove northeastward in route to the Twin Cities. She finally arrived at Cannon Falls, Minnesota where she topped her tank with gasoline and went to a restaurant for a quick bite to eat. As she was eating, she realized she had not eaten the previous night and paid for an order of eggs with bacon to take with her.

Back on the road, she entered St. Paul from the south and merged on Highway 10 on the northern side of the Minnesota state capital. On several overlooks of the Mississippi River, she quickly realized how diminutive the river was in central Minnesota. Tyisha could not believe this was the same river she had crossed at Memphis, Tennessee.

Driving northwestward, Ty finally crossed the Mississippi River at Little Falls, Minnesota. Highway 10 diminished into a two-lane highway past Little Falls, but Tyisha chose to stay on Highway 10.

She had never seen so much beauty. Lakes and rivers were everywhere. The scenery had almost lulled her into a trance as she watched a waterfall when she came around one of the few curves. In a particularly wooded area on the side of the highway a black bear with her two cubs sauntered in front of Ty. Ty hit her brakes and could not control her car. The trailer whipped violently from side to side. When she finally got the car to stop,

Café con Leche

she looked back to see the mother and her cubs had not altered their course and were entering the woods on the other side of the highway.

"Thank you, Lord, that there was nothing coming on the highway and your angels are riding with me. Without them, I would have surely wrecked, but I am safe as are the little bears. May I continue safely on toward the ministry You have given to me."

Tyisha drove her car onto the shoulder and looked at her hands that were stuck to the steering wheel like they had been glued there. She tried to remove them, but she was shaking like she had during and following the tornado. She sat there in her car for a few minutes more, before she could exit her car and walk to the nearby waterfall. The fresh air did her good and she dipped her face into the cold water of the stream. Within minutes she was feeling refreshed and thanked God for the bears that had nearly caused her to wreck her car.

With the near wreck behind her, she continued on northwestward on Highway 10 with a slight tremor still in her hands. By Lincoln, Minnesota Tyisha's nervous condition was a former state and she returned to being awed by the natural beauty of north-central Minnesota. It was afternoon, but Tyisha drove on. The towns flew by-Wadena, Frazee, and Detroit Lakes. It was late afternoon when Tyisha entered Moorhead, Minnesota from the east. She crossed over the Red River of the North into Fargo, North Dakota. She had read about the river since it was a rare river flowing northward into Canada. Most of the rivers in North Dakota and Minnesota flowed south, but not the Red River.

In West Fargo, North Dakota Tyisha pulled her car into a gas station. While the attendant filled her gas station, she went into the office of the station and bought a bag of potato chips and a bag of peanuts out of a vending machine. Next to the machine was a cola machine which required the purchaser to put in his or her quarter in the machine before it would allow the removal of a bottle of soda. Tyisha bought a Grape Nehi guiding it through the labyrinth to the opening of the machine. After paying the attendant, Tyisha got on Interstate 94 and headed westward. The Interstate went all the way west to Montana and Ty would love to have driven as far as she had to go, but her body and mind were not willing. There were still a couple of hours of daylight left in the day, but Ty decided she would drive as far as Valley City, North Dakota and spend the night there.

A sign on the Interstate about three miles from the exit to Valley City advertised a hotel in the center of the town. It sounded like it was worth investigating, so Ty drove across the Sheyenne River "The City of Bridges." For a moment, Ty thought she was home again. The river did not flow, it oozed.

The center of the town was just ahead, but her lane was totally blocked. There were people stopping their cars in front of her and many others were parked on the side of the street. She was clearly not going any further until the cars ahead of her moved, so Ty pulled her Oldsmobile as far to the right as possible and decided to go forward on foot to see why the traffic had stagnated. Only a narrow lane could move in the middle of the street.

Tyisha had noticed that people in Iowa and Minnesota had pretended not to stare, but they could not help themselves. She concluded that they looked at her with curiosity since she was not blonde-haired and blue-eyed, like so many she had met in the last couple of days. She wasn't sure whether she liked the stares of curiosity more or less than the apathy she had experienced growing up in the south where many did not even acknowledge her existence.

Walking toward the center of Valley City, Ty saw a large group of people gathering ahead. When she reached them, she asked in her southern accent, "Can someone tell me why the street is nearly blocked?"

A young woman, in a typical Nordic accent replied, "Every year, some of da Negro children from Chicago come here and spend da summer with local farm families. Many of us never seen a Negro so some drive for miles just to see dem. Dey is supposed to arrive any minute."

Holding her tongue, Tyisha did not reply as she wanted to: "Well, you are looking at one of dem."

With her long, semi-straight hair, peanut butter skin and green eyes from her mother, high cheek bones and medium width nose from her father, she could pass for a mix of Mandan Sioux Indian and a white European from the "Peace Garden State."

Tyisha was not an expert on the Mandan Sioux peoples, but she did recall reading about the Lewis and Clark expedition. William Clark's father had a slave simply known as "York" who Mr. Clark had willed to his son, William. Captain Clark had made York a full member of the expedition, but he never received pay.

Café con Leche

The Mandan Sioux tribe had agreed to allow the Lewis and Clark expedition to live and work on the far side of the Missouri River from one of their main villages. Not only did they tolerate the presence of the Europeans, but they also helped to feed them and protect them. The Mandan leaders became fascinated by York's black skin and attributed great spiritual power to him. Because some of the local folks confused Tyisha with a Mandan Sioux Indian, she would let them, but never deny her heritage if confronted. Maybe the Mandan Sioux tribe was right about York's black skin. Her faith and spiritual growth were the result of her affiliation with blacks.

Tyisha nearly ran back to her parked car and after several attempts, she was able to turn it around and head back to the access to Interstate 94. Tyisha had completed almost a quarter mile of her retreat when she saw four buses coming toward her. She pulled as far to the right side of the lane left by other parked cars, and the buses passed without slowing down. Tyisha looked up at the buses as they passed at the little black children, some looking scared and others expectant. As the last bus passed, Tyisha said to herself, "The zoo on wheels is coming to entertain all of those fine white folks." Just for a moment, Tyisha had a sudden affiliation with the black race. It took her a few minutes, but she calmed herself and remembered that the Lord Jesus Christ died for all men with no regard as to their race. He loved the little white children on the side of the street as much as He loved the little black children on the buses. Her anger subsided and she realized its source-Satan. Tyisha was on her way to start a ministry to children in western North Dakota and they were white.

She went west to the 8th Street exit and continued north toward the location of the hotel. When she finally arrived at the hotel, and got out of her car, Ty discovered huge mosquitoes. When she told the clerk at the hotel about the mosquitoes, he responded, "So, I see you have met our state bird." He thought he told the funniest joke of the day and laughed at his own attempt at humor.

Ty took her bag up to her room on the second floor of the hotel, locked the door, and walked down the street to a "mom and pop" restaurant a couple of blocks away. She had looked at her highway maps and was sure she could finish her trip the next day.

She started feeling another adrenaline rush overwhelming her and decided to go for a walk before going to bed. She crossed the street and followed Central Avenue south to the place it terminated at 4th Street. Just across the intersection was a footbridge across the Sheyenne River to the campus of Valley City State College. Tyisha decided to walk across the river to the campus and walk around a bit, so she crossed the river, looking down at the brown water filled with alluvial soils. She might have stayed longer, but the mosquitoes were becoming intolerable. Tyisha decided to forego the planned tour of the campus and walked back the way she had come to her hotel room. A deep and restful sleep was not far behind. She was only a day from the beginning of her new life.

***

The rays of the morning sun slowly broke over the eastern edge of the Sheyenne River valley and brought Tyisha to her feet. She quickly showered and dressed and checked out of the hotel. She decided she would go westward as soon as possible, so she accessed Interstate 94 and drove toward Montana.

Ahead on the hill above the exit to Jamestown, North Dakota stood a huge statue of an American bison, a symbol of a nearly eradicated species. Ty pulled into the town and bought gas for her car and ate a good breakfast.

Back on Interstate 94, Tyisha came to the twin cities of Bismarck and Mandan, North Dakota. To Tyisha, growing up in southern Alabama, every snake was poisonous. She had seen cottonmouths and rattlesnakes all around her grandfather's farm and especially near the river. But, according to some of her research, there were only poisonous snakes west of the Missouri River and none east of the river. She did not know if this bit of trivia was fact or fiction, but she hoped she would not have to find out.

Bismarck was named after the German chancellor by the same name and had been made the first capital of the Dakota Territory including both North and South Dakota. When North Dakota became a state, Bismarck became the capital of the new state.

The plains and wheat fields of the eastern part of the state quickly changed to a drier and more desolate environment. Ty had never seen a butte, but they became more prevalent the further west she drove. She

Café con Leche

could feel a sense of excitement now. It seemed she had driven more than the miles from southern Alabama; she was driving to a new life.

Pulling into Dickinson, North Dakota, Tyisha topped off her gas tank one last time and bought three candy bars for the last leg of her journey. Ty caught herself speeding more than once and had to slow down, despite her desire to get to her final destination, Williston, North Dakota. When she reached the junction with Highway 85, she left Interstate 94 for the last time. Driving north, she passed through the savannah plains prevalent in eastern Montana and western North Dakota. The highway was normally flat and straight, so when Tyisha could see well in front of her, she often drove up to seventy or even eighty miles per hour. After a couple of "political curves," those artificial ninety-degree curves around the property of a wealthy or influential landowner, Tyisha finally entered Williston on the north banks of the Missouri River. Williston sat on one of the most northern points of that long tributary of the Mighty Mississippi.

She had arrived and her exhaustion was replaced by an excitement over the possibilities. Finding a room for the night was secondary and she was willing to spend the night in her car, if need be. Her stomach was rolling, so she opted to eat her last candy bar and planned to have a full meal in the morning.

Tyisha was becoming tired of sleeping and waking up in a motel room and she was looking forward to finding a small house to call home. She hung up her clothes and placed her suitcase on a stand in the corner of her last motel room. Lying across her bed, she read Matthew 18:14, "Even so it is not the will of your Father which is in heaven, that one of these little ones should perish."

She was a teacher, a noble profession, and one she felt a ministry ordained by God. She had been called of God to uplift and train her students to succeed in an inhospitable world. The Lord had literally helped her re-commit to the ministry ahead and she could not wait to begin.

The long arduous trip from Tuskegee had cost her roughly $640.00, leaving her $3160.00 in her account. She would need much of it to pay for a rental and any deposits, including the cost of living until her first paycheck. How had Aunt Lizzie known just how much she would need years later? Only the Lord could have used Aunt Lizzie to prepare and guide Tyisha in the way He would have her go.

As Ty drifted off to a peaceful sleep, she had a sense that her restlessness was finally waning, an anxiety she had carried with her since childhood. She was home! She had that rare feeling that she was exactly where the Lord wanted her to be and exactly when He wanted her to be there. A life of torment was becoming a life of atonement (at-One-ment) with her God, and she liked it.

CHAPTER 6

She didn't awaken to a new place or in a new room; Tyisha awoke to a new life. After weeks of waiting, she was finally here in Williston, North Dakota. Surely there would be no racial prejudice here.

After a wholesome breakfast of eggs, bacon strips, and a couple of sausage patties at a local restaurant, Tyisha went to one of the real estate offices listed in the local phone book. The lady in the second office looked around the door frame when Ty entered the door. There was no receptionist.

"Can I help you?"

"Ma'am, I am new here and looking for a place to rent. Do you have any local listings?"

"You came to the right place. We service several local homeowners and rental owners. We take a small percentage of the total monthly rent and in return, we keep the property rented, clean it and make it presentable to the next renter. Let me show you a few of our listings in the Williston area. By the way, I am Lydia."

Lydia reached behind her on a table inside her office and came back out to the front office and placed a Rolodex on a desk near where Tyisha was standing.

"I am going to be the newest teacher at the Redeemer's Salvation School. Do you know where it is located?"

"I should. I am a member of the church. Christian Christensen is the headmaster and he's a member of our church. You should come to our church since it is one of the few 'Spirit-filled' churches in Williston. We would love to have you worship with us. We meet in the gymnasium of your school.

I don't have an appointment until 2:00 p.m. this afternoon. Let me take you and show you a few rentals in driving range of your school."

"Lydia, I have nothing but time. By the way, I am Tyisha."

"Wonderful! Your school is located near Chinaman Coulee northeast of town, and I have two or three rental properties on that side of town. Come and ride with me."

Ty had no idea what a "coulee" was, but she was sure she was going to find out. She had never heard the term in the south.

Lydia grabbed her purse and car keys and the two walked to the front of the building and entered Lydia's Lincoln Continental. Lydia first drove them to a four-unit apartment building on 42nd Street East. To be polite, Ty looked at the apartment, but did not have any desire to live in a building reminiscent of her college dormitory.

Using a great deal of subterfuge, Ty hinted that she was really looking for a stand-alone house. She was not predisposed to take on the upkeep of a yard in south Alabama where one might be mowing the lawn for ten months of the year. But in North Dakota, it was unlikely she would be mowing over three or four months a year.

"I have a listing of a small house with a nominal size yard about three miles from your school. Would you like to look?"

"Sure. I am sure I have more time than do you."

They drove the gargantuan car to a little single-story house with a wheat field behind it. It literally sat on 22nd Street West near the western edge of Williston. It was quiet, and the yard was a manageable size for one person. As they went through the front door, Ty was instantly impressed with the floor plan. The kitchen and living room were divided by an arched doorway. The only bedroom was large with several windows and the bathroom just down the hall was large and had a bathtub, something Ty had always wanted. She had been forced to wash in a shower, but only after her uncle

Café con Leche

had finished his shower. There were several closets and even a small room for a clothes washer, but no dryer. In the back of the house, were two "T" poles in the ground with wires stretched between them, for drying clothes.

"How much are they asking per month for this house?" Ty was afraid to hear the answer since her total monthly salary was only $620.

"The lady who owns this house is the widow of our deceased Presbyterian minister. She told me only last week that she is willing to rent it for $100 per month for a Christian who would care for it and serve our Lord. Tyisha, you are that person."

"Lydia, we don't have to look further. This is the house for me. Can you please contact the owner and arrange for us to meet?"

"Let's go back to the office and I will call her from there, okay?"

"Let's go!"

As they drove, Lydia renewed her invitation to Ty, asking that she come and get involved in her church. Ty agreed to come to worship with her and her congregation the following Sunday.

Once back at the office, Lydia telephoned the old widow.

"Mrs. Edgerton, I have a lady here who would like to rent your house. She is a Christian and will be teaching at the Redeemer's Salvation School this year. She would love to meet you. Is that good for you?"

"Honey, you know it is. I have been praying the Lord would send me the right person and I trust you to bring me that person. Lydia, how about we meet at East Lawn Park at 5:00 p.m.? Is that good for you?"

Tyisha shook her head in approval and Lydia replied, "We'll see you then."

***

Lydia recognized Mrs. Edgerton's old car and saw it parked on the side of Reclamation Drive on the northeast side of East Lawn Park. She pulled her car alongside Mrs. Edgerton's and the two ladies, with young Miss Tyisha McFarren walked to a park bench nearby.

"That's an unusual name, 'Tyisha.' Is that a Mandan name?"

"No, Ma'am. My mother was a southern woman and my father, whom I never knew, was a black man. 'Tyisha' means 'alive and well' in Arabic and was a common name in Atlanta, Georgia where I was born. You can just call me 'Ty' like everyone else."

Lydia had given Mrs. Edgerton a thumb-nail-sketch of Ty's background, but it was obvious Mrs. Edgerton wanted some answers to her own questions.

"Young lady, are you a Christian?"

"Yes, Mrs. Edgerton, I am saved by the blood of the Lamb and baptized all the way under the waters of Chewacla Creek north of Tuskegee, Alabama. Ma'am, I am here to do more than simply teach. The Lord has opened this ministry for me, and He has promised to be with me every day.

I believe He drew me to your house, and it seems to be perfect for me. As you probably know, this is my first professional position after college, and I don't have much money. I promise to be a conscientious and meticulous renter and to always pay my rent in a timely fashion."

"Now, Ty, my daughter will go over there and clean the floors and make sure everything is ready for a new renter. Can you move in day after tomorrow?"

"Oh, thank you, Mrs. Edgerton. If you don't mind, can I give you the first month's rent and get a key from you, so I can go through the house and get an idea regarding the furniture I need to buy?"

"Sure, you can, Ty." Mrs. Edgerton moved toward Lydia and Tyisha and hugged both women. "Sisters, I sense we are all here to do the will of God. Lydia, I want to thank you for finding such a fine young renter. Tyisha, I cannot thank you enough for coming to us to teach our children the Word of God. I feel like I am helping to accomplish the will of our Lord.

Here is the key to the house, Ty, and you can move in any time after tomorrow. Is that good for you?

"Oh, yes, Mrs. Edgerton." Tyisha went into her purse and got her check book. She wrote a check for the rent to Mrs. Edgerton and the ladies all parted company.

On the way back to the real estate office where Ty's car was parked, Lydia reinforced that Ty would always be welcome at the church meeting at the Redeemer's Salvation School. Ty promised to see Lydia at the church worship service the following Sunday as she got out of Lydia's car and into her own. The two ladies agreed to meet before worship on Sunday in front of the school/church.

When Sunday morning came, the two ladies sat together and partook of the Bible study that preceded the worship service. Tyisha recognized at once that the hymns were not the ones she had sung as a child in the Deep South, but the theology was compatible. The old man in the front of the sanctuary and his periodic outbursts were distracting, but not intolerable. At the end of the service, Lydia introduced Ty to many of the congregants as "our newest teacher." Most simply thought she was some mixture of Mandan Sioux and something else, but never guessed she was mulatto. She was treated warmly by the local Christians and thought she might really like this place.

***

Each small town has its share of "special people." Williston, North Dakota was no different. Most people gave these persons a wide berth on the street or treated them as if they did not exist. They were an irritant to most people and present in almost every local institution.

The Williams County Poor Farm was located five miles north of Williston on the same road as the Redeemer's Salvation Church, so the manager brought his charges every Sunday to the nearby church. Besides, for three hours, he and his wife got a break away from the high-need residents.

One of the older men was obviously suffering from coprolalia, or uncontrolled cursing. Johnny Noles by name, he would sit directly in front of the pulpit and curse non-stop throughout the pastor's sermon. Most of the long-term congregants had grown use to the eccentricities of the "special member" and paid no attention to his outbursts in the worship service.

The children in the congregation would sit in the back of the sanctuary and play "hangman" or "tic-tac-toe." When Johnny Noles was present in the worship service, the children dropped all other distractions and started watching his antics. Johnny would pull out his pocketknife, open it and insert the blade into his left ear and twist it to remove ear wax. The children would let out an audible "ooh" halfway expecting to see the point of the blade exit the right ear.

Another "special member" was Mr. Tony Bilson. Tony was one of many who had been injured during childbirth by a doctor too anxious to use forceps. He had sustained a slow blood bleed in his cranium that had affected both eyes, but his left eye more than the other. Light coming into the dark sanctuary obscured any image, so he would roll up his left hand like a telescope to focus the image and block out any light.

One afternoon, as Tyisha sat in her car in front of the Post Office, she sensed someone was staring at her. She looked left, and less than six inches away, Tony had his hand rolled up and pressed against the glass. After he had recognized who was in the car, he pecked on the glass and warmly waved at her. Tyisha, though initially frightened, recognized Mr. Bilson and returned his wave. The old gentleman sauntered down the street in his halting gate.

Tony and Johnny and some other residents at the Poor Farm hitchhiked into Williston each day and took up their positions at major street corners. They spent hours waving at passersby car drivers and yelling at those they personally knew. They whistled at others. Sometimes, they would approach drivers and offer to clean their windshields with the same rag they had used on ten previous cars. Most of the residents of Williston knew the residents of the Poor Farm and had a great deal of tolerance for them. They would kindly agree to the offer and give the men a quarter for their effort.

Only a few weeks after Tyisha had arrived, Tony had been making his daily vigil to his corner in Williston and had stepped in front of an oncoming car. He was killed instantly. Tyisha had known the old man with the terrible eyesight only four weeks, but she cried at the loss of the old man who had recognized her in Williston. Tyisha went to his funeral at their church with the ten other local folks who would miss Tony.

Fortunately, the cemetery was directly across the road from the school/church and was on level ground. Since the funeral director had difficulty finding six pallbearers, Tony's casket remained on a flat casket trolley and wheeled across the road for the graveside ceremony. After saying a few words about Tony and his impact on all four of those that had made the trip to the graveside, the pastor read I Thessalonians 4:13-18 emphasizing "For the Lord himself shall descend from heaven with a shout, with the voice of the archangel, and with the trump of God: and the dead in Christ shall rise first." He assured those gathered at the graveside that they would all see Tony again, but his vision would be perfect. After a short prayer, the entire group filed away toward their cars in the school parking lot, all except Tyisha.

Café con Leche

After the others had departed, four large men from the funeral home came to the hole that had been dug for the casket and lowered the casket across two large wooden beams lain across the hole. The men draped two ropes around the casket inside the beams and began to lower the casket. The smallest of the four men dropped his rope end and the casket fell into the hole with a crash. Nearly in unison, the four men looked around to see if anyone had seen their faux pas. Tyisha was behind a large tree and not in their direct line of sight, so they assumed they had not been seen.

The leader of the crew said to the others, "That crazy old man never did know which end was up." They all laughed and hurriedly started throwing dirt on top of the casket leaning against the wall of the hole.

Ty watched from the confines of a tree and secretly cried. Even Tony, with his diminished intellect and poor vision, deserved more respect than these men were giving him. When they had finished, they walked away one way to their van, and she walked the other to the only car left in the school parking lot.

***

When she arrived home, she called her friend and sister, Lydia. "Lydia, remember we were supposed to go out and eat together tonight?

"Sure, Sis, I was going to get ready in a minute."

"Lydia, I just came from a funeral, and I just don't feel like going anywhere tonight. Would you be offended if we went another night?"

"We can go anytime you want. You know I just want to be with you when you want me there. I will try to always be here for you, and I am sure there will be times you need a friend. Call me when you feel up to going somewhere together. I'll talk to you later and see you at church on Sunday."

"Thanks, Lydia, I'll be calling. See you Sunday."

After Lydia hung up the phone, Tyisha made herself a ham sandwich with real mayonnaise. She sat down and ate her sandwich and drank her soda on a TV tray in front of her little 13" black and white television. She was melancholy after her day and could not imagine how her fellow man had so little respect for the most disabled among us.

***

Some dates and times just seem to change the course of the rest of our lives. Such was June 5, 1968. Tyisha sat eating her ham sandwich when the station out of Bismarck was interrupted by a news announcer who had tears in his eyes. He said that the network was just getting word from its Los Angeles bureau that Robert Kennedy had just been shot and killed after speaking to a crowd in the Ambassador Hotel. It was too early to know the details. Mr. Kennedy was a candidate for President and had just won the California presidential primary.

Tyisha bowed her head and cried. This young man seemed to be the one to end the Vietnam War, to calm the racial turmoil, and to encourage Tyisha's generation which seemed to have lost its faith in the future of America. Now, he, like his brother, was gone and all of the hope associated with him was dead.

Suddenly, in her sadness, Tyisha realized that the hope of mankind was not in a man, but in their Creator. Robert Kennedy's death was just another example of the depravity of man and reminded her that God had loved her and all of those that called on Him. He had sent his own Son to bring salvation to them and she was one of those that had been bestowed with this greatest of gifts.

After a fitful night, she awoke and listened to the details pertaining to the assassination of Robert Kennedy. It seems a Palestinian man named Sirhan Sirhan had shot Mr. Kennedy numerous times with a .22 caliber pistol. Two huge men, Roosevelt Grier and Rafer Johnson, had escorted Mr. Kennedy from the ballroom and through the kitchen where he was killed. Five other bystanders were also shot.

Tyisha began to cry in earnest and her tears literally dripped from her chin into a cup of coffee she was holding. She knew, intellectually, that the loss of any man was not the end of mankind. But Ty couldn't control her tears. She had placed so much hope in this man that his loss was overwhelming. The tears started to flow again, as she felt guilty. She had placed more hope in a man than in her Savior.

"Oh Father, forgive me for without intending to do so I have had another god and placed him before You. Forgive that young man, Sirhan Sirhan. May he know your love and your grace and come to know your salvation through your Son, Jesus Christ.

Café con Leche

Father, prepare me to serve You. May I make my students know my love for You and in so doing, let them be changed and prepared to serve You in their own lives. I haven't taught a day of school or even met the students, but already I know You are preparing me for some future service to You. Your will be done in my life."

CHAPTER 7

Ring, ring, ring. The alarm clock's bells awakened Tyisha at 5:00 a.m., much to her chagrin. Her quiet house, surrounded on two sides by a wheat field, was conducive to a good night's sleep.

Tyisha drug herself out of bed and headed toward the bathroom. Slowly, she took a bath and fixed her hair. It was wavy, but not difficult to brush. After completing her attire with a pair of blue jeans, a white cotton blouse, and a pair of low-cut Converse deck shoes, she felt ready to go out into the world.

Most of the Christian schools in the upper Midwest states and Mountain states mandated their new teachers attend a teacher's meeting the summer before the school year began. In 1968, the teacher's meeting was scheduled to be conducted in Rapid City, South Dakota. Mr. Christensen, the school headmaster, had promised the school would pay back all expenses Tyisha incurred for attending the teacher's meeting.

Williston, North Dakota had become unbelievably small and isolated over the past month. Tyisha had gone to a local fair, driven to Bismarck to see a movie and a lunch at a local restaurant, and even gone as far as Lake Sakakawea to do some walleye fishing. She had heard about the legendary fish but had never had the opportunity to capture one in Alabama. Since most of the local population thought she was some mixture of white and

Café con Leche

Mandan Sioux, she had decided to explore the Fort Berthold Reservation. Tyisha would never forget her chance meeting with an old man with long white hair sitting in front of a general store. She had pulled in to fill her gas tank when he said to her, "Sister, you look allot like my mother." Tyisha thought she had been complimented and thanked the old man.

Yes, the teacher's training was coming at just the right time and Ty had planned well for it. She had filled her car's gas tank and packed her travel bag the day before. The car was loaded, and she was underway by 6:15 a.m.

Driving south on Highway 85, Tyisha rolled down her windows and unfurled her brown wavy hair. It was late July and the high temperatures had been 80 degrees, invigorating to someone who had been raised in southern Alabama.

Occasionally, she saw a mound higher than the badlands of southwestern North Dakota. Known to the local folks as "buttes," they were barely more than mole hills, and the plains seemed to go on forever. Even White Butte, the highest point in North Dakota, was barely noticeable from Highway 85.

The buttes became more prevalent in South Dakota. The bright red sides in the late afternoon sunlight and the verdant green pine trees on the flat tops, made what had been mundane, beautiful and Ty recognized the Creator's hand. Ahead of her was a large looming storm cloud as she hurried toward Spearfish, South Dakota on the northern edge of the Black Hills. The further south she went, the darker the gloom of an approaching storm and the more frequent the buttes.

Ahead, Tyisha could see the town of Spearfish and finally recognized that what she had thought was an impending storm was the famous Black Hills. They rose straight out of the plains and were covered with dark green pine forests.

It was nearly 5:00 p.m. and Tyisha had been driving nearly the entire time except to obtain a small meal and gasoline for her car. She pulled into a family-style restaurant in Spearfish and decided to rest as well as to eat her last meal of the day. She believed she was only about an hour from Rapid City where the organizers of the teacher's meetings had reserved her room. Tyisha checked into her hotel in Rapid City and laid her bags inside her room. She was so tired, even after her respite in Spearfish, that she took a quick shower and went directly to bed. In the midst of her nightly prayer praising God and thanking Him for a safe journey, she dozed into a deep and rejuvenating sleep.

***

Finally, the time had come for the much-awaited teacher's meeting. Tyisha arose, dressed and went to a nearby bakery by 7:15 a.m. She bought an éclair and ate it as she returned to her hotel where seven buses were waiting outside in the parking lot. They had been leased for the precise purpose of transporting over 200 Christian teachers to the meeting approximately ten minutes away. The meetings were scheduled to begin with a general assembly in a high school gym and then the participants were to break up into smaller groups in some of the high school classrooms.

The buses pulled in the semi-circular drive in front of the high school. From her vantage on the fourth bus, she watched the other participants disembark from the preceding three buses. Most were about her age, one was black, the vast majority was white and female, but there was one young man that immediately caught her eye. He walked directly below her window seat on the bus. He was well over six feet tall, 235 lbs. and possessed an athletic physique. Tyisha knew she shouldn't look again at the young man but couldn't help herself. The young man was her male twin. He had wavy brown hair, blue eyes, dark skin though not black, and average facial features somewhere between white and black bone structure.

Tyisha continued watching out the window interrupted only by a lady who stopped in the aisle by her. "Miss, are you getting out?" The lady continued to wait for Tyisha to get out in the aisle and move forward to the front door of the bus. Quickly Tyisha regained her sense of surroundings and walked out of the bus and into the gymnasium with the other new teachers. On a table next to the main entrance to the gym were hundreds of nameplates, one for each of the participants. Tyisha put hers on her lapel and continued to a free seat near the front of the stage. There, three rows forward and four seats over was the source of her attention. The young man stared back at Tyisha. She had been caught! She decided to catch another quick glimpse, and when she did the young man was smiling back at her. He, too, had attempted a quick glimpse.

After two guest speakers told the group that their children were gifts from God and had been placed in their care for a short time, they gave the

Café con Leche

crowd their first twenty-minute break of the day. Before Ty could stand up, a young man stood next to her and said, "Hello, Ms. Tyisha (as he looked at her lapel.) I am Jeremiah Hall representing the Savior's Christian School in Pierre, South Dakota. Would you be willing to eat supper with me tonight?"

"My, Mr. Hall, you certainly are forward. Why, I could be married or engaged to be so. Don't you think you might want to know a little more about me? For instance, I am a born-again Christian and do not date anyone who is not."

"A young bi-racial man in southern Alabama has most paths blocked. I learned when I was young to trust God and to follow Him through every door that was open. May your fears be allayed. I, too, am a born-again Christian and have been since my freshman year in college. Now, will you eat supper with me tonight?"

Tyisha thought a moment and replied, "I normally would be reluctant to go anywhere with a total stranger, but somehow, I think you may know more about my walk with the Lord than most folks. Okay, let's go eat tonight at 7:00 p.m. at DiCarlo's Ristorante. So, we can afford the cost, we will each pay for our meals. (Tyisha had done her homework and had planned to eat at the renowned restaurant long before she had met Jeremiah.) I am in Room 212, so you can come to the room to pick me up."

Jeremiah looked at the floor sheepishly. "Just one problem, I rode here with another teacher from my school and have no car."

"That is not a problem. I drove down here, so come by the room and we will drive to the restaurant. See you then."

Tyisha walked away trying to be nonchalant. She could feel Jeremiah watching her all the way out of the gymnasium.

The next five hours consisted of a meal provided by the organizers in the high school cafeteria and another twenty-minute break in the afternoon. Tyisha endured the day's scheduled events with her mind solely on the night to follow. She had detected a southern black drawl in Jeremiah's speech, but she was unsure as to its origin.

***

It was 6:45 p.m. and Jeremiah could wait no longer. He had been dressed for his date with Tyisha since 6:00 p.m. and had set at the only table in his little hotel room for the past forty-five minutes. Jeremiah's high school football coach had made famous a saying, "If you ain't ten minutes early, you're late!" Jeremiah justified his early arrival at Room 212 by telling himself he was only applying the wisdom of his old high school coach.

Knock, knock, knock, Jeremiah rapped his knuckles on the door of Tyisha's room. Before he could lower his right hand from the action, the door opened, and Tyisha stood before him. She must have been awaiting his arrival just inside the door.

"Come on, slowpoke, let's go eat. I'm starving."

Tyisha nearly skipped down the hall toward the exit nearest her car, with Jeremiah attempting to catch up. Although Jeremiah offered to drive, she made it clear that she was quite capable of driving "her" car and got in on the driver's side. They drove toward the restaurant, chitchatting about small topics-the spokespersons of the day and how the ideas presented could be applied to their classrooms. All along, they withheld the more profound topics for the mandatory post-meal discussion.

Jeremiah had made a reservation at the popular restaurant and when they entered, they were led to a table far too near the public restrooms. He saw the disappointment evident in Tyisha's face and Jeremiah immediately asked the maître d' cuisine if they could be seated "closer to a window with a view of the Black Hills?" The maître d' immediately complied, and they were led to a window on the west side of the building watching the sun go down over the nearby hills.

Their waiter approached them and took their drink orders; she asked for sweet iced tea and he ordered the same. To avoid an unnecessary trip by the waiter, they proceeded to order their meals. Since they were in beef country, Tyisha asked for an 8 oz. rib-eye steak with a loaded baked potato and a small chef salad. Jeremiah ordered a monster hamburger with cheese and a loaded potato on the side.

The waiter no more than walked out of earshot and Jeremiah looked at Tyisha and said, "So, Miss Tyisha, where do you call home?"

"I'm not like some of the folks I have known-unsure where to call home. I was raised in Suzie, Alabama down near the junction of Alabama, Florida, and Georgia. When I was a child, my mother raised me in Atlanta until she was near death from cancer, and she moved us back to Suzie. After my mother's death, my grandparents raised me in Suzie where I

Café con Leche

attended a segregated black school until I went to college at Tuskegee. While I was in school, they were both killed in a car accident. My uncle calls me a 'black bastard.' I guess this is because my father was black, but I have no idea where or who he is.

My best friend when I was a child was an old woman named 'Aunt Lizzie Mitchell.' She was wonderful to me and helped me accumulate the money to both go to college and take my first job. I am here because she believed in me and helped me every step of the way.

But my life has been most affected by my mentor when I was student teaching. Miss Jorgina Boudoir had been personally involved in the civil rights marches in Alabama and knew Dr. King. But her greatest attribute was she walked with our Savior every day and she shared the Lord with me. The Lord has led me to a new life, one with hope and a future. I never believed tomorrow would be better than today when I was a child-maybe only survivable. The Lord has shown me that He has a plan for my life and right now, it is to love my students and show them the Lord that Miss Jorgina lived before me. She was killed in Alabama in a car accident, but I will never forget her or the Lord she introduced to me.

Now, you know something of me, tell me your story."

The waiter returned with their meals and Jeremiah looked at Tyisha, winked, and said, "Let's eat first. You are going to be surprised at how much our lives have overlapped."

After the meals were placed before the couple, Jeremiah instinctively bowed his head and said, "Miss Tyisha please bow with me."

Tyisha complied as Jeremiah ardently prayed to their God. "Father, I have heard and felt some of the pain Tyisha has exposed to me this night. Guide my response to her. Let her hear my heart, my walk with You and my hopes of serving You in the future. Now, bless the food before us and our fellowship. In the name of our Lord, Jesus Christ, I pray it. AMEN."

Looking up from the heartfelt words, Tyisha saw two small tears in the corners of Jeremiah's eyes. He put up his finger to his lips signifying silence. "Let's eat a moment and then I will tell you anything you want to know about me." They ate their meals almost in silence, but Tyisha's interest only intensified. Who was this mysterious young man to whom Tyisha was drawn like no man in her history? Why were his words and more importantly his drawl so familiar to her? What caused his tears?

No more than they had taken their last bites of their meals, the waiter appeared and asked if they would like to order any dessert. They looked at each other and then both declined. The waiter walked away.

"Don't make me wait any longer. Tell me your life story, especially about your speech and why it is so familiar."

"Miss Tyisha, how would you like me to address you?"

"Jeremiah, just call me 'Ty' like most folks do."

"Well, as you can plainly see, I am half white and half black. But though your mother was white, and father was black, my mother is black and my father was white.

My father was a football legend in Madisonville, Alabama and still holds most of the records for sprints, basketball and football touchdowns scored at the local high school. He was ranked as the number one prospect in football in Alabama his senior year. He accepted a scholarship from Syracuse University 'Orangemen' to play football the following year. He did well in his first two years on the team, but in his third year a defensive back hit his knee from the side and broke it. His football career was over.

Dad had been dating my mother for over a year, but they had never told her parents or my father's parents. My mother's compassion for my father helped him adjust to a life devoid of football. Although he had been a Christian since childhood, it was her obvious love for him that led him back to serving the Lord. They realized they had more than just lust for one another. They were in love. A couple of months beyond a surgery on his knee, they went across the Niagara River and were married in 1942 in Canada. They returned to Syracuse on the shores of Lake Onondaga and my dad finished his B.S. degree at the university. He went on to obtain his Master of Education degree. I was born in Syracuse in 1943 and lived there until my father took a teaching position in Madisonville, Alabama in 1947. In those days, Madisonville was a hotbed of racism. One of the local ladies wrote a famous novel about it. I have no idea why my father wanted to go back there because he certainly was not a racist.

We lived there until my daddy found out he was dying with testicular cancer that had spread to his liver. That was the reason for my tears earlier. I knew you understood that grief because you lost your mother the same way. He died a horrible death and alone except for my mother and me. His family would have nothing to do with him since he had married a black

Café con Leche

woman. Those that nearly worshipped him in high school for his athletic prowess would not acknowledge his presence. He tried to keep my mother and me out of the fury that he endured every day. On several occasions, attempts were made to have him fired from his teaching position, but the President of the School Board was his friend and former fullback and had considerable sway with the rest of the Board. Even his former fullback could not stop the ravages of his cancer and we lost him when he was only thirty-six years old.

My mother had been a Christian woman who had found a home with her brethren in the local African Methodist Episcopal Zion Church. By the way, that is where I was baptized.

I had always attended school at the segregated black school but was never accepted by the teachers or other students. Fortunately, I inherited my father's athletic skills and could outrun every other student in the sixty-yard dash. It didn't make me popular with the student body, but they respected athletic achievement, and I was becoming a good halfback in football.

The constant shunning my mother had endured for years in that little racist cesspool became more than she could take. We would be walking down the sidewalk near our house and people would walk to the other side of the street rather than meet us. She was a college graduate at Syracuse University, very nearly an 'Ivy League' school, and she could find no work in Madisonville after my father died.

She took the first job she could find as a building janitor at a hospital in Columbus, Ohio. I was a high school student and joined the football team. By the time I was a senior, I was recruited by some large schools and small schools, but my heart was set on going to Syracuse like my father. I hoped and watched the stands for any scouts from Syracuse, but there were none. Then I found out Syracuse had a halfback by the name of Floyd Little and a fullback named Larry Csonka, both 'All Americans.'

It was a humbling experience for me, but God knew what I needed more than me. The University of Iowa, Clemson University and Oklahoma State University all looked closely at me, but I kept coming back to the smallest school, Alabama State University in Montgomery, Alabama. I just felt the coach, who loved to win, talked allot about religion and lived very little of it. He was offering me the kind of experience I wanted-religious without being too committed. Thank the Lord, my roommate was a "saved" man of God. So, you see we went to college only thirty miles apart. Now, you can understand why my speech is so familiar to you. I am an Alabama boy at heart.

I did well as a running back in college, but by my sophomore year I became convinced that football would likely take me little further, and football became a means to obtain my education. I received my B.S. in Education in 1967 and was hired by my school this year. My mother is still living in Ohio but would never come to see me as long as I was south of the Mason-Dixon Line. I still go see her, but now that I am living in South Dakota, I hope she will come to see me. You would love her. She has been hurt so deeply, but the Lord has healed her in so many ways.

I am teaching because that is what the Lord has provided for me now. But, for years, I have sensed the Lord wants me to serve Him in other capacities. I know He has already chosen a wife for me who will be my complement.

Now, you know something of who I am and why I asked you here tonight."

It was time for Ty to shed the tears. All those years of loneliness on her rock, of feeling that she alone had been forgotten by her peers and hated by her own family were suddenly miles away. She sat across from a man who had experienced so much of the pain she had felt. God had brought them together in this place so far from Alabama and whether she was experiencing spiritual feelings or romantic feelings she didn't know, but it felt good. There had been few times in her pitiful life when she could honestly say she felt 'happy.' This was one of those times.

Ty turned toward the window looking toward the Black Hills as the last rays of the sun filtered through the peaks. The scene was intoxicating, but the real reason for her action was to hide her tears from Jeremiah. She did not want him to think his words had caused her pain. Just the opposite, she sensed at that very first meeting that God had led her to another wayfaring sojourner that truly understood her pain and could help her heal. Becoming a Christian was just the first step in atonement, and she so wanted to be whole. She would be cautious, but she suspected Jeremiah was a cog in the wheel toward completeness.

When Ty had regained her composure and dried her eyes, she turned around and said, "Jeremiah, thank you for sharing your life with me. Your

Café con Leche

honesty is refreshing. I must tell you what I know about the will of God for my life. I have felt for some time that the Lord had something special in store for me at these meetings more than just educational theory. Who knows, this meeting may be 'something special.' It will be late by the time I get my clothes ready for tomorrow and get my shower. You have given me so much to consider. How about we meet for breakfast tomorrow morning at 7:00 a.m. and catch a quick bite at the restaurant just down the street?"

"Sure, that sounds great. I would love to eat breakfast with you."

They called to the waiter and asked for their bills. When the waiter arrived with the bills, Jeremiah grabbed them both and paid for them. Ty verbally protested, but not too loudly. They drove back to the hotel and Jeremiah exited the car first, going around to the driver's side and opened the door for Tyisha. She slowly stood up, keeping her dress over her knees.

Jeremiah closed the door of the car behind Tyisha and said, "Ty, I have thoroughly enjoyed our time together and hope we can have future experiences like tonight." Jeremiah stepped away from the car and shook Tyisha's hand. Ty stood there disappointed. She was sure Jeremiah would do something romantic: kiss her cheek or forehead, but none was forthcoming. Jeremiah turned and grabbed Tyisha in the strong embrace of a large man and kissed her hard on the lips before she could protest. He then turned and walked toward the hotel lobby.

The kiss, though not sought, was surely not unwanted. Tyisha was still standing next to her car in shock, but a good shock. She said nothing but was literally shaking like a leaf with emotion. When she regained control, she walked to Room 212 and prepared for the following day. Sleep was not easy for Ty that night. She laid in her bed thinking about the words Jeremiah had said to her at supper and asked the Lord to help her be discerning and not to allow her emotions to lead her. Emotions change with the weather, but she wanted to seek the man the Lord had prepared for her and to know the will of God for her life. It was nearly 1:30 a.m. before Tyisha went to sleep; the few hours she slept were peaceful and full of anticipation about what might lay ahead.

CHAPTER 8

Room 212 faced due east and the sun came through the cracks in the curtain on the window. As the sun rose over the plains of western South Dakota, Tyisha awakened with a sense of anticipation. She was smiling, even before she rose from her bed.

After dressing for the day, she asked the Lord to give her the words to say to Jeremiah. She asked if Jeremiah was the man who had been prepared for her since before the foundations of the world. "It is just breakfast," thought Ty, but it seemed so much more. Ty wondered if the next meal might help define the rest of her life.

The elevator door opened, and Tyisha was almost running toward the restaurant and the breakfast scheduled with Jeremiah. As she entered the restaurant, Jeremiah was sitting in a booth and stood as Tyisha arrived. She sat down in the opposite bench as Jeremiah waited for her.

"How did you sleep?"

"Well, though I did not sleep much. And you?"

"Miss Tyisha, I mean Ty, I have to tell you that last night created more questions than answers. I spent much of the night wondering what happened to cause you such pain and I love the fact Christ Jesus is the 'Great Healer' in your life."

Café con Leche

The two young teachers ordered short stacks of waffles and had a short prayer before their meal. It was 7:15 a.m. and they had to board the school bus by 7:45 a.m., so they kept the discussion light and laughed about their shared experiences at Cheaha Mountain, DeSota Canyon and Cahaba, the first permanent capital of Alabama. After eating, they walked to the bus and sat together in route to their training classes of the day.

It was a day seldom witnessed in southern Alabama. There had nearly always been a haze from the overpowering humidity from the nearby Gulf of Mexico. But today the air was fresh and clean and so clear one could see every peak of the nearby Black Hills. There was a hint of change in the air.

Neither Tyisha nor Jeremiah knew where their new relationship was going, but they both knew the Lord was their Master and they were His servants. They were determined to follow Him and seek His will.

Once inside the high school gym, they walked inside with the rest of those who had been on the bus with them. Most sat in the folding chairs setting near the right side of the stage where the speakers were scheduled to give their orations. Tyisha and Jeremiah sat at the back of the block of chairs and spoke briefly before the first speaker made his climb to the stage. Shortly after the speaker began, Jeremiah looked over at Tyisha and said, "Ty, may I hold your hand?"

Tyisha had not held the hand of her boyfriend in high school and here was a young man whom she had just met asking her to hold his hand, and in a public place no less. Slowly, Tyisha moved her left hand over toward his right hand and gently intertwined her fingers inside his. She caressed them and unabashedly massaged them. This small romantic gesture just felt right to both and they didn't care who else saw them.

"How is that for an answer to your question?"

Jeremiah did not answer, but simply smiled at Ty. He had thought his question extremely forward and did not expect she would respond as she did. He was a bit shocked and pleasantly surprised by her sign of affection.

The two listened as much as they could but found themselves whispering to one another to the chagrin of other attendees nearby. Since neither was wealthy and the meal the night before had consumed much of their per diem, they decided to eat the evening meal at a nearby fast-food restaurant.

It was early, but they both had much to discuss, so they took Tyisha's car to the nearby McDoogle's restaurant. They sat in the plastic seats mounted on the steel frames across from each other and looked in each other's eyes. Tyisha was sure the old saying was true; "eyes are the windows of the soul." For the first time in her life, she had found someone who really understood the pain of her youth. He had roots to a town less than a hundred miles from her own and had lost a parent to cancer.

After taking Ty's order, Jeremiah went to the front counter and ordered their food and drinks. Shortly, he returned with a tray and their meals. After a prayer, they looked at one another, enjoying their time together.

With her mouth half full, Ty said to Jeremiah, "Why did you come all the way to South Dakota to teach?"

"I just wanted to go anywhere north of the Mason-Dixon Line. I had lived in Ohio for a year and never felt the animosity, the hatred I felt in Madisonville.

We had a lady at Alabama State University that helped graduates with placements. She is a devout Christian, so I asked her to only consider Christian schools on my behalf. She found several Christian schools where she thought I might fit in. I finally decided to take the position offered at the Savior's Christian Elementary School. Now, you know how I got to Pierre, South Dakota."

Tyisha thought for a moment and then looked at Jeremiah. "Why couldn't we have met in Alabama? Our walk has been so similar. I am in Williston, North Dakota for nearly the same reasons.

Jeremiah, you know I want to see if the Lord wants more for us than just a couple of days at a teacher's meeting, but tomorrow at lunch, the meetings are over, and I will be driving back to North Dakota, and you will be riding back to your school in Pierre. Neither of us have the money to travel to see the other on a regular basis. I really don't know how we will continue this relationship."

"Ty, I, too, want to see where the Lord takes this relationship. He will show us His will and if He has future plans for us, He will make a way for it to mature and bloom.

Do not worry about what tomorrow holds. We are together right now and let's make the most of our time together."

Café con Leche

Tyisha agreed and they continued their very personal discussion almost oblivious of the other customers.

The young couple drove back to the hotel and left Ty's car in the parking lot. Neither was ready to go to bed, so they walked to the nearby downtown area of Rapid City. Try as they would to live for the minute, both were dreading their imminent departures.

Occasionally, as they walked hand-in-hand, they would stop to look in a store window. Suddenly, Jeremiah stopped and looked in the window of an electronic shop. There were television sets lining the back wall on two levels. But his eyes lit up as he was suddenly aware that he was looking at the answer to their problems-a display of ham radios on a shelf underneath the televisions.

One model was listed as $69.00 and was affordable for Tyisha and Jeremiah. They planned to get up the next morning and be at the store door when it opened at 8:00 a.m. Hopefully, they could still be at the last two blocks of the teacher meeting starting at 9:00 a.m. But whether they were on time or not, the purchase of ham radio units was more important than anything else at the moment.

"Ty, remember how I said my mother would not come down south of the Mason-Dixon Line? She got her license to be an amateur radio operator and I did as well. We found we could contact one another at least once a week or as called for by each situation.

While playing football in Montgomery, Alabama, I learned a saying from the personnel on the nearby Maxwell AFB. 'It is easier to get forgiveness than permission.' I already have a 'call sign' assigned by the government.

You can call me, and I can call you, all the while making application for your amateur radio license and obtain your call sign. If you ever get caught, you can always say, 'Gee, I didn't know.' Ignorance is a great defense."

***

The sun was yet to make its first appearance over the South Dakota plains when Tyisha arose. She had a strange sense of anticipation and dread at the same time. She was looking forward to seeing Jeremiah and dreading saying "Good-bye."

After dressing for the day, Tyisha packed up her luggage and locked the door to her room. As planned the previous evening, Ty and Jeremiah met at the hotel desk at 7:00 a.m. They jointly checked out and made sure the clerk billed their individual schools.

As usual, Tyisha drove her car and they arrived at the electronics store by 7:30 a.m. Jeremiah had placed his luggage in the trunk of her car, to be transferred to his fellow teacher's car when they parted company. As soon as the door opened, the blind was raised and an "open" sign was turned around, Ty and Jeremiah rushed in the door and directly to the ham radio displays. They told the clerk what they needed the units for, and the young man pointed to one that was "on sale." He felt it would meet their needs and it only cost $59.00 per set. Each bought a set and rushed to get back to their last day of teacher's meetings, arriving at the school gym at 8:55 a.m.

All through the last two blocks, they sat together, catching furtive looks at the other throughout the morning. They had only met three days earlier, and something had happened to both young lovers that neither had ever experienced-they sensed the Lord was working a great healing in both of them and they liked it.

The noon hour finally arrived, and the organizers of the teachers' meeting ended the meetings as they had begun, with prayer. The speaker asked the Lord for safe travels for all who would be going back, in some case hundreds of miles, to their schools. No more than he spoke, "I pray it all in the name of our Lord and Savior, Jesus Christ," some of the participants were already heading for the exits. For the ones with the furthest to drive, they had one goal in mind-go as far that afternoon and early evening as they could.

Ty and Jeremiah stood in an embrace that they hoped would last them until they met again. Soon all the other teachers had left the auditorium leaving them alone.

"I dreaded this moment," Jeremiah said to Ty. "But, if there is one thing we now know, it is that the Lord has more for both of us and hopefully that He has drawn us together to do His will.

I wish we had met years ago in Alabama, but we were not ready. This is the time the Lord has brought us together. We shall follow His leadership wherever He leads. I can't see where that is right now, but I want to go there with you."

Café con Leche

Tyisha, who was not a short woman, looked up at her taller love and said, "And, I with you." She had few words to say and was overwhelmed with emotion.

"Ty, my luggage is in your trunk, and I know my ride is waiting. Can I get it from you?"

As the two walked out to the parking lot, Jeremiah looked at Ty and said, "Get your ham radio hooked up and we'll call each other every night or two." They set up the radio frequency to use as they got to Ty's car.

"Okay, Ty, the clerk at the electronic store said we needed to have 'handles.' I'm 'Capital Christian.'"

"Then, I am going by "High Plains Sister."

"That suits you, Ty."

A car drove up next to them and the driver honked at Jeremiah. It was time to go, and Jeremiah took his suitcase to the trunk of the waiting car and put it in. He walked back to a Miss Tyisha, who was nearly shaking with grief.

"Don't cry Ty. If we are meant to be 'one,' the Lord shall bring us together. Now, you go and pray the Lord's will be done. I will do the same and this is not 'good-bye,' but 'hasta luego.' Jeremiah hugged Tyisha to him and knew they would have to remember this moment for awhile. He kissed her forehead and walked backward into the waiting car. He and his friend drove away toward Pierre, South Dakota. Jeremiah's every sentence seemed to focus on Tyisha to the point his friend put the radio on just to have a choice of what he wanted to hear.

***

Tyisha waited inside her car until every other car had left. She silently cried. All her adult life she had thought of herself as 'damaged goods" and never dreamed she would find true love. She couldn't fully love herself, so how could she expect a man to love her? But the unthinkable had happened. She knew two things; Christ loved her, and Jeremiah loved her. If they had only met earlier! Now, to be apart from Jeremiah after finally finding a man who could understand her walk caused nearly unbearable pain. Pain, yes, but with a hope she had never experienced.

She finally gathered herself and started the long drive back toward Williston, North Dakota. She simply wanted to go as far that afternoon as she could so the trip back home was achievable the following day. She retraced her trip from the route she had chosen four days earlier. Driving past Spearfish, South Dakota, she turned northward up Highway 85 crossing the Belle Fourche River and the town by the same name. As she continued northward, the beauty of the Black Hills and the pine-sided mesas diminished in size and number.

It was getting late in the day, so Ty drove into a motel on the edge of Buffalo at the junction with Highway 20. Before going into the lobby to register for a room, she looked at a road map of South Dakota and noted that a town named "Bison" was not far from her location. It seemed strange to have towns named "Bison" and "Buffalo" so close together.

After obtaining a room, she asked the clerk to recommend a local eating establishment and he recommended a small family-style restaurant near downtown Buffalo. After putting her luggage in her room, she drove to the restaurant to eat supper. After three evening meals with Jeremiah, the food did not seem to fill the hole in her heart. She returned to her room, and, after a quick shower, she set her alarm for 6:00 a.m. the next morning and went to sleep.

Ty had slept better than she had believed possible. She awoke with a desire to get home and begin to ready her room for the school year ahead. She was looking forward to seeing her friend, Lydia, and spending some time with her before the upcoming school year began.

She drove her car into a nearby gas station and while the gas tank was being filled, Ty went into the gas station and bought her breakfast out of a vending machine. After paying for her gas, she drove through the sleepy little western South Dakota town and continued north. The few buttes that existed no longer had pine trees on their sides but looked like ghostly sentinels over the silent plains. They were a strange sight for a girl from the South.

Closing in on home, she was running low on gas. She pulled in to fill up her gas tank one more time at Watford City, North Dakota. Across the street was a small grocery store, so she went in and bought one of their last chocolate éclairs, a pint of chocolate milk, and a sandwich of sugar-cured ham and American cheese. Maybe it was not the most nutritious of suppers, but it was filling, and it was there. She ate with one hand and drove with the other ever northward. She shortly crossed the upper portion of the Missouri River and was reassured that she was close to home.

She drove into her driveway on the edge of Williston, unloaded her car and went inside. She started reading the instructions to the ham radio even before she had begun an evening meal. She vowed to herself to have the radio installed and running by the end of the night. Tyisha, who was not mechanically inclined, amazed herself when she had the radio installed and took it on its "maiden voyage." She turned it to the pre-agreed frequency and attempted to call Jeremiah.

"High Plains Sister calling Capital Christian, High Plains Sister calling Capital Christian." She waited, but there was no reply. Just as she was about to go into the kitchen to fix a late-night snack, the radio crackled in her ear.

"High Plains Sister, this is Capital Christian, come back." As Tyisha responded to Jeremiah, they nearly laughed-two mulatto kids from Alabama sounded like a couple of crusty old truck drivers. It had only been two days since they had been together, but Tyisha took comfort in the unique inflexion of Jeremiah's voice.

"Tyisha, I have thought of little else since we were together. Come back."

"Jeremiah, me either. Come back."

"Have you started decorating your room at your school? Come back."

"Yes, I have hauled a few things over, but I am going to begin in earnest tomorrow. My friend, Lydia, agreed to help me before I ever came to the teachers' meeting. I'm going to call her tomorrow and ask if she can help me tomorrow night. Come back."

"Great minds seem to think alike. I am going to take a carload of charts, pictures, office supplies, treats for the kids and name tags for their desks, alphabet poster, handwriting posters, colored chalks, etc. Come back."

"Tomorrow, we begin doing the service to which the Lord has called us. It is 11:30 p.m. and I know you need your rest. I have yet to eat any supper, so we had better cut it off for tonight. I have so enjoyed hearing your voice and I will be counting the days until we can see one another again. Come back."

"And I know you are right, but I hate to say good-bye, High Plains Sister. You sleep well and we will talk again tomorrow night. God bless you, Tyisha. We are apart by hundreds of miles, but you are in my every thought and prayer. Come back."

"Please be well, as you prepare to change the lives of children for the Lord. You will be in my every prayer. Come back and Goodnight."

With this parting, she turned off the radio, and resumed fixing a quick sandwich before going to sleep. She smiled as she said her evening prayer to the Lord. She asked Him to continue blessing this new and wonderful relationship with Jeremiah and to show her that Jeremiah was the one who had been prepared for her since before the foundations of the world. Exhausted from the trip and installing the radio, Tyisha faded off into a world of dreams so much more peaceful than the real world she had known. Jeremiah was in each one.

***

Lydia and Tyisha took a three-day trip to see the endless wheat fields of northern North Dakota and the International Peace Garden on the Canada/United States border. This was Tyisha's last "hoorah" before the school year began and she would have precious time to travel to tourist attractions after that.

The two young women intentionally traveled into the Province of Manitoba just so Tyisha could say that she had been to Canada. Ty did not know, this child of the rural south, that she would visit many countries in her life.

The International Peace Garden was everything it was purported to be-beautiful flower beds, green forests reminding Tyisha of the pine forests of her home, and meandering paths and roads throughout. The two women walked along the paths and talked about the beauty all around them, the real estate market in Williston, North Dakota and Tyisha's fears of having complete control of her first classroom. Tyisha could not hold back and told Lydia all about Jeremiah and how she felt the Lord was in the midst of their romance. Both ladies, sisters in the faith, continuously gave God the glory for their many blessings.

They arrived back in Williston on Friday evening. This was Tyisha's last weekend of freedom before the bedlam called "education" began on the following Friday. Lydia kept talking about their church and the services on Sunday, but Tyisha could barely keep her mind on anything but all the

Café con Leche

ideas she wanted to implement in her class. She could visualize a world map on the cork board next to the doorway and handwriting examples above the windows in her room. She planned to print and write her name on the chalkboard in red, white and blue chalk. Upfront on the corner of her desk would sit a conspicuous Bible and she would start each day with a passage of Scripture and a prayer. She vowed to always be available to her students and listen to any need they had. Tyisha wanted to teach her children reading, writing and arithmetic, but she knew from her own experience that life can be tumultuous, at best, and children often need the help of an elder as a guide.

Sunday morning came and her last worship service before the academic year began. Lydia came in the gymnasium and sat next to Tyisha. Before the service began, Lydia leaned over and whispered in Tyisha's ear.

"Are you ready for tomorrow? Have no fear, God will be with you."

"Yes, I am going to prepare my classroom tomorrow and Tuesday and then go to teachers' meetings on Wednesday and Thursday before the students arrive on Friday. I think my biggest worries are the Nordic names of the students. Please pray for me. I need your prayers and you need the practice."

Tyisha winked and hugged her sister in Christ. Lydia was her first real friend since Sister Jorgina passed away. It was so different from her childhood to have a true friend, someone who loved her despite the color of her skin.

The pastor, who was also a teacher in the school, stood before his congregation and asked them to stand and pray with him. Dutifully, the congregation stood and bowed with their pastor.

"Lord, once again you have called us to serve You by preparing the children to be Your servants. This week, 450 young malleable minds will enter these halls. We must make everything second to their needs and they must know that 'God is love' through our love for them.

Father, guide our hands and let our mouths only produce encouraging words. May we train our students to see the world through Your eyes and help us live lives worth emulating. Inside the classroom or out in the world, may we be worthy of the title 'Christian.' And may all our efforts bring glory to You. It is in the name of Jesus Christ that we pray it all.

Remain standing as we sing *Great is Thy Faithfulness.*" The pastor returned to his chair as the Music Director changed places with him at the podium and led the congregation as they sang the old hymn. Two more hymns were sung before a young Mandan Sioux sang a special song, *Amazing Grace,* leaving many of the older Christians in tears.

Tyisha tried to focus on the words of the pastor during his sermon, but she was constantly distracted by her plans to decorate her class to honor God. Her mind wandered to the stories her mother had told her about her maternal great grandfather, Newman Shelton. Like her great grandfather, Tyisha had been born to trouble. He was born in a small town in southern Alabama where his father was the local city adulterer. Newman's father was killed by a jealous husband who found his wife embracing the adulterer. Four months later, Newman's mother died with cancer. Newman stood at the graveside and cried as the rest of the attendees walked away. He had no idea where he would live or even what he would eat that night. One family which had been at the funeral was nearly halfway home when the husband looked at his wife and said, "We've got to get that little fellow and raise him for Kate. She deserves that much. Besides, we can use the extra help on the farm." They returned to the cemetery and found little Newman sitting on his mother's grave and crying uncontrollably. There was no social agency for children, so they simply took the boy home with them.

From the first time Tyisha's mother told her about her maternal great grandfather, Tyisha wondered why her mother thought it so important to tell the stories. Now she knew. Tragedy had befallen her great grandfather from his earliest days, but he had never allowed those painful experiences to determine his personality. He was the "white slave" of his adoptive family and worked like a mule but became a noted Christian in his church. He had married a woman from a prominent family, and they had four daughters, one of which was her grandmother.

Tyisha giggled as she remembered one of her mother's stories about her grandfather just as the pastor said, "millions who do not know the Lord are going to Hades for eternity." Lydia looked over at her and smiled. Thankfully, none of the other worshippers heard Tyisha's faux pas.

Back in her own little world, Tyisha remembered why she had giggled. Great Grandfather Newman was known for his quick wit, as was his entire family. One of her mother's favorite stories about him had been told to Tyisha repeatedly when she was a girl.

Café con Leche

It was the first days of the winter and a bit cool. Newman sat on his front porch whittling a piece of wood when one of his grandsons drove up in his brand-new pickup.

"Hey, Grandpa, I'm going over to Dothan to show off my new truck. You want to go with me?"

"Why sure I do, son." The old man that had a bad leg from an errant surgery, pulled himself up into the new pickup. At that very moment, his wife Anna, came onto the porch and yelled at her husband.

"Newman, where do you think you're going? There ain't a stick of wood in this house."

In the blink of an eye, Newman retorted, "Well, woman, I ain't taking the axe."

Tyisha had always wished she could have met her Great Grandfather Newman Shelton. His children and all who knew him loved him. Those events that had made lesser men bitter and angry had been transformed into love by a loving God. Tyisha's mother had been impregnated by a black man in the Deep South, raised a daughter by herself in Atlanta and worked every day of her life until she could no longer do so. She had every reason to hate her situation, but her faith in God never waned. She loved Tyisha when no one else did.

Ty could not forget her mother's parting words. Her mother died at her grandparents' home. With Tyisha by her bedside, she said "Tyisha, your life is going to be full of pain and crying. I had so hoped to be your mother and protect you from most of it, but I cannot. The Lord told us to 'seek and ye shall find.' You seek Him and you will find Him. He will send His Holy Spirit to you and comfort you through the hard times life will give you. I love you and always have. Goodbye, my darling."

Within moments, Ty's mother was in a coma and died only hours later. Tyisha had hidden between the bales of cotton in the barn for days and cried. The memories of her mother's passing were abruptly interrupted by the end of the worship service and Lydia and the other worshippers stood to their feet. Tyisha arose late, but not noticeably so.

After the service, Tyisha and Lydia went to a local restaurant for a lunch together. They talked a bit about the service, at least the parts when Tyisha had been taking part, but Lydia could tell Tyisha was highly distracted and made an excuse to cut the meal short.

Tyisha went home and her thoughts returned to the beginning of classes, now less than a week away. It seemed the wait had been much too long. Now, all her training at Tuskegee and her work alongside her mentor and Christian sister, Miss Jorgina, was on the verge of becoming real. She knew she was ready and couldn't wait to get started.

Most nights, she spoke to Jeremiah via the ham radio. Even though he was about to begin his first year of teaching, his nature was to be an "encourager," and he made her feel like she had taught for twenty years. She was ready.

***

Monday came and Tyisha was prepared. She had loaded up her car with a few visual displays she had been creating in the past two months along with others she had inherited from Miss Jorgina after her tragic death. She waited impatiently for 7:00 a.m., when the school would be open and her classroom available for transforming.

Tyisha had originally been told she would be teaching the first-grade class, but the fourth-grade teacher had unexpectedly decided to move to Texas and live out her days in a warm climate with her daughter's family. It was somewhat challenging for Tyisha to make the change but agreed to do so to help Mr. Christensen in a crisis.

By 10:00 a.m., it was difficult to find a square foot of painted wall that was not covered by a poster, painting, or chart. At the front of the room, was a chart listing the "rules of the class."

"Love your fellow students as yourself. Respect both your fellow students and teacher. Apply yourself to learn every day to the best of your ability…" Tyisha was proud of her class rules and had borrowed heavily from Miss Jorgina.

At the back of the classroom, was a large chart with the multiplication tables from "1" to "10." Next to it was a diagram of the human body. On the left side of the room was a poster showing a Biblical timeline from Adam and Eve through Satan's eternal inundation in the "lake of fire." On the right side of the chalk board at the front of the class were seven Biblical quotes from the Old Testament prophets predicting the coming of Christ. Opposite of each prediction was Christ's fulfillment of that prophecy. Tyisha was proud of her room and the teaching aids she had added to the milieu.

"Sister Tyisha, we are having lunch in the lunchroom in ten minutes. Please join us. It is catered from a local restaurant with authentic Norwegian food. See you there." The headmaster, Mr. Christensen walked on down the hall with his prepared speech to the next teacher. Tyisha had been up much of the night before and needed the break from her work. She had much to do yet, but she had another day to finish her preparation.

There in her plate before her was klub (grated potatoes with chopped ham and rolled into a ball), pølser (deer sausage on the side), fårikål (mutton and cabbage stew), and krumkake (a waffle cone filled with a whipped cream) for dessert. Everything was delicious; Tyisha got a second helping of the pølser.

After lunch, Tyisha returned to her classroom and started making up her grade and attendance book with the names of her students she had been provided earlier in the day. By the end of the day, she felt more confident that her room was close to being complete and that she was nearly ready for her students.

Tyisha completed her preparatory work by 1:00 p.m. the following day and went home early. Lydia was coming over for supper and Ty wanted to have everything ready to eat when she arrived. The menu included bison steaks, baked potatoes topped with bacon bits, butter, and chives sprinkled on top. For dessert, she had prepared a pumpkin pie a day earlier topped with whipped cream following the supper. The meal was an amalgamation of foods from her new home and from her southern roots.

After a prayer of thanksgiving for the food, Lydia and Ty went into her small living room and sat on two chairs on either side of her coffee table. The two young ladies relished their independence and the changes of the last few years to society. It was the time of Gloria Steinem and Virginia Slims. It seemed every woman had read the book *The Second Sex* by Simone de Beauvoir. Along with the civil rights movement, the War in Vietnam and the loss of leaders like Martin Luther King, Jr. and Robert Kennedy, the whole nation was more divided than it had been since the Civil War. The two friends only had two things holding their friendship together; their mutual faith in God (they were sisters in the faith) and their hopes for equality of women everywhere. These two aspects overcame all other considerations. The fact that Lydia was Norwegian and Tyisha was biracial, Lydia was from the far north and Lydia was from the Deep South just didn't matter all that much. They enjoyed each other's company and they had determined to make their relationship work if possible.

By 9:00 p.m., the two friends hugged each other and parted company. Lydia made her long trek to her empty and dark apartment across Williston, and Tyisha washed her dishes and laid them on a towel to dry next to the kitchen sink. When she finished, she called up Jeremiah on the ham radio and talked just a few minutes. Tyisha wished him well since the classes for both were scheduled to start the following Friday. As usual, they concluded their conversation with their mutual assurance of love for the other and their commitment to follow the will of God for their lives.

CHAPTER 9

The next two days of teacher's meetings were nearly a repeat of those in which Tyisha had met Jeremiah. Despite that, Tyisha tried to focus on the speakers and feign excitement. She endured both Wednesday and Thursday so she could finally get to Friday.

All her preparation and education was over; it was time to teach. She could not blame her failures on Miss Jorgina or any of her professors. She was ready!

Tyisha was in her classroom by 6:00 a.m. and wrote her name, "Miss Tyisha McFarren" on the chalkboard at the front of the classroom. She had created a sitting chart and the name tag of each student was placed on the corresponding desk. "Søren Kierkegaard," named after the Danish philosopher no doubt, "Sabina Eiker," "Gabriel Brustad," "Tarik Hegdahl," and "Wichahpi Kallevig." This little Mandan Sioux girl had a Norwegian father and Native American mother. Her picture depicted her as a beautiful little girl who was small for her age. Ty couldn't wait to meet her.

Her entire class consisted of only fourteen students and was the perfect size to produce a close relationship with the children. Ty could barely wait for them to arrive and to begin the year. It was only 7:00 a.m. and Ty's enthusiasm caused her to physically shake. She sat down at her desk and pretended to look at her lesson plan that she knew verbatim, waiting for her students to arrive or her shaking to abate whichever came first.

By 7:55 a.m., all her students had arrived and were talking to their peers about the occurrences of the summer months and so excited they barely noticed the presence of their new teacher. When the first bell to start the day rang loudly, Tyisha forcefully told her students to take their seats. Miss Jorgina had taught her a bit of wisdom and it was time for Ty to employ it fully.

"Miss Tyisha, you remember this: It is always simpler to ease up on your students than to tighten up on them later. You start out hard on them."

Tyisha brusquely introduced herself in her best adult voice. She explained the rules of her class and said each one was based on a precept in the Bible. She explained her grading scale and attendance policies and promised to be available to any student needing additional assistance.

Despite the words of Miss Jorgina, it was just not in Tyisha's nature to be "professional." She already loved each one of her students and she barely knew their names. Lydia had tried to help this southern girl pronounce the Nordic or Native American names of her students, with some success.

"Sabina, Gabriel, Tarik, Wichahpi (Tyisha pronounced the first name of each of her students), your teacher is a believer in the Lord Jesus Christ, like many of your parents. I want to love my God and all who He places in my class. Now, do not think that my love for you is license for you to misbehave. If you do not obey me or the rules of this class, there will be consequences. If your behavior is serious, I may refer you to Mr. Christensen. For smaller offenses, I will handle the problem in the classroom.

As I said earlier, I am a Christian. I was raised in the church, but no one there was concerned about my spiritual state. It was not until I did my student teaching in Tuskegee, Alabama that someone finally spoke to me about the sacrificial death and resurrection of Jesus Christ. She was my mentor in the classroom and testified of the Lord's love for me. After accepting the salvation of Jesus Christ, I was baptized in a creek just north of Tuskegee.

Each day we are in class, I want to teach you about academics, but more importantly, I want to testify of the Lord. I have dealt with some

Café con Leche

huge problems in my life and the Lord is healing all my wounds. Usually, He brings me relief through other people. I want you to feel like I could be one of those people for you. Should you ever need to speak to me about anything, simply tell me and I will arrange to meet with you either before or after school.

Let's have fun this year. Learning can be enjoyable and when the year is complete next May, I want us to look back with awe at how much we have learned about Math, Science, the Bible, and our Lord."

Following her opening exhortation to her students, Tyisha went ahead in her opening lesson in multiplication tables, knowing that they were essential for her students to learn long division. Her first day was rewarding to her and most of her students, who referred to her as "Miss Tyisha" in class. Tyisha knew in her soul that she was right where and when the Lord wanted her to be.

***

Ty settled into a routine of sorts, but she liked it. It helped her to deal with the stresses of being apart from Jeremiah and to feel like she was doing exactly what the Lord had prepared her to do.

At least four nights a week, she devoted herself to lesson plans, test creation and lessons based on the Bible and calendar. She taught the children about Joshua leading the Children of Israel into the Promised Land, about Columbus' discovery of the Americas, and how the author of *Amazing Grace* was a saved slave trader.

Tyisha had finally received her ham operator's license, so she and Jeremiah used every opportunity to speak to one another. It was becoming obvious to each of them that what had started as affection had developed into true love. They each recognized that God was in the midst of their relationship, and He had a plan for their lives and their relationship. Tyisha wanted so much to announce her love to Jeremiah, but southern girls were told it was his announcement to make.

It was 9:00 p.m., Friday, November 15, 1968. Tyisha would never forget the time or the date. She was literally quivering trying to hold back her feelings to meet societal norms. She was unsure she could when Jeremiah came on the radio at the previously agreed time.

"Tyisha, I have been fighting back the words hoping to wait for the Christmas break and speak to you in person. I cannot fight this feeling any longer. I know it is not that romantic to ask you on the radio, but I love you and can't think of a future without you. Will you marry me? Over."

Jeremiah barely finished his last word when Tyisha nearly screamed in the microphone, "You know I will. I love you, too, and was hoping you would ask weeks ago. Over."

"Tyisha, I can't believe it. This is like a dream for me, and I had no idea I would ever find true love, but your voice gives me joy each time I hear it. I am almost in shock, thinking I will have a lifetime to hear that voice.

I guess we need to set a date for the marriage and start working toward that date. Since we are both working hard in the classroom, I suspect we should look at next summer sometime to give us a bit of time to work on the wedding. Is that good for you? Over."

"I am like you, Jeremiah, somewhat in shock but a good shock. Anytime, anywhere is good with me. I just want us to start our life together with God at the center of our marriage. Wherever the Lord leads you, I want to be alongside to be your helpmate. Over."

"I wanted to go home for Christmas to see my mother. Could you go with me? She will love you, Tyisha. Over."

"I would love to go with you. I will be out of class on Friday the 13th of December. Yes, Friday the 13th. If I have my bags packed, I can probably make it to Bismarck and spend the night there. Hopefully, I can be to Pierre by 2:00 p.m. on the 14th. Is that good for you? Over."

"Sure, that is great! Tyisha, the Lord has chosen the exact dates for the Christmas break for our school. We go back to class on January 2, 1969. That means we can leave my mother's house and get back here by December 29. That will allow you to return to Williston and get some rest and prepare for the second semester. Will that timing work for you? Over."

"That is perfect, my love. I will start working on that trip this weekend and I can't wait to see you and meet your mother. She did a great job and I just wish my mother could still be alive. She would love you. I need to get to bed, so I will close for tonight. Finally, I can speak my heart. I love you, Jeremiah and cannot wait to be your wife. Goodnight, darling. Over."

With that final word, the young couple parted company. Tyisha felt somewhat guilty. She had lied to her husband-to-be and told him she

Café con Leche

had to go to bed. It was after 10:00 p.m., but Tyisha could not wait until morning. She had to tell her friend about the huge change coming in her life.

Tyisha dialed Lydia's number, knowing she often turned into bed by 9:30 p.m. The phone rang in Tyisha's ear.

"Hello." Tyisha could tell from the tone of her voice that what she feared most had occurred. Lydia had been asleep.

"Lydia, I am so sorry to have called you this late. I just had to tell someone, and you are my closest friend."

Lydia jumped up from a reclining position and nearly screamed in the phone, "Do you mean what I think you mean?"

"He asked me tonight and I said 'yes.' I am going with him to meet his mother in Ohio over the Christmas break, and we are planning a summer wedding next year. I can't wait. It seems so obvious to me now that he is the one the Lord has prepared to be my husband."

"Have you decided where to have the wedding?"

"Not yet, but he has family from his father still in Alabama. They don't want anything to do with Jeremiah. Also, his mother will not go south of the Mason-Dixon Line. My only living relative, an uncle, has told me he would have me arrested if I ever come back to the home where I was raised.

So, no, we have not decided on a place for the wedding. I don't care if we are married by a Justice of the Peace or a Magistrate Judge. I just want to start my life with Jeremiah as soon as possible."

The two young women talked awhile longer, but both were tired and even the joy of the news began to subside. They finally said "Goodnight," and tried desperately to sleep.

CHAPTER 10

Just down the main hallway from Tyisha's classroom was the classroom of Mrs. Rike Bingenheimer. She had an advanced racist bent and had thought Adolf Hitler was "misunderstood." After all, every major invention of mankind was developed by white people, right? Even the atom bomb was created by Germans, though they were actually Jews. Mrs. Bingenheimer's racism had deeply affected her theology. For her, God was white with blue eyes. He had not "created all people equally" and had formed the most blessed to look like Him. The darker the skin and eye color indicated a diminished blessing by God. The hypocrisy in her views was depicted by her maiden name "Schwarz," which means "black haired" in German. True to her name, Mrs. Bingenheimer had darker hair than Ty's, much to her chagrin.

Mrs. Bingenheimer had guessed that Miss Tyisha's dark complexion was not from Mandan Sioux heritage, but from a black bloodline. There was no place in the Kingdom of God for a mongrel like Tyisha. Mrs. Bingenheimer decided that the parents of the students and the administration had to know just who was teaching their children. She did not know what lie she would divulge to them, but Miss Tyisha was bound to commit some infraction of the school rules. Better yet, maybe Miss Tyisha would run afoul of North Dakota ethics and laws, and then she would preside over the undoing of the popular young shapely Miss McFarren.

Café con Leche

At arbitrary times, Mrs. Bingenheimer walked by Ty's classroom, but to her disappointment never witnessed anything untoward. Then came that day when a situation presented itself that was a gift from God. Unexpectedly, it was right in front of her. She could barely believe her eyes. It was better than anything she could have concocted on her own.

On three separate occasions, Gabriel Brustad, had come to Tyisha's class and asked to stand at the back of the class. Tyisha knew the Brustad family and had seen them in church since she had lived in Williston. On numerous occasions, Ty and Lydia had seen the brutish Mr. Brustad rudely escort one of his three children out of the church service. Moments later, he returned pulling a sobbing child by the ear. Corporal punishment was his first and only form of correction.

Gabriel came to school that Monday morning, but it was obvious he did not want to be there. He thought about every step and slowly entered the classroom. Even before Tyisha asked, he had gone to the back of the classroom and leaned against a bookshelf. He stood there in obvious agony until the lunch hour. Tyisha released the other children to go eat lunch with another teacher's class. When they were out of the room, Tyisha came close to Gabriel.

"Gabriel, did your father hit you again?"

Gabriel simply shook his head to affirm the question.

"Where did he hit you?"

Once again, Gabriel did not respond verbally, but pointed to his back and rear end.

"I do not want you to do anything you do not wish to do. Gabriel, are you willing to pull off your shirt and let me see your back?"

Still, not speaking, Gabriel unbuttoned his shirt and pulled off his T-shirt. His modesty made him remove the latter reluctantly.

Tyisha let out an audible "Oh, my God!" reacting to what she was seeing. Gabriel flinched at the outburst of his teacher. He had open oozing wounds across his back and large welts from multiple strikes with an object. Blood was drying on the inside of the undershirt, but the wounds were still draining.

"How did you get these bruises and wounds?"

"My father said I can't tell anyone, or he would give me a worse beating." Without trying, he had answered Ty's question.

"What did this to you, Gabriel?"

He no longer tried to conceal the person who had done this, and his revelations seemed cathartic. "My dad used a 2x4 board on me, because one of his sows ate her entire litter of pigs."

Tyisha could not control herself any longer and pulled the little boys head to her breast and kissed the top of his head. Tears rolled down her face as she remembered the abuse she had sustained as a child. Even little Gabriel was moved by his teacher's tears, and he shed some of his own.

Through her tears, Tyisha said to her student, "Gabriel, you go home today as if nothing has happened and tell no one what we have discussed. Tomorrow, I will go to the principal the first thing in the morning and let him know your situation."

At that moment, Mrs. Bingenheimer walked by the door in the main hallway. As had been her custom over the past few weeks, she peered in to see a half-dressed boy with his head at his teacher's bosom. She could not see Gabriel's wounds on his back, and she did not want to see more. She rushed away to be with her children for the remainder of the lunch hour. Mrs. Bingenheimer was nearly gleeful as she thought of what she would tell her fellow churchmen at the Bible study later that night. When she arrived home that night, she ran through a couple of variations of the story she was about to tell.

Years ago, if a gossip wanted a falsehood to circulate through the community, they started the lie in a barber shop or hair salon. Now, the same could be accomplished faster by telling the same lie to a group of church folks and feign concern for the person who was the target of the lie.

Monday night was Mrs. Bingenheimer's turn to host her rotating Bible Study. Each time she hosted the women, her husband took their children to the local restaurant to eat. The father and children looked forward to these Bible Studies since Mrs. Bingenheimer was not much of a cook.

With the house to herself, she ran through her story including facial expressions. The doorbell rang and the first of the ladies arrived. It was Mrs. Aleksandra Østerberg. She was more efficient at sending a message than the United States Postal Service. Living on a farm near Williston, her telephone was connected to a party line with nine other customers. Each morning the members of the party line club got on their phones at exactly

8:00 a.m. for the express purpose of sharing the tidbits of gossip each had acquired in the past twenty-four hours.

Mrs. Østerberg was only the most proficient of the gossip mongers. There was also Cedolphine Dahlström, Oddlin Forfarg, and Steinbjørg Jenssen, each with skill at disseminating untruths. The ladies stood around the kitchen of Mrs. Bingenheimer and feigned their concern for their pastor.

"You girls know that I am not one to talk, BUT I was driving by the Pine Mesa Motel yesterday morning and saw our pastor's truck parked outside of Room 112." Mrs. Forfarg nearly cried as she intimated their pastor's obvious affair.

"I always wondered about him. No one is that spiritual." Mrs. Jenssen could hardly make her allegation with her mouth so full, food shot out with the pronunciation of every "s."

Not to be outdone, Mrs. Dahlström looked at the other women of God and said, "Did you all notice how our pastor liked to hug you? There just seems to be something 'rar' (strange) about him."

The ladies forgot to mention that their pastor was bi-vocational. During the school year, his salary from the school and the church were sufficient for his financial needs. However, during the summer he did not receive the school remuneration and he served as a handyman to make some extra money. On the day before, the inhabitants of Room 112 had been awakened by the sound of a water leak under the sink that quickly flooded the room. The young pastor was called, and he responded in his pickup which he parked outside of the room.

The ladies at the Bible study liked their assumption of events better than the truth. Apparently, they had never heard the old saying: "Never assume because it makes an 'ass' out of 'u' and 'me.'"

Mrs. Bingenheimer was fascinated by the latest fiction regarding her pastor and fellow teacher, but she had news of her own and wanted to get her own gossip before the highly trained disseminators of falsehoods in the Bible study.

"Ladies, it is getting late. Oddlin has the lesson tonight, so let's go into the living room." Mrs. Bingenheimer led the group into the living room where ten chairs had been set up in a circle.

After all the ladies were seated, Mrs. Forfang stood and began to exegete Romans 1. She was also a teacher at the school and did a masterful job of taking Paul's words and making them understandable using applications to the ladies' lives. She read the entire chapter and then explained it. Finally, she neared the end of the lesson by reading the last five verses.

28 And even as they did not like to retain God in their knowledge, God gave them over to a reprobate mind, to do those things which are not convenient;

29 Being filled with all unrighteousness, fornication, wickedness, covetousness, maliciousness; full of envy, murder, debate, deceit, malignity; whisperers,

30 Backbiters, haters of God, despiteful, proud, boasters, inventors of evil things, disobedient to parents,

31 Without understanding, covenant breakers, without natural affection, implacable, unmerciful:

32 Who knowing the judgment of God, that they which commit such things are worthy of death, not only do the same, but have pleasure in them that do them.

"Paul is obvious in this passage. Many of the early Christians were returning to the lives they had lived prior to their acceptance of the salvation of God. Well, I think we all know someone like those Paul is describing. There may even be one or two in the pews with us at church." With that, Mrs. Forfang turned the rest of the Bible study over to Mrs. Bingenheimer.

"Ladies, do you have some prayer requests tonight? I will begin the season of prayer and all of you are invited to join in the prayer time. We will close if there is a lull. Cedolophine, you close tonight, please." Mrs. Dahlström nodded in agreement.

"We need to keep Mrs. Hegdahl in prayer. You know she and her husband are dealing with the trials associated with a daughter who is pregnant out of wedlock."

"I have been troubled all day and really wondered if I should bring this to your attention. But I know that many of you have children in the school and deserve to know what I saw." Mrs. Bingenheimer made her best

Café con Leche

attempt to look contrite and reluctant. "We need to pray for Miss Tyisha McFarren. She has recently come to our school, and this is her first year to teach. Today, as I walked by her room, I saw her with a little boy scantily clothed. She pulled the boy's head to her bosom and was kissing him on the head. At the very least, her actions were inappropriate with a student and at worse they were pedophilic. I worry about the safety of the other children in her care. After all, what do we really know about this young lady?"

Every lady looked at Mrs. Bingenheimer with genuine shock. Several of them had children of their own in the Redeemer's Salvation School. One of Miss Tyisha McFarren's students, Tarik Nilsen, was the nephew of Mrs. Steinbjørg.

"You will have to proceed without me. I have to get home and call my sister and let her know her son is in danger." With that, Mrs. Steinbjørg grabbed her Bible and rushed out of the house. Mrs. Bingenheimer looked distraught on the outside but was almost giddy on the inside. Her plan was coming together perfectly.

The remaining participants decided to forgo their planned season of prayer. This news was too crucial to waste time in prayer. They all rushed to their homes in hopes of being first to contact others in their gossip chain. Mrs. Bingenheimer watched the last lady leave her home. She stepped back inside the door and realized the others would do her job for her. "My job is done, here." With that statement she waited for her husband and children to return home.

***

The first call awoke him at 1:00 a.m. followed in quick succession by three more calls by 3:30 a.m. Each was from an irate parent of a child in the Redeemer's Salvation School, and one was from a parent of a boy in Miss Tyisha McFarren's class. Their stories almost sounded rehearsed. The calls uniformly began with the parents berating Mr. Christian Christensen for hiring a pedophile and placing the children of the school in danger. The phone calls each ended with an ultimatum-either Miss McFarren is dismissed at once or the parents would seek the dismissal of Mr. Christensen. No words of reason seemed to sway the parents' anger, so Mr. Christensen stopped trying, replying to their slurs and attacks with a simple "uh-huh." Most of the calls ended with a click in his ear as the parents summarily hung up the phone angrily.

It was that telephone call at 7:12 a.m. that concerned him more than all the others.

"Chris, are you up?" Jon Johanssen was the President of the School Board and didn't care if his headmaster was up or not. He had been called by many of the same parents and all were demanding action. Many had threatened to remove their children from a school where they were endangered.

"Yes, Jon, I have been up since I received the first phone call at 1:00 a.m. This is about Ms. McFarren, isn't it?"

"Ya, Chris. I was afraid I would have to come to your house and wake you up. Every member of the Board has been called and we have decided to have a special Board meeting tonight at 7:00 p.m. We want you there and let's put this thing to bed. You find out what you can and give us a report on your findings tonight. By the way, we don't need Ms. McFarren there and she does not need to be informed of any allegations just yet. If any action is warranted against her, we will wait until our attorney can review the allegations and propose any action."

"Jon, I will see you this evening and hopefully get to the bottom of these allegations."

Both men hung up the telephone and after several more telephone calls, Christian Christensen finally discovered that the allegations had originated with his teacher, Mrs. Rike Bingenheimer.

***

Gabriel Brustad was devastated. Sure, the physical wounds were painful, but they would heal. His emotional pain would not. His only hope for healing was from the Great Physician, Jesus Christ. Tyisha was living evidence of the power of God to heal. The following morning, Tyisha left her class in the care of another teacher on her free hour. As she left the class, she hugged up Gabriel one last time before going to the office of the school to report the abuse of her student.

"Can I see Mr. Christensen?"

The school secretary seemed to enjoy taking charge and treating the teachers as if they were insignificant. "He's at a State Administrators

Café con Leche

Meeting and won't be back in school today. I will be glad to leave him a note if you like."

"No thank you. Something must be done today." Tyisha hurriedly returned to her classroom and told Gabriel to try to endure to the end of the school day. Within a couple of minutes, the remaining students of her class returned to the classroom from the playground. Miss Tyisha completed teaching the curriculum that Friday afternoon in dread of what was to come that night.

After the last bell and the students were released to waiting buses and parents, Tyisha closed her room door, sat at her desk and cried. She had sent Gabriel home on the bus, and she wondered if she had done the right thing. If his father found out Gabriel had told his teacher about the abuse, there could be unwanted consequences.

Tyisha regained her composure and drove to the Williams County Sheriff's Office. Once inside, she told the desk sergeant that she needed to report a crime. She was referred to a Detective Hann.

Detective Hann asked Tyisha to follow him into a small room furnished with a metal table in the middle with two chairs on either side. Tyisha sat in one chair and the detective sat on the other side.

"Madame, can you give me your name?"

"My name is Miss Tyisha McFarren, and I am a teacher at the Redeemer's Salvation School."

"What can I do for you today?"

"I have a little boy in my class that has been beaten by his father and this is not the first time since the school year began. In this latest beating, my student was struck repeatedly with a 2"x4" board. One strike was at the base of his neck and could have killed him.

You would be speaking with the headmaster, Mr. Christian Christensen, but he is not in town this day and I feel the threat to the child deserves immediate attention."

"Miss McFarren, please give me the details starting with the name of the victim and show me on this chart where the injuries are located on the student's body."

"The little boy's name is 'Gabriel Brustad.'" Ty took the diagram of the human body provided by Detective Hann and drew lines to indicate the location of the injuries on Gabriel's back.

99

"Miss McFarren, is this little boy the son of Dag Brustad?"

"I don't have any documentation with me, but I think that is his father's name."

"Okay, leave your contact information with the desk sergeant and we will be back with you as soon as we have investigated. Also, leave your school contact information. Thank you for coming in today and bringing this to our attention."

Tyisha knew she had just been dismissed and she had a gnawing feeling that the detective had decided to do little or nothing about the beating Gabriel had taken. She dutifully stood and walked to the front desk to give its occupant her contact information. In the meantime, Detective Hann remained in the interview room and pretended to write more notes.

After completing the task, Ty left and went to see her friend, Lydia. She had to share the events of the day and Jeremiah was not close by. Tyisha had not spent the weekend with Lydia since Thanksgiving, when she had spent the holiday with Lydia and her parents. She knew Lydia would be sympathetic to the trauma Tyisha was experiencing and Lydia asked Ty to spend the weekend with her. Ty readily accepted.

***

As soon as Ty left, Detective Hann walked over to the desk sergeant, who had his head buried in a magazine.

"Do you know who she wanted to make a complaint against?"

The desk sergeant looked up with a blank look on his face. "She said Dag Brustad beat his kid again."

"Sheriff Eich took his family on a ski vacation to Colorado and his last words to me were, 'Don't contact me while I am on vacation, unless Williston is on fire, and only then if the office is in danger of burning.' Dag Brustad has been a County Commissioner for five terms, and I know Sheriff Eich would never pursue this case. I will go out and tell Mr. Brustad that the allegations have been made again, but that is all I am going to do without the express orders of the Sheriff. Besides, what a man does in his own home is his business."

The desk sergeant shook his head in agreement. With that, he took the allegations, wadded them up and threw them in the trash can under

Café con Leche

the desk sergeant's desk. Detective Hann went back to his office and telephoned Mr. Brustad and told him about the new allegations.

***

Jon Johanssen gaveled the meeting to order. Miss Tyisha McFarren had not been invited. It took three loud strikes of the gavel before the seventy-plus parents began to sit down. Their anger was palpable. By now, several had tried to telephone her, but with no response. Some had even gone to her home to threaten her with physical harm if she did not immediately leave their bucolic community. They were equally frustrated by her absence. Now, they demanded action on the part of their leaders. En masse, they had decided on the guilt of Ms. Tyisha McFarren. After all, the allegations had been made by good Christian women whom they all knew.

"This evening, we are here to discuss the allegations that we now know were begun by Mrs. Rike Bingenheimer. She has given her testimony to the school headmaster, Mr. Christian Christensen, today. We are honored to have her here with us tonight and she has agreed to recount what she saw yesterday in the classroom of Ms. Tyisha McFarren. With that foreword, Mrs. Bingenheimer please come to the microphone."

"Thank you, Mr. Johanssen." Mrs. Bingenheimer approached the front table, and the microphone was handed to her. She stood at the end of the front table in full view of the hungry crowd who seemed to hang on her every word.

"You folks know me, and I have sat next to many of you over the last twenty years in the pews of the Redeemer's Salvation Church. You know that what I am about to say gives me no pleasure." She had practiced her contrite facial expressions all day in a mirror at home. In truth, she was ecstatic, and her plan was working far better than she could have hoped.

"Yesterday, at the lunch hour, I walked down the main hall toward the cafeteria. As I passed the room of Miss Tyisha McFarren, I saw her with her student, Gabriel Brustad. Young Gabriel had his shirt off and his teacher had buried his head in her breasts." There was an audible inhalation of the crowd who were in total shock at this description of events. This was going better than any plan Mrs. Bingenheimer had concocted, so she continued to verbalize her hyperbole.

"Miss McFarren was holding young Gabriel's head in place and kissing his head. It was obvious she engaged in inappropriate behavior with one of her students or possibly she is a pedophile." Another gasp went around the room, as Mrs. Bingenheimer returned to her seat. At least five parents patted her on the back as she sat down. What a lady, to have the moral strength to come forward with such dire allegations against a fellow teacher.

Mr. Johanssen returned to his center chair with the microphone. The entire crowd had grown suddenly quiet awaiting their leader's proclamation.

"Now you have heard the allegations, as has every person sitting at this table. Most of you know the gentleman sitting at the far end of the table. Mr. Olsen, would you please stand up?"

Alf Olsen was the school's attorney and a member of the church and School Board. He had been contacted earlier in the day by Mr. Johanssen and the allegations were relayed to him. He stood up and waved to the crowd. After a moment, he returned to his seat.

Being the moderator for such a raucous bunch was hard enough, but Mr. Johanssen stood for a third time before the demanding crowd. An onlooker might have thought the crowd was demanding "Crucify Him!" Instead, almost in unison, the crowd yelled "Fire her!" Mrs. Bingenheimer joined in with the verbal melee. As soon as he could speak, Mr. Johanssen banged the gavel loudly. When the crowd quieted, he continued.

"The Board has decided to take immediate action in this matter, but to do so by following both moral and legal procedure. Mr. Olsen has told us that he believes the allegations are serious enough to call for Miss McFarren's immediate dismissal, but before he can be sure, he wants to revisit her contract. Since tomorrow is the Lord's Day, he will not work on the matter, but he assures us he can have a legal opinion for us by the end of the school day on Monday.

We share your concern. Our first obligation is to educate our children within a Christian curriculum. But if our children do not feel safe, no education will occur. By 5:00 p.m. on Monday night, we will decide how to continue with Miss McFarren's termination. Until then, we beg of you not to do anything rash."

One of the parents of a little half-Mandan Sioux student, Wichahpi Kallevig, stood and was nearly shaking. She was a Mandan Sioux from

Café con Leche

the nearby reservation who had met Wichahpi's father at a local grocery store when they were both teens. She could not wait until Monday; she needed answers now.

"I cannot allow my daughter to go back into the classroom of this she-devil! My husband and I will be in to withdraw our daughter from the school on Monday morning."

Other parents screamed they would follow suit. It was obvious the school was on the verge of chaos and perhaps the end of the private school that was always on the edge of collapse. Mr. Johanssen returned to the microphone to try to quell the outrage of the parents.

"Please, we are doing everything our State of North Dakota laws and the policies of our own school require. We can do nothing more than we have told you. Now, let me make a proposal that I think can allay all our fears. If you choose to keep your children out of school on Monday, we cannot blame you. In fact, Mr. Christensen will not even count the absence of your children, will you Mr. Christensen?" Mr. Christensen almost injured himself nodding in agreement with his boss. "Let us go home tonight knowing that all which can be done is being done. We will protect your children."

With that parting and hopefully comforting statement, Mr. Johanssen closed the meeting. The crowd reluctantly parted and spoke loudly about their foe, Miss Tyisha McFarren, on the parking lot outside the school gym. More than one conversation included the phrase "tar and feather."

***

It was a beautiful Lord's Day as the sun beamed through Lydia's guest bedroom window and onto the face of Ty. She slowly sat up on the side of the bed and thanked the Lord for the day and another chance to serve Him. After a time of prayer, she picked up her Bible that was almost always with her and began to read the first chapter of James. After reading the entire chapter, she read again the twelfth verse:

> 12 Blessed is the man that endureth temptation: for when he is tried, he shall receive the crown of life, which the Lord had promised to them that love him.

Tyisha was baffled. She had been reading the Book of Hebrews and begun to read the writings of the brother of Jesus, James. She could not shake the feeling that verse twelve was especially relevant to her life. She read through the verse two more times. What was the Lord trying to tell her? Certainly, her life had been full of trials. Could there be more now that she had turned her life over to Christ?

She deliberately walked around the house barefoot so not to awaken Lydia, who was still sleeping. She sat in the garden behind the house on a bench and prayed the Lord would show Himself to the congregants gathered at the church. Tyisha waited as long as she could before awaking Lydia. It would take longer to get ready with two young ladies and one bathroom.

Two hours later, Lydia and Tyisha sat down in their usual seats three rows in front of the pulpit. For some strange reason, the other worshippers who usually sat next to them were four rows back. They sat alone throughout the service with no other worshipper closer than twenty feet. Lydia leaned over and whispered in Tyisha's ear, "Who did we offend? Did you remember your deodorant?" Both young ladies giggled.

At the end of the service, the pastor went to the back of the congregation after a closing prayer and blessing. As the congregants filed out of the gymnasium, the pastor shook the hands of each one. In turn, the congregants told him flagrant lies like, "Pastor those were the very words I needed to hear today" or "I just feel the Holy Spirit is in our midst every time you come to the pulpit." The "Pharisees" finally left, and Lydia and Tyisha approached the pastor.

"Pastor, we have been out of touch with the community this weekend. It is obvious to us that the church has decided to shun us, but we don't even know why."

"Lydia, I can only talk to you. Just being seen with Miss McFarren could cost me my job as a pastor and teacher. I am fighting ridiculous accusations about my fidelity to my wife, and I cannot do without the finances we receive from the congregants."

Tyisha could not believe what she was hearing. She had been in the Williston, North Dakota area for over six months and had never done anything deserving this sort of treatment. She walked to her classroom where she opened the door and sat at her desk. Little did she know she was sitting in that familiar chair for the last time.

Café con Leche

Lydia finally arrived. Everyone, including the pastor, was gone from the building and the two sisters in Christ began their conversation by hugging one another.

Tyisha began by asking, "What in the world happened to cause such a reaction?"

"The pastor lied to me and said he didn't know what happened. He said that many of the worshippers had been to some kind of secret Board meeting last night and you played prominently in the discussion. That is all he claimed to know."

Lydia and Tyisha went to eat at Lydia's parent's home, who were members of another church in town. By the time of their arrival, Lydia's folks had been fully briefed as to the accusations against Tyisha. Tyisha had become their "pseudo-daughter" and they wrestled as to how to break the news to her.

After eating lunch, Lydia's mother broke the silence. "Tyisha, several of the parents have been told you sexually abused one of your students." The news came as a total shock to Tyisha. She felt as if the air had been drawn from her lungs. How could anyone think such evil about her? She had sensed that teaching was the ministry to which the Lord had called her.

"Bert and I just felt you had a right to know so those hypocrites don't 'blindside you.'"

Tyisha thanked both of Lydia's parents for the lunch and the information. She excused herself and drove her car out in the country. After a couple of hours of prayer, she returned home. Usually, she called Jeremiah at 7:00 p.m. on Sunday nights, but she had to talk to him and tell him the pandemonium that had transpired that weekend. She didn't want anyone else to hear their conversation, so she picked up the telephone and called his home number.

"Hello." Jeremiah had clearly been in the midst of a Sunday afternoon nap.

"Jeremiah, I am sorry to call you now, but what I have to say just won't wait." Her voice was quivering as Tyisha almost cried.

"Ty, are you alright?"

"No, my whole world is coming apart."

Tyisha recited the whole episode-how her student had come to school beaten, how she had reported it to the Sheriff's deputies and how she was being accused of sexually molesting her student.

"Wow, Ty, I was hoping you would just call me and tell me how much you love me." Jeremiah's attempt at humor failed miserably.

"Jeremiah tomorrow doesn't hold anything good for me. Lydia is praying for me here, but I need to know that you are praying for me."

"Tyisha, I pray for you every day. Don't worry. You know you haven't done anything wrong. If the worst happens tomorrow, the Lord will be with you. He never promises to prevent all trouble from coming your way. He only promises to be with you through the hard times and to bless you with more blessings than you can contain.

You get a good night sleep and call me just as soon as you know something more definite. Remember, you are not alone. I will organize some Christians here to pray for you and I know Lydia is praying for you there. More importantly, the Holy Spirit is with you and will give you the words to say when needed. Don't worry, Tyisha, I will start the prayer circle this very evening. God's will be done. I love you and will be waiting impatiently for your response tomorrow. Good night, darling."

With this farewell, Jeremiah hung up the phone, but he could hear quiet snubs on the other end. He wished he could take the attacks of the satanic brethren, but all he could do was to pray and to ask other Christians to pray for Tyisha.

Jeremiah began to call fellow Christians in Pierre, South Dakota. Some worked at the school, others were in his church and still others had simply encountered him over the past six months since he had lived in South Dakota. Ten Christians volunteered to pray for Tyisha, whom they had heard about from Jeremiah, especially the following day when she went to see the headmaster.

CHAPTER 11

Tyisha had tried to sleep all night, but the severity of the allegations against her had kept her awake until the morning. How could any rational person think she would do harm to one of her student? Didn't people know that she loved each and every one of them? Maybe that was the wrong term. Perhaps it was better to say that she was "very fond" of them.

When it no longer mattered, she exited the bed and got ready for school. She wanted to get to school well before the arrival of the students. She knew the headmaster arrived by 6:30 a.m. and she wanted to be waiting at his door when he arrived.

True to plan, she arrived at the school before the sun was rising. The school custodian had already unlocked the front doors nearest to the headmaster's office, so Tyisha went in and found Mr. Christensen was already at his desk.

"Mr. Christensen, I have to tell you what happened Friday in your absence."

Mr. Christensen looked up at her casually and pointed at a chair. Tyisha stepped over the other chair and sat down directly in front of the desk.

The headmaster pretended not to know anything about the child abuse and allowed Tyisha to recount the events he knew more about than he wanted to.

"Last Friday, little Gabriel Brustad was hurting so badly he could not sit down at his desk. He has come to school at least three times with bruises, but this was the worst beating I have ever seen him sustain.

I had him take off his shirt so I could see the extent and location of the bruises. I was so emotionally distraught by what I saw that I pulled little Gabriel up to me and kissed the top of his head. There was absolutely nothing sexual about my action, nor his.

I came to your office to relay the events on Friday, but you were not here all day. So, as soon as school was dismissed, I traveled to Williams County Sheriff's Department and filed an official complaint against Gabriel's father. A Detective Hann took the information and promised the Department would investigate."

Mr. Christensen had already contacted the Williams County Sheriff's Department about the incident. Detective Hann had not been on duty, but the Desk Sergeant was, and he denied any knowledge of the complaint and said no one matching Miss McFarren's description had been in the office. He verified he had been on duty on the preceding Friday.

"Look, Miss McFarren, I almost believe your rendition of events. However, there was a respected witness who observed your interaction with young Mr. Brustad. The depiction of the event is extremely different than your own. Reality is ninety percent perception. Many parents want the school to err on the side of the safety of their children and they want nothing less then your dismissal.

Now, an emergency meeting of the School Board including the school's attorney was held on Saturday evening. It was the conclusion of the Board that you had violated your contract. Your contract states, and I quote, 'I will not commit any immoral acts or bring shame on the Redeemer's Salvation School.' The Board has concluded that you have violated both stipulations and they have terminated you at once."

Mr. Olsen who had promised not to consider the legal stipulations of Tyisha's contract on the "Lord's Day" had lied for the sake of his public image. He not only had looked at Tyisha's contract but gave his legal opinion to the members of the School Board that she could be fired on the

Café con Leche

ground of "Moral Depravity." What is more, he recommended that they write such a scathing letter to be placed in her personnel file that she never obtains another teaching position in a private or public school.

"I am so sorry to have to deliver this message, but the decision was not mine. Right now, I want you to go to your room and take down your posters, etc. and clear out your desk. I have already made arrangements for a long-term substitute to finish the year in your place. Your final check will be ready for you by the end of Wednesday, but do not come for it in school hours. It is best if you simply leave the school without further contact with your children. I will be by your room in about 30 minutes and at that time, be ready to leave the school."

Tyisha sat there dumbfounded for a minute. She could not believe that the promise held by the Redeemer's Salvation School just a few months earlier had been taken from her. Now, it was the source of her personal hell. She began to think that perhaps Mr. Christensen's mother had misnamed him.

Returning to her room for the last time, she tore off the walls all her teaching aids in minutes. It had taken days to originally mount them. She stopped at the custodian's closet next to her room and emptied a box of bottles of floor wax. Hurriedly, she threw the contents of her desk into the box and as she finished, Mr. Christensen entered the classroom door. Dutifully, Tyisha followed her headmaster for the last time to the front door. He was the perfect gentleman and Christian par excellence as he grabbed the bundle of posters and transported them to her car. He just wanted to see Tyisha leave and the problems that went with her.

Holding back her tears until Mr. Christensen loaded her car and turned back to the school building, Tyisha could do so no longer. The first students were arriving for the day, but Tyisha didn't care. She cried as hard as ever, like she did after her mother died years earlier. She drove away in her old Oldsmobile and went directly to Lydia's office.

She sat in the car in front of the real estate office, shaking like a leaf in a breeze. Finally, Lydia drove up in her own car and parked next to Tyisha.

"Tyisha, I have been praying all morning. Do not worry the Lord is your Sustainer and Provider."

"Thanks, Lydia, but prayer can't help me now, I was just fired."

"Oh no, Tyisha doesn't the School Board know what they are giving up? You were not only a good teacher, but I could feel your faith each time we prayed together. The students are the real losers in this mess. Just wait, Ty, the Lord has something even better for you. Do you want me to take the rest of the day off and go home with you?"

"Thanks, Sister, but I think it is better if I just go home and try to make some sense out of what has just happened."

Lydia came over to Ty's car and hugged her hurting sister through the car window. The embrace lasted several minutes, before Lydia moved apart from the car and Ty drove toward her home.

When she arrived, she decided it would be fruitless to unpack her box or posters and take them inside. After all, she would be packing up her car shortly. She had no plans. She didn't know where she would go or what she would do, but it was obvious she had to go somewhere and do something.

Inside the house, Ty picked up her Bible and asked the Lord to show her what to do. She simply opened the Bible to an arbitrary location and looked at the scripture in front of her.

> But as for you, ye thought evil against me; but God meant it unto good… (Genesis 50:20)

"Wow, how is the Lord going to fix this mess? I am so hurt, Father, but I know You can heal me. Even when I can control my tears on the outside, I am crying on the inside. You know how hard I have worked to become a teacher and now, in a moment, it is all being taken from me. I doubt if I can ever teach again anywhere. Lord, why did You bring me here just to send me away? Lord, bring back my joy. In Jesus name I pray it all, AMEN."

Before Tyisha fully opened her eyes, the telephone rang. It was Jeremiah calling at his free hour.

"Tyisha, I just couldn't wait until the end of the day, so I called your school. They wouldn't tell me why you weren't in your room, but the secretary did admit you were probably at home. So, tell me about your meeting with your headmaster this morning." With that, Jeremiah waited for a response. There was none. Tyisha was trying to avoid crying, but she could not.

With tears streaming down her face, she simply said, "They fired me! I have nothing." She could not continue.

Café con Leche

"Tyisha, listen to me. You don't have to say a word. I have been thinking about our situation ever since you called me yesterday. We have been planning to have a June wedding after the school year. Since you were coming here at the end of the semester and we were going on to Ohio to see my mother, maybe we could alter our plans a bit.

I can't wait to be your husband and June seems a lifetime away. Would you be my wife at Christmas break?"

Tyisha went from being heartsick to elated in a matter of seconds. "Yes, yes, I want to be your wife and I will marry you in December or June, in Ohio or Alabama. Besides, what else do I have to do?"

"Honey, I have been planning for this wedding and I think we can survive for the rest of the year. I'll get an income through next August and any funds you can add to our budget will be welcome. The Lord has planned everything ahead of our needs. My roommate was just promoted at his shoe store and has been selected to manage a new store in Yankton, South Dakota. He is leaving tomorrow. He promises to move all his personal belongings by Saturday. The house has plenty of room for us and it will be ours. I know that you are hurting right now, but I want us to make a new beginning here. The same Lord that brought us together will heal us. Only believe.

I can't wait to see you. I know the rest of the week will be busy for you, but I also know that all the pain you have experienced today will be lessened by time. I will do my best to provide all the love you need for healing, and God will do the rest. I only have one question-will I be allowed to drive your car to Ohio?"

Tyisha was already feeling better and responded, "Let's see how things go before I commit." She giggled and Jeremiah felt better knowing that she would be better, and her faith would survive the valley.

After telling Tyisha how much he loved her and promising to pray for her through the time of trial, he hung up the phone. Jeremiah rushed from the teacher's lounge and literally ran in to his class where his students were waiting.

"Students, I know all of you are fidgety with the Christmas Vacation quickly approaching. But that is no reason for your teacher to be distracted. However, I have a good reason. When you return to school in January, you will have a married teacher."

The class nearly erupted in congratulations, eight of his students left their seats and patted their teacher on the back. When order had been restored, Jeremiah continued.

"I will be going to be with my mother in Ohio over the holiday where my fiancée and I will be married. I will introduce you to her next semester. Until then, I apologize for being late. Now, let's turn to page 12 of our Reader."

As soon as the school day ended, Jeremiah drove home and grabbed a soft drink out of his refrigerator. Though it was cold, he went out on his back porch and looked over the Missouri River. As he drank slowly, he worried about Tyisha five hundred miles north on the same river. He wanted to be with her and hold her and whisper in her ear. He wished he could be there to give a piece of his mind to a certain headmaster and School Board members. He felt impotent, but then he remembered that both he and Tyisha were seeking to serve the Lord. God would not forget them, and He would make all things right, if not now, then when He was ready.

Jeremiah and Tyisha were entering into the most holy relationship-marriage. Jeremiah was determined to base their marriage on faith and love and nothing less. No matter how deep the valley seemed right now, only faith in God could provide the strength to endure to the end.

Jeremiah's soft drink was beginning to form ice on the top, and he was cold, so Jeremiah returned to the warmth of his home. Though he was empathetic with his fiancée's situation, he could not wait until he and Tyisha were wed, and Ty no longer lived near those wretched people who had treated her so cruelly in Williston, North Dakota.

***

Tyisha spent every available moment with Lydia. Both knew they would soon be living apart and neither wanted the separation. In six months, they had become best friends and sisters in Christ. Neither had ever experienced a closer relationship.

The half-filled boxes were strewn throughout Tyisha's house as she quickly ran room to room collecting personal belongings-pans and pots in one box, clothes in another, and whatnots in still another. As Tyisha packed, she kept out clothing she would need for her trip to Ohio and wedding and return trip to South Dakota.

Café con Leche

With all her personal items packed, she prepared for Wednesday. It promised to be the busiest day of the week. Lydia was coming to take her to see Mrs. Edgerton, the owner of Tyisha's house. As Lydia drove up on the hard-packed snow to the side of the house, Tyisha felt ashamed to be there. The two young ladies had come to tell Mrs. Edgerton about the events of the week and to break the news that Tyisha would have to break her lease and was leaving the next day.

Mrs. Edgerton's house, if one could describe it as such, was ten feet wide and twenty feet long. It was wrapped in black tar paper and had a rusty tin roof. Tyisha had seen chicken houses that were more substantial in the south. She dreaded delivering the news of her imminent departure to a lady who clearly depended on the income Tyisha was providing. But she had no choice. She had to leave, and she knew the Lord would support the old lady as He had before Tyisha had come.

After Lydia knocked on the door, they heard the old lady slowly coming to the door. Lydia had called Mrs. Edgerton earlier, but this forewarning did not seem to comfort the old woman. Mrs. Edgerton opened the door that was not square and had half-inch gaps on the right and top of the door.

"Girls, come on into my humble abode." Tyisha's house was three times as large and in much better condition. It was obvious that Mrs. Edgerton had rented out the house where Tyisha lived, because she needed the income and could never rent the house where she lived.

It was a typical frigid North Dakota December day. As Lydia and Tyisha entered the house, they could still see their breath. Inside the house, asbestos insulation was showing around the edges of newspapers that covered the inner walls of the house. An old threadbare sofa and chair sat in the 'living room.' A toilet was next to the bed in the 'bedroom' and from her seat on the old sofa, she could see the edge of a wash basin hanging on the wall. Tyisha could see the bed; an old full-size mattress hanging over the edge of a much smaller frame. The mattress suffered from a hole in the middle deeper than any valley in North Dakota. In the corner of the main room sat a small wood stove and next to it was a neatly stacked pile of lumber offal, all cut to different lengths. From the temperature in the room, it was obvious Mrs. Edgerton used it sparingly.

Mrs. Edgerton saw the two girls staring at her stove and broke the silence.

"Lydia, you know Jack Ingram, the owner of the Williston Lumber Yard?"

Before Lydia could answer, Mrs. Edgerton continued.

"Well, of course you do, he has lived here all his life. Jack was raised in the house next to ours and he was our son's best friend. His folks actually had less than we did, and he ate most of his meals at our house.

Now, forty years later, he has never forgotten. He brings me a load of scrap lumber pieces every week to heat my home and always has a couple of bags of groceries with him. Look how uniform the pieces are. I think he cuts up perfectly good lumber just to help me through the winters.

After my husband died fifteen years ago, I could not afford to live in the house where Tyisha lives now. In all those fifteen years, not one of the church members or the pastor of the Calvin Presbyterian Church has ever come to see me. Not one has brought an old Christian sister a stick of wood, a bag of groceries or taken me to a doctor."

Suddenly Tyisha felt ashamed. For six months she had planned to visit Mrs. Edgerton and maybe take the old lady out to eat, but she never had. She knew that good intentions would never take the place of good deeds. Now, she would never have the opportunity to do what she had planned to do.

Tyisha began. "Mrs. Edgerton, I don't know what you know about the situation I am in. Thank God, I met the love of my life while at teacher's meetings in South Dakota, and he is helping me through the hardest trial of my life. This past Monday, I was fired without a single chance to defend myself from baseless allegations.

I have already paid my rent for December, but I want you to keep it in totality. Also, I would be honored if you would take my furniture I have bought since last June. It is not worth the money I am obligated to pay until next May, but maybe it will offset some of the money owed. Lydia will even arrange for it to be delivered to you after I am out of the house."

Tyisha looked at Lydia who was nodding her head in agreement.

Finally, Mrs. Edgerton slowly walked toward Lydia and Tyisha and hugged them both.

"Thank you so much for coming to see me. I get awfully lonely. Sisters, the Lord supported my needs before you came, Tyisha, and He will provide for me as long as He has need for me in this life. It has been an honor to know you.

Café con Leche

Yes, I have heard about the disparaging remarks made by our fellow Christian about you, but I felt the Spirit of the Lord on you the first time we met. I know you are hurt, but there are some good people in Williston, North Dakota. Please don't think the worst of all of us due to the few who have done this evil to you. Now, you go and start your life anew with your young beau. Mr. Edgerton and I were married for sixty-nine years, and we learned to love each other almost as much as we loved the Lord. You make Christ the center of your marriage and love Him as you do one another."

"Mrs. Edgerton, you showed me the love of our Lord the first week I was here and now you are continuing to love me when I have been so unloving this week. I love you and Lydia; you are my sisters." Tyisha hugged both women as Lydia and Tyisha left the little shack. To Tyisha's surprise, it was Lydia who had a tear in her eye.

Together, they returned to Tyisha's house so she could drive her own car. They planned to have supper together that night at a local restaurant, but Tyisha had several things to do first. She drove to the school at the end of the school day and waited until all the students and teachers had left. When she was sure only the school offices were occupied, she went in and asked the secretary for her last check.

"You have your nerve after what you have done." Tyisha stood at the counter almost in awe. Just the week before, the same lady had taken her to lunch. She had never considered that caring for her students could generate such a hostile reaction.

The lady walked over to a desk, picked up the check and almost threw it at Tyisha. Tyisha's immediate human reaction was to say 'I am going to jump over this counter and pull the hair out of this fat, blue-eyed bimbo' but she did not. Instead, Tyisha simply said, "Sister, each of us will stand before our Lord in judgment and then you will know the truth." Tyisha turned and walked away.

Tyisha got in her car and drove to a nearby gas station that had rental trailers. After a hitch was attached to her back bumper, a trailer was hooked on. She paid the owner and drove back to her home, where she began to load the trailer. Lydia drove up just as Tyisha was placing the last box inside and locking the back door.

They took Lydia's car to a family restaurant in Williston. Both sensed this was their last meal together. They tried to keep the mood light, but they were not parting company by choice. After the meal, they prolonged the night as long as possible, but the time came when they had to part. Lydia drove back to Tyisha's house, which looked so forlorn with no curtains or lights on inside. They sat inside the car for twenty minutes, before Tyisha finally announced she had to go in and get some rest. The following day was certain to be trying.

"Lydia, you have been the best friend I have ever had. I hoped we could live close by for years, but that is not to be. The Lord has given you the gift of love and hospitality. Never lose them.

Tell your folks 'Good-bye' for me and thank them for their support and the good meals. I will be leaving here early in the morning so I will not be able to see you before I leave. Please pray for me and safe travels. Jeremiah and I will be getting married in Ohio just before Christmas. We will be returning to his house in Pierre, South Dakota before January 3 when he goes back to school. I will be sure to send you our new address.

Sister, this is not the way I wanted to part, but it is a mixed blessing. I have lost my career as a teacher, but I have gained the husband I always longed for. I love you and your support through this ordeal has kept me going. Don't worry I will call you as soon as Jeremiah and I are established in South Dakota."

Both ladies knew a phone call would never take the place of an occasional hug or laughter at their own expense. Tyisha leaned over and hugged Lydia one last time. The embrace lasted for several minutes, before Tyisha opened her door and went inside with tears flowing down her eyes. The next morning came quickly following a night almost devoid of sleep. All packed and ready to leave, she threw her sheets and blankets into the back seat of the car. She dreaded driving on Highway 85 after five big snows. She was still a girl from the south and only slowly learning to drive on frozen precipitation. The snow trucks had thrown most of the snow off the highway, but it was still a daunting task to drive hundreds of miles on partially covered pavement.

It was dark when Tyisha pulled out of her drive and headed south toward Lake Sakakawea and the sun didn't show the light of a new day until she was well into the wheat fields of western North Dakota. She looked into her mirror with mixed emotions. She had a sense of reluctance

Café con Leche

as she left Williston and anticipation as she thought of a life with Jeremiah in service to the Lord.

Tyisha drove all the way to the junction with Interstate 94. She noted that her trailer seemed to be traveling well and did not wander side to side. It was lunch time when she arrived in Bismarck. She pulled off the Interstate and ate at a fast-food restaurant before going across the street and having her car filled with gas.

Back on the Interstate, she continued east to the intersection with Highway 83. Turning south, she followed the highway to the border with South Dakota. It was getting late in the day, and she was exhausted. The trials and tribulations of the last week had left her severely weakened. Barely into South Dakota Tyisha approached the small town of Mound City. She had hoped to drive all the way to Pierre, but knew she was too tired to make it. Whether it was a vision or exhaustion, she knew not, but Tyisha saw the vestige of her old friend, mentor and sister-in-Christ sitting on the passenger side of the Oldsmobile.

Tyisha started to gasp, but before she could make a sound, her eyesight corrected, and she could see the sign of a motel just ahead of her.

As was her habit, she rented a room in a local motel on the side of the highway and asked the motel clerk to direct her to the nearest restaurant. After placing her luggage in the room, she went to eat a quick supper. Fortunately, the miles left to see Jeremiah were doable. She hoped to be in Pierre by 2:00 p.m. when Jeremiah was due to be out of school for the Christmas holidays. Tyisha planned to return the trailer to a local dealer and be at Jeremiah's home when he returned from school. She hoped he would feel like driving when he got home, and they could make a couple of hundred miles eastward toward Ohio by the end of Friday. Every mile she drove toward Jeremiah, the less she thought about the hurt she had experienced in Williston.

***

Dag Brustad was a huge man who had been considered the town bully since he was in elementary school. He grew up near the Springbrook community, northeast of Williston, where his father left him more than 8,000 acres of wheat producing land.

Even the Williams County deputies were afraid of him. He had no conscience and could commit any crime. Mr. Brustad was jovial when it served his purposes and highly intelligent. He could be quite charming when he wanted a person's vote or to make a deal.

The people of Springbrook and the surrounding area were tired of being frightened every time the huge man brought a load of wheat to the elevators. He seemed to take great joy in scaring the little children and adults alike of the agrarian community.

The whole community had heard about the multiple beatings of little Gabriel Brustad and how he was still bruised and battered by the most recent attack. At least ten of the local populace had reported the beatings before to the police authorities but nothing had been done, leaving Mr. Brustad with a feeling of invincibility.

Folks from the village and surrounding countryside had a clandestine meeting in a local barn. The group was raucous at the beginning, but eventually concluded that the only remedy was to remove Mr. Brustad from the land of the living. The self-appointed leader of the meeting, a Mr. Teddy Jackson, was a former county deputy. He told the participants that they had to use shotguns to avoid detection and they had to take a vow to never give any information that could identify anyone else in the plot. Each one of the attendees readily took the vow and promised to be prepared to commit the crime on the following day. Dag Brustad always came to the little store next to the elevators on Fridays to buy supplies for his farm and livestock. They took the vow one at a time. Some were farmers, others worked at the grain elevators and the one woman was Dag's wife.

Like clockwork, Mr. Brustad arrived at the small store at about 10:00 a.m. He sat there in the cold in his pickup listening to *Kiss an Angel Good Mornin.'* Dag loved Country music and the fact it was dominated by white artists made it even more appealing. He never knew his favorite song was performed by a black man and he would never find out.

He was so engrossed in his music that he did not notice his wife and nine of his neighbors were slowly encircling the back and sides of his pickup. In unison, they pointed their shotguns at Mr. Brustad and shot him multiple times at close range. Some had five-shot pump shotguns, others had over and under shotguns and still others had double-barrel shotguns. The loud retorts did not end until all shells had been emptied into the pickup.

Café con Leche

Teddy Jackson opened the pickup driver's door and pulled the nearly decapitated body from the truck and onto the ground. Those with remaining shells approached and emptied each shot into the long-dead body. The smoke slowly drifted upward as the conspirators walked nonchalantly into the store. Teddy Jackson walked over to the telephone on the wall of the store and telephoned the Williams County Sheriff's Office. He told the desk sergeant that he had just discovered the body of Dag Brustad next to his pickup in front of the store in Springbrook. Mr. Jackson told him he would be waiting for the deputies sent to investigate.

As soon as he hung up the phone, Mr. Jackson sent the others on their way to their homes and jobs and waited for the officers to arrive. When the deputies arrived, three of them, they found the former Dag Brustad in an almost unrecognizable state. They had to send off a blood sample to the state laboratory to prove their victim was, in fact, Dag Brustad.

Every person in the small village at the time of the murder was interviewed by the deputies, but none of them heard or saw anything. Since there were literally thousands of shotguns in Williams County, they concluded Dag Brustad was killed by one very angry assailant or multiple assailants. The deputies knew that the victim had almost an inexhaustible list of people with motive to kill Mr. Brustad. With no evidence or witnesses to the crime, the FBI was called to investigate, but none of the inhabitants' memories improved.

The folks of Springbrook were almost giddy after the elimination of the reprobate, Dag Brustad. Mrs. Brustad's neighbor rented her 8,000 acres for enough money to allow Mrs. Brustad and her children to survive and even thrive. Besides, it was her land now and when Gabriel and his younger brothers matured a bit, they could farm the land.

At the graveside service for his father, Gabriel knew there were adults in the crowd that expected him to cry. He just couldn't generate any tears, so he feigned shock.

Gabriel began to heal, inside and out, but always felt responsible for the termination of his teacher, Miss Tyisha McFarren. He had no idea where she had gone, but no one had treated him with the love she had shown him. He didn't know much about God since his father was a Churchian, but in his childlike faith he prayed that the Lord would guard and protect Miss McFarren.

CHAPTER 12

It was Friday morning and Tyisha got up ready to travel. She was tired of saying 'Good-bye' and she couldn't wait to see Jeremiah. She had not been in his presence since they were at teacher's meetings in the earlier summer, and she needed his deep faith now more than ever.

Pulling her trailer out of the motel's parking lot, she continued south on Highway 83 to Selby, South Dakota. She stopped at the first gas station and had the attendant fill her car. Across the street was a small diner. Tyisha got a ham and cheese sandwich 'to go' and ate with one hand as she drove with the other.

She travelled non-stop to Pierre and followed the directions Jeremiah had provided to her arriving at his house at 12:45 p.m. As he had promised, he had left the back door to his house unlocked. She went in and took a moment to do research into the living habits of the man she planned to marry. She was pleasantly surprised. Jeremiah's roommate had been moved for over a week and Jeremiah had cleaned the two rooms his roommate usually occupied. The entire house was clean and neat. There were no clothes strewn over furniture or in piles on the floor. She was duly impressed. His neatness and organization were to be envied.

Tyisha had work ahead of her. She unlocked the front door and after four attempts, she backed the trailer up the drive so she could carry the contents the shortest distance into the house. Box after box, she carried the contents of the trailer into the house and into an unoccupied back bedroom.

When she finished, she pulled the trailer to a local dealer and turned it in. By the time the trailer hitch was removed from the bumper, and she drove back to Jeremiah's house, it was 2:20 p.m. She almost had a head-on collision with her fiancée, who was returning from his school. She got out of the car and ran to him. He exited his own vehicle and the two young lovers hugged indefinitely in the middle of the street until Jeremiah's neighbor yelled out of his own car, "Hey, you two want to do that somewhere out of the street?"

Jeremiah yelled back, "Sorry, sir, we'll move right now." Jeremiah moved his car into the drive and Tyisha moved her car to the curb and allowed the neighbor clear passage.

"Ty, I have my luggage packed and ready. Let me go retrieve it and lock up the house. We have a lot to talk about, but let's drive east as we do so. I'll be right back." With that Jeremiah ran into the house to lock it up and retrieve his bags.

By the time he returned, Tyisha had turned her Oldsmobile around in the direction of Highway 83 and eventually the intersection with Interstate 90. They filled up at a local gas station and headed toward the destination-Ohio.

With vehicles few and far between on Interstate 90, Jeremiah seemed tense, and Tyisha could feel his emotion as he held her hand. Finally, Jeremiah looked over at Ty and said, "Honey, I know you have just been through a horrific event and that the changes that marriage are going to create, cause plenty of stress right now, but I have to add another."

Ty squeezed Jeremiah's hand and pulled hers lose. "It's a good thing I am sitting down. Do I want to lie down to hear this?"

"No honey, it is nothing that should come as a shock to you. You know how I have given my life to the Lord and have vowed to follow Him wherever He leads. Over the past three months, He has shown me in multiple ways that He wants me to take His gospel to the world. In other words, He wants me in missions."

This came as no shock to Tyisha who had detected movement in Jeremiah's faith and commitment during their nightly radio conversations. She was not offended by Jeremiah's comments; in fact, she was excited. She had only one goal now that her career had been taken from her and that was to marry Jeremiah and be his wife wherever the Lord took them. She couldn't wait to get started.

"Jeremiah, I can't claim the Lord has called me to missions, but I know He has called me to be your wife. I want to go anywhere, anytime you go. I trust you to follow the will of God and I want to help you achieve His purposes."

"For weeks, I have wondered just how I was going to broach this subject with you. Just as I was about to get the courage, you had the crisis at your school. Then, we had the tension of a wedding six months early. Now, here we are driving to see my mother and have that wedding.

I never dreamed you would be amenable to my calling, but I should have known the Lord would prepare you to hear His call just as He has prepared me."

They resumed holding hands as Jeremiah continued eastward. They spent the night at a motel in the middle of Sioux City, South Dakota. After a quick meal together, they went back to their individual rooms with the hope of needing only one room in four days.

By 6:00 a.m., Tyisha and Jeremiah were the first customers at the same restaurant where they had eaten supper. They ate hurriedly and got on Interstate 29 south. They traveled through eastern South Dakota and then into western Iowa across the Missouri River from Omaha, Nebraska, through one corn field after another. As they entered northwest Missouri, the land began to change to more hilly terrains.

Jeremiah, who was something of an amateur historian regarding criminals looked at Tyisha and said, "Ty, we are entering the land of famous criminals. St. Joseph, Missouri was the location of the murder of Jesse James. He and his brother, Frank had a notorious gang that robbed banks and trains in the Midwest. They were from Kearney, Missouri just forty miles further south.

Just outside of Platte City, Missouri, Bonnie Parker and Clyde Barrow's gang had a major shootout with the local police and FBI, including an armored car from Kansas City. They got away and continued their crime spree.

To the east, is a little town entitled 'Excelsior Springs.' It is famous for providing rest and relaxation for criminals from the challenge of robbing and

Café con Leche

killing. To the south is a town called "Liberty." The Clay County Bank on the square was the first bank to be robbed in daylight by the James Gang.

Kansas City had a 'powerbroker' named 'Tom Pendergast.' Back in the 1920's and 1930's, he controlled the city's politics and even criminals. Criminals who wanted to rob a bank had to get his 'blessing' before committing their crime. He gave us Senator Harry Truman who later became President Truman."

"Wow, Jeremiah, where did you learn so much about an area almost a thousand miles from our home?"

"When I was little in Madisonville, I had no friends, black or white. I had to find ways to fill my time. I loved to read, and my parents both encouraged me to do so. One of my favorite topics was famous criminals and how they became criminals. This area of northwest Missouri has quite a history of criminals dating back into the 1860's."

Just south of St. Joseph, Missouri, Jeremiah began to feel the grip on his right hand lessen. He looked over and saw his bride-to-be leaning on her door. She was snoring so loudly that he could hear over the sound of the wind. Jeremiah did all he could not to laugh. After the hardest week of her life, and there had been many, Tyisha was finally able to sleep. Jeremiah allowed her to do so.

Driving south of Platte City, Jeremiah caught occasional glimpses of downtown Kansas City. He had never seen such an impressive sight in Alabama, not even in Birmingham, certainly not in Pierre, South Dakota. He merged onto Interstate 35 and took the loop around the downtown area and exited onto Interstate 70 east toward St. Louis. He was thankful it was only 2:30 p.m. and the traffic was light. He found himself continuously wandering outside of his lane, distracted by the tall buildings just inside the loop of Interstate highways.

Winding through the eastern part of Kansas City, he quickly saw the exit to Independence, Missouri and the President Harry Truman Library. Tyisha continued her "snore fest" through the entire metropolitan area. She only awoke when they crossed the Highway 13 intersection. Jeremiah pulled the car off and filled up with gasoline at the first gas station. Meanwhile, Tyisha slowly gained her bearings.

"Hon, I'm getting hungry. Are you ready for a break and I'll drive us further east after we eat?"

"I thought you would never wake up. Columbia, Missouri is ahead, and we can find someplace there to eat. I hope we can still get to St. Louis by 9:00 p.m. so we can make it an easy trip to Mother's house tomorrow."

"That sounds great. I'll take a little nap until we get to Columbia." Tyisha leaned against her door and closed her eyes. The stress was fast leaving her; the further they were from Williston, North Dakota, the more her stress seemed to diminish. Just in the last few days, her personality was quickly changing. She had asked the Lord to forgive all of those who were responsible for her termination. She was sad regarding their ignorance. Sin always has consequences, whether it is forgiven or not. Her enemies' combined sins would cost them far more than they were willing to pay.

The car hit every seam in the highway and the monotonous "thump, thump, thump" quickly caused Tyisha to fall into a deep sleep. Sitting there on the passenger side of the car with her head resting against the window frame, Tyisha heard the voice of her old friend and sister-in-Christ, Miss Jorgina Boudoir.

"Ty, you have forgiven those who sinned against you in North Dakota, but you still have hate in your heart for your grandparents and uncle who sinned against you in Alabama. Girl, you are right to forgive them. Now, forgive all of those who have hurt you, so the Lord can use you to do His work."

She awoke with a startle from the lights next to the highway shining in her eyes. Tyisha's anger was subsiding and had begun to do so the moment she forgave those who had sinned against her. She was now focused on the future, not the past, on a life with Jeremiah led by their God.

She quickly returned to a deep sleep as Jeremiah drove through the dark ever eastward. After more than an hour, he exited the Interstate on Highway 63 and went to a restaurant frequented by the students from the nearby University of Missouri. Tyisha roused as they entered the parking lot in front of the restaurant.

Following a good evening meal, Tyisha took the wheel of the car and returned to Interstate 70 and headed east toward St. Louis. By the time she arrived in St. Louis, she went downtown on the Boone Parkway and crossed the Mississippi River below. To the south was moored *The Admiral*, a large tourist boat. She could not take her eyes off the huge "Gateway Arch," a national monument completed in 1965. Tyisha looked in her rearview mirror and was awed by the giant stainless-steel arch backlit by downtown St. Louis.

It was 8:30 p.m. and Tyisha was getting tired. She continued to the exit nearest Scott AFB and got the first motel room she could find. Jeremiah had fallen asleep and had snoring issues of his own. She woke him up and they got their overnight bags to carry into rooms 11 and 12. They didn't even care about getting any food since it was 9:00 p.m. and they were exhausted after a full day of traveling.

Before he went to sleep, Jeremiah telephoned his mother from his room and told her that he and Tyisha planned to be at her house by evening the following day. He could hear the excitement in her voice. She told her son that she had arranged with her pastor to perform the wedding service in her church a couple of days after their arrival. Also, Mrs. Hall told Jeremiah that she had a friend at church that was employed at the Scioto County Courthouse. He had promised Mrs. Hall to take the personal information she had provided for Tyisha and Jeremiah and have the government forms complete, so all they would have to do was to come in on Monday, show identification and sign them in his presence.

Jeremiah thought about it for a moment and thanked his mother for all her hard work on his behalf. He was sure he and Ty could "tie the knot" and still be able to have a short honeymoon before returning to Pierre. He hoped the headmaster of his school would give him a "business day," on January 3, if warranted, especially since it was a Friday. Not much would be accomplished on Friday, whether he was there or not.

Mrs. Hall, beaming with pride for her son, said, "Jeremiah, I have a surprise for you when you get here. I telephoned your old coach at Alabama State University and got the contact information for some of your old teammates. Some are coming to your wedding, and a few will be in the wedding. Also, your cousin 'Nisy,' is coming from Indianapolis and will be Tyisha's bridesmaid." "Juanita" was her real name, but she could never pronounce her name as a small child. Hence, she had been nicknamed "Nisy" by members of the family.

"Mom, I know you must work, so don't go overboard organizing my wedding. We will be there tomorrow night and then we can finalize any plans for the wedding. I can't wait to make Tyisha my wife. Wait till you meet her. She loves the Lord and is going to be a wonderful helpmate for me. I can't wait to tell you about the ministry to which God is leading us.

We have a long trip left to us tomorrow, so I better get a few hours of sleep. We'll see you tomorrow night. We love you Mom and we're looking forward to seeing you. Good night, Mom."

Mrs. Hall hung up the phone but knew she would not be able to go to sleep. She was so proud of the man Jeremiah was becoming. His father would be proud of him, as well. She knew the obstacles he had overcome. Somehow, he had found the Lord at a young age, and that relationship had grown. Now, Jeremiah had found a quality young Christian woman who wanted to share her son's life and his call of God.

All those years ago in the heart of the Deep South, Mrs. Hall's husband had died and left her to raise a biracial son when everyone around them despised them. She, a black woman, had to leave that town to find some degree of peace. Her son continued to attend college nearby, but only his football skills made him acceptable to his peers. Now, Jeremiah was a teacher and following the leadership of God in his life. The pain, crying and sorrow were worth it all just to see how far her son had come. She lay down and thanked her Lord for all the miracles He had worked in her life. She knew her husband would approve of the job she had done with their son. Mrs. Hall fell asleep with a deep sense of peace and joy.

***

Since most of them were employed across the Deep South, they had all agreed to meet in the parking lot in front of their old college dormitory. The entire offensive line had decided to go to the wedding of their old teammate, Jeremiah. When they had played football, Jeremiah was a star. He was the one that people came to see and all the sports reporters wanted to interview him after each game. Jeremiah had never failed to give credit to the line for opening a hole or for a crucial block that sprung him around the end of the line. His line loved him and would do anything for him.

The former right guard was a huge man six feet seven inches tall and weighing over 330 pounds. For comfort, he had purchased a Chrysler Imperial car. It was the only vehicle they could hope to fit in. One at a time, they entered the huge car, but the last one, the former tight end,

Café con Leche

weighed 250 pounds. He could only make it into the vehicle by readjusting the other occupants.

No matter how hard they tried or inhaled in unison, the driver could not turn the steering wheel without obstruction. The former center had enough and told the others he was going to drive his own vehicle, a 1966 Mustang. He and one other member of the line got out and entered the little car. This allowed sufficient room for the other members of the team to have some space in the oversize Chrysler Imperial. Still, the 440 cubic inch Wedgehead engine had to use every cubic inch to propel the huge car up the higher elevations of northern Alabama and Tennessee.

The Imperial with the Mustang following pulled off the highway at Cullman, Alabama where the enormous men got a quick meal at a place entitled "Hilda's House." A sign on the front of the building said in chalk, "T'day's specialty: Pickled Pigs Feet, Green Beans, Peach Pie and Ice Cream for Dessert." After the big men ate, they reentered their cars and drove down old Highway 31 toward the north. They stopped at the last service station on the way out of town and pulled up next to the gas pumps.

"We don't serve your kind around here," said the shriveled little man who had been a former member of the KKK.

All six huge men exited their vehicles and walked toward him. He had a sudden change of heart when he saw the size of the men and the clear anger on their faces.

"Well, the boss ain't here, and we just won't tell him. Sir, pull your car up here and I will get her filled for you."

The gas attendant filled both cars and was happy to see both cars drive out of sight.

The young linemen, all of whom had graduated and were in excess of twenty-one years of age, thought about stopping early and seeing some of the nightlife of Louisville, Kentucky. To the shock of each one of them, they all returned to their rooms ready for bed and not one had drunk alcohol to excess. Only the center was a professed Christian. The others were just exhausted from their trip. Maybe they truly were growing up.

Early the next morning, the group awoke and ate at a local restaurant. After filling their cars with gasoline at a local service station, they drove northeastward on the new Interstate 71 with four or five portions still to be completed. After crossing the Ohio River at Cincinnati, the two cars turned

127

southeastward on United States Highway 52. The highway was roughly contiguous to the Ohio River and was a scenic drive. There were farm fields on both sides of the roadway and only an occasional small town east of Cincinnati. They drove down the highway all the way to Portsmouth, Ohio, the setting of the wedding and Jeremiah's mother's home.

In the front of Mrs. Hall's home, they were awed by the view from her front door. It sat on the east side of Portsmouth and had an unobstructed view of the river bottom. When Mrs. Hall answered the door, she saw six huge men on her front porch. Her first thought was, "I hope the carpenters braced the floor."

Mrs. Hall was a hugger. One at a time, she hugged each member of Jeremiah's team. A couple of the young men were embarrassed by the exuberance of this woman the age of their mothers.

The center, a Mr. Rory Calente, was the designated speaker for the group. "What's for supper Mrs. Hall?" The very idea of trying to feed this bunch nearly gave the middle-aged woman a heart attack. The whole group erupted in laughter at the shock on Mrs. Hall's face.

"Actually, we have already paid for motel rooms for the next three nights and we want to take you, Jeremiah and Tyisha out to eat tonight. We have never met Tyisha, but if Jeremiah has chosen her as his wife, she must be quite a gal."

From inside, they all heard Jeremiah, "Mom, who is at the door?" Jeremiah stepped out on the front porch and the "lovefest" began all over again. His old team members wanted to take the hugging inside, so a passing motorist did not see them. Seven large men hugging one another always brings unwanted attention: especially seven black men in 1968 whether north or south of the Mason-Dixon Line.

"So, Mr. Hall, where is this beautiful 'God's choice for you?'" The rest of the team members all nodded at Mr. Calente in agreement.

"We picked up the marriage license this morning so it's too late to back out now. Ty is out with my cousin and her bridesmaids doing some last-minute shopping. They'll be back anytime."

"Okay, but we're beginning to think she is a figment of your imagination. We're going back to our rooms and get some rest. How about we meet at 7:00 p.m. and go out to eat at a restaurant of your choice? You make the reservations. Is that good for you all?"

Café con Leche

Jeremiah and his mother looked at each other and nodded in agreement. Jeremiah was not even married, and he was learning it was a mistake to compel Tyisha to anything without consulting her first.

"Guys, let me get with Tyisha when she gets home, and we will get back to you about time."

"Dude, that's fair. We're at the Riverview Inn, rooms 8, 10 and 11."

"We'll call and guys it is so good to see every one of you. Thank you for coming to be with us on this special day. I know Tyisha will come to love you almost as much as I do. We look forward to spending a few quality hours together."

"We all do, too. We'll get some rest and wait for your call. Talk to you later, Mr. Groom." With this farewell, the six football players left in their cars for the motel and a well-deserved rest.

***

By previous agreement, the entire wedding party had decided to meet at an Italian restaurant entitled "Luigi's Ristorante." It was an old establishment dating back to the 1890's and had a great view of the Ohio River below.

The six huge linemen pulled into the side parking lot of the restaurant in the Chrysler Imperial and the Mustang. Nearly simultaneously, Jeremiah parked next to them in Tyisha's Oldsmobile. A fourth car arrived, and the three occupants exited the small Chevrolet Nova. The driver, Miss Juanita Jefferies, was Jeremiah's cousin from Indianapolis. She was tall, had an athletic build, and was a "knock out." All six men from the Alabama State football team nearly turned their heads in unison to view the young beauty.

Before Jeremiah could introduce his cousin and her friends, Rory Calente moved toward Miss Jefferies.

"Hello, I'm Rory Calente. I was Jeremiah's roommate and his main blocker on the Alabama State football team." The other team members almost erupted with, "Yeah, right!"

To heal bruised egos and to avoid any contention between his old friends, Jeremiah recommended they go inside, especially since the wind coming off the river was frigid, and the Southern men were starting to slur their words and shiver.

"Hey, guys, why don't we go inside before we freeze?" The entire wedding party went inside the front door of the restaurant into a room where the maître d' stood, looking at his list of reservations. Jeremiah walked up to him and said, "I am Jeremiah Hall, and I made the reservation for twelve for 7:00 p.m." The older man looked up from his desk and saw the huge mass of mankind in front of him. He began thinking quickly. Without verbalizing a word, he thought to himself, "There are two big oak beams down in the wine cellar and a rock foundation corner right under tables 11 and 12."

He looked at Jeremiah and said, "I hadn't considered the size of your guests. Please give me a moment to make the proper arrangements." With this he walked away and moved tables 11 and 12 together and their place settings.

"Right this way ladies and gentlemen." He led them to the two tables and asked them their drink orders. He left and was replaced by their waiter, a young man named "Franco." After ordering multiple orders of lasagna, spaghetti with Italian sausage, and cannelloni, the formalities seemed to fade away. The fellows sat at one end of the tables and rehashed great plays on the football field. Mrs. Hall, Tyisha, Juanita and the other two ladies sat on the other end talking about the wedding in two days, the color of their dresses they had purchased earlier that day, and the pillow treatments Tyisha was planning in the bachelor's den back in Pierre, South Dakota. She had not told Jeremiah of her plans, nor would she.

"Man, Jeremiah, you would have loved this honky in Cullman, Alabama." Immediately, both groups perked up their ears as Antonio Feldman, the former right guard on the team, recounted the racism of the gas attendant.

"You all know that Tyisha and I have lived in the northern Midwest for much of the last year. There is one thing we have both discovered. Racism is not geographic. It is everywhere and in a whole lot of people.

I keep up with Syracuse University because it is where my father played football and met my mother there. Syracuse has been having race riots and there have been injuries to both police and rioters alike. The rioters broke into a huge Sears and Roebuck store and stole anything that wasn't nailed down.

There was a white family from Missouri who moved into private housing near the University. The father was a student there and their daughter, who was nine, went to a public school nearby. On the first day of school, a large black girl who had been retained four times, told the little girl, "Honky, I'm gonna get ya." That same day as the little white girl left the school grounds, the much larger black girl attacked her. She knocked the little girl down and began kicking her, breaking three ribs. The father went to the Registrar's office to disenroll from his Ph.D. program. The following day, he filled up a rental trailer, and drove his family back to their home in the Midwest where his daughter healed in the relative peace of the Ozark hills.

Tyisha and I have been living in North and South Dakota since last spring. We have seen the racism there, as well as in the South. The American Indians are barely tolerated in some places by the white settlers. The few Asians are not treated much better.

Guys, we aren't any different. Do you all remember that game with those white boys from Quachita Baptist University? I knew they couldn't run with me, so I took every opportunity to make them look bad. I scored five touchdowns that day and enjoyed every one of them. It was allot more fun to score on those white farm boys than to score against Grambling."

Rory chimed in, "Yeah, man, do you remember the coach's pep speech before that game? I almost remember it word for word.

'You have a great opportunity tonight. You can teach a bunch of white honkies how to play this game. You can hit them so hard linemen that they will want to let the second stringers come in for the second half. Jeremiah, you can outrun anyone out there. You get around their linebackers and show them nothing but your rear. Johnny, you can catch the ball and run with it like no player I have ever coached. I don't want you runnin' a single play for less than twenty yards. Now, by halftime, I don't want to have to give you some speech about catchin' up. You make these white boys know they have been in a game, and I want to win by thirty points.'"

"And we won by 63 points! Man, now that was a game." Marquis Dubois was another of the "bookends." At six feet seven inches tall and 330 pounds, he was a handful on the field. Usually quiet and reserved, he became exceptionally animated when the topic was a football game.

Jeremiah interjected that they had missed his point. "Listen guys, we are as racist as the guy in the gas station. We tried to hurt white guys on the football field because we could. It wasn't enough to just win, but to crush white guys, because they were white. My dad was a wonderful athlete, and he was white. I don't run like the wind because I am part black or part white, but because he was my father. I sometimes feel ashamed to call myself a Christian and hate any man. He didn't and he suffered from the hate of others all his married life."

Tyisha, who was sitting next to Jeremiah, reached her right hand over and squeezed Jeremiah's left hand.

"Remember, honey, we are all a work in progress. From the day we accept the Lord as our Savior, we are being honed and improved until the day we are fully atoned and living eternally with Him." Everyone at the table stopped their conversation and listened to Tyisha. She continued, "My mother was a wonderful person. She loved me more than the culture she lived in, more than the wishes of her own parents. And she was White. Evil and good come in all colors of skin, but God loves us all." Rory, Juanita, Mrs. Hall and Jeremiah were the four other Christians at the table, but all were impressed by the words of this young Christian.

Franco was accompanied by another young man as they hoisted large platters over their heads with several meals on each. As they passed them around the table, the smells wafted in the noses of all the wedding party and the huge men wondered if it would be unseemly to order more food in the presence of the beautiful Juanita.

The conversation over food was more light and friendly. They talked about the upcoming wedding and Jeremiah's friends made a toast to the new couple. All of them voiced their amazement that Jeremiah had found any woman that would marry him, let alone one as beautiful and Godly as Tyisha. Of course, the toast was in jest, and they all laughed, even Mrs. Hall who was typically more stoic than the rest.

Mrs. Hall had readily accepted Tyisha as her son's bride and even thought of her as the daughter she wished she had. She was so happy Jeremiah had found a woman of God to marry.

"Children, you are going to love my pastor. He has more soul than any man I have ever known other than Jeremiah's father. He loves the Lord and lives for Him every day. He wants all of us to come by the church tomorrow afternoon so we can run through the entire wedding before the actual service the next day. The church organist will be there. I have called several of the church members and twenty or more are planning to attend the wedding. God is providing.

Café con Leche

I know my new daughter and my son will make this event the beginning of a new life, one in which God is glorified and they become 'one flesh.' I feel blessed just to be a small part of this wedding and I thank all of you for helping.

We'll see all of you at my church tomorrow at 2:00 p.m. Jeremiah knows the way and he will give you directions. I have to work tomorrow until noon, so I need to go home and get some rest. It has been a pleasure to meet all of you since Jeremiah has told me so much about all of you. You all have a great stay and enjoy every moment of this blessed time." With that, Mrs. Hall excused herself and made arrangements to pay for the meals of her guests, Rory and the rest of the football line had already paid. In her absence, Jeremiah gave directions to the church to all the guests. They stood, nearly in unison and began hugging each other and saying their "Good nights." Rory Calente hugged Juanita Jeffries longer than most, embarrassing the young lady.

The wedding party departed the restaurant, all talking and jubilant, and departed in their individual cars. Juanita and her friends were staying in the Hall home. After the other two girls went to bed, Juanita asked her cousin if he would join her in the kitchen. They quietly went down the hall to the far end of the house accompanied by Tyisha.

"Jeremiah, tell me more about Rory Calente, when did you meet him, where is he from? He told me that he drives a Mustang and wants to drive me home after your wedding and send his friends along with the other guys. Should I go?"

"Cousin, Rory was the first guy I met at Alabama State. He was already unpacking his bags and was my roommate for the next four years. Rory likes to talk about his exploits on the football field, but he wasn't lying when he said he opened most of the holes that sprung me free. We developed a real rapport. In the huddle, I just had to look at him and he knew he needed to open a hole, crush a middle linebacker, or throw a short block on a 'student-right' play. He is one of the most dependable guys I have ever known. If he told you he would be the lead blocker, you knew he would be there, and the defender would not.

I know there are more handsome men out there, and certainly smaller ones, but there aren't any better ones. And the best characteristic about Rory is he is a 'born-again' Christian. In the middle of the night, I would catch him on his knees and looking out the window toward his home in Meridian, Mississippi and praying. He was so homesick, but he came back each summer for football camp. I can almost hear his words in his prayers. 'Lord, you know how I miss my father and mother and how they don't have the money to come and visit or see any of my games. Give me comfort and bless them. May I be a blessing to all of those you place in my days and show them Christ Jesus through me. Amen, Father.'

That big mass of humanity has a heart like no man I have ever known, except for my own father. When his mother and sister called him from the neighbor's home and told him his father had died at forty-six years of age, Rory cried uncontrollably for an hour. I have seen him give poor children near the campus a dollar for food when he thought no one was watching.

Juanita, I could recommend a dozen men to you as dates, but Rory is the only one I can honestly say would make a great mate for life."

"Wow, Jeremiah, I just wanted to know if he had any history as an axe murderer. Only kidding! Thanks for the ringing endorsement. Maybe I'll take Rory up on his offer.

Tyisha, I have got to tell you that none of Jeremiah's family would ever find a woman who was willing to marry him, let alone a beautiful lady with your qualities. I'm not as much of a churchgoer as I should be, but I admire those who really live for God. You and Jeremiah have that faith that my momma is always telling me about. You're going to have a great marriage."

Juanita and Tyisha had been together for the entire day shopping for dresses for the bridesmaids and a wedding dress for her, but Tyisha had never heard Juanita vocalize anything as honest and heartfelt as she just heard.

"Thank you, Juanita. I love your cousin and have since we first met in Rapid City, South Dakota. I would be lying if I didn't admit I was initially attracted to him on a physical level, but what sold me was his faith in God. Like him, I believe the Lord has a plan for us and Jeremiah wants to follow the Lord. I want to follow Jeremiah wherever he goes."

This last statement did not sit well with the beautiful young Juanita who was an avid follower of the outspoken feminist, Gloria Steinem. Still, she bit her tongue. This was Jeremiah and Tyisha's time and though she

Café con Leche

did not agree with her cousin-in-law-to-be, she knew this was not the time to argue the role of a woman in a marriage.

"Young 'uns' [Juanita was a month older than Jeremiah], it's getting late, and I want to look beautiful for the rehearsal tomorrow. We old folks need our beauty rest." Juanita stood up from the kitchen table and kissed her cousin and his fiancée on the forehead. She walked down the hall toward the bedroom assigned to the young women in the wedding, as Ty and Jeremiah watched her leave.

Tyisha stayed awhile longer, but she told Jeremiah that this was the last time Jeremiah could stay in his own mother's home before the wedding. After the rehearsal the next day, he had to stay with his friends at their motel until the wedding. He reluctantly agreed.

Since this was likely their last chance to share a kiss before the wedding, Jeremiah and Tyisha shared a kiss for the centuries. Each one felt the love of the other and thanked God for bringing them together. At its conclusion, they walked slowly down the hall, hand in hand, as Tyisha quietly entered the bedroom designated for the bride and her bridesmaids. Jeremiah left her at the bedroom door and returned to the couch in the living room where he was sleeping. As he lay down, he thanked God for the many blessings coming to fruition in only a couple of days.

CHAPTER 13

Mrs. Hall hit the nail on the head. Her pastor was a real hoot. He was a former Air Force chaplain who had survived the conflict of applying the humility of Jesus Christ in a world abounding in rank and self-promotion. His faith in God had been unfazed by his years in a world where faith was a hindrance, and he could not help himself; he had to hug everyone at least once. Steve Braun was a sixty-four-year-old man who had "overcome" most things in life. He had lost his wife to a diabetic-induced-stroke, to whom he had been married nearly forty years. While on the mission field serving the needs of indigent children, Rev. Braun had been fired from a position based on false allegations. Though he had a Master of Divinity degree and a Master of Social Work degree, he was "black-balled" by the children's welfare association of his mission. When the couple and their teen daughter returned to the United States, the closest Rev. Braun came to serving in a church was as janitor of the Jaraida United Methodist Church. Somehow, through all the valleys of his life, Rev. Braun had kept a sense of humor and his love for God was known to all who met him.

It was Tuesday, and Rev. Braun had promised to do a "run-through" of the wedding service for the Hall wedding party. He stood in the narthex awaiting the wedding party and when the Alabama State line appeared first, he couldn't resist a sharp barb at the expense of their size.

Café con Leche

"Guys, you all look hungry. Food is already on the tables downstairs in preparation for our meal tonight, should you feel faint."

"Yeah, funny, preacher," responded the humongous Rory Calente. Before he could react, Rev. Braun had a bear hug on Mr. Calente. The others sought a place to hide as Rev. Braun hugged each in turn.

"Welcome to the Lord's house. All who enter here will be loved by others who have known his forgiveness and salvation. This is the place where we come to celebrate what the Lord has done, is doing, and promises to do with His children. Tomorrow, we celebrate the Lord coming to us and tomorrow afternoon, we will celebrate His presence in the marriage of Tyisha and Jeremiah.

Now you young men go on into the sanctuary and I will wait for the others. As soon as they arrive, we'll get started."

Rory Calente, who had slowly become the leader of the linemen, led them into the sanctuary. They all followed, four still in shock from the pastor's over-zealous affection. Hadn't they all endured the affection of Mrs. Hall the day before? After the men were out of sight, those in the wedding party from the Hall home came in the front doors of the church. Mrs. Hall, who was used to the physical affection of her pastor, was first to meet Rev. Braun. Anticipating the hug to come, Mrs. Hall hugged her favorite pastor. Jeremiah noticed his mother hugged the pastor with a little more enthusiasm than most other Christians. More alarming, the pastor seemed to return the affection to Mrs. Hall.

She whispered in his ear, "Thank you for doing this for my boy and my new daughter at such a busy time of the year."

The pastor returned the whisper with one of his own. "To serve Christ, I would do anything. Conducting a wedding is joy for me."

Rev. Braun had been nicknamed as the "marryin'/buryin' preacher." He had decided years earlier, as an Air Force chaplain that weddings and funerals provided great opportunities to witness of Jesus Christ. People would come to those two Christian events that would never come to the regular worship services in the church. His evangelical bent made him look forward to all weddings between Christians.

After thoroughly hugging the rest of the wedding party, being careful not to offend the young ladies, Rev. Braun led them into the sanctuary. He guided the men to stand next to Jeremiah, who was on his left at the front of the stage area. Conversely, he placed the bridesmaids on his right, leaving space for Tyisha. Walking to the back of the sanctuary, he said to her, "My uncle Ted, another widower, is coming later tonight and he has agreed to 'give you away' if that is agreeable to you?"

At first, she thought the proposition was humorous. The thought of an old white man pretending to be her father was almost laughable until she remembered she was as much white as black. Her mother would approve.

"Sure, pastor and thank your uncle if I don't get a chance to do so."

Rev. Braun gave a wave of his hand to the organist who began playing the wedding march. Rev. Braun held Tyisha's right arm under the forearm and began the slow, methodical walk toward Jeremiah and the rest of the wedding party. The pastor took his place behind the groom and bride and said to Tyisha, "When you arrive in this place, I will ask Uncle Ted 'Who gives this woman to be married to this man?' Uncle Ted will respond, 'I do." He will then return to the pews to sit near Mrs. Hall.

Rev. Braun led them through the entire ceremony, including the kiss at the end of the vows which Tyisha and Jeremiah found to be their favorite part of the ceremony.

It was nearly 4:00 p.m. and the pastor kept looking at his watch. Finally, he said, "I think we are all clear as to the wedding service I will use, so let us stop for the afternoon and we will meet here again at 1:15 p.m. tomorrow. That should give us plenty of time to accomplish any last-minute errands before we perform the ceremony for real. All of you go home, get a good night's sleep and do not feel any undue stress. Tomorrow is a time to celebrate what the Lord has done and will do in the lives of Tyisha and Jeremiah. It is an honor to have just a little part in their lives and serve the Lord at the same time. God bless all of you and I will see you tomorrow." With that, the pastor departed out of the sanctuary via a side door to his office. After Rev. Braun departed, Jeremiah and Tyisha led the rest of the wedding party downstairs, where some ladies of the church had prepared and served their wedding dinner.

After a short kiss and promise to see each other the next day, Jeremiah led the men to their cars in the parking lot while the women climbed in Tyisha's Oldsmobile to return to the Hall home for some last-minute preparation.

Jeremiah tried his best to find a comfortable position in the 'back seat' of Rory's Mustang. So, he succumbed to being miserable for the next ten minutes until they got to the motel. In route, they stopped at a fast-food restaurant and grabbed a "bag supper" just in case the big men got hungry before bed. They returned to the motel to eat their late feast.

The desk clerk at the motel brought in a cot for Jeremiah to sleep on. The room was no bigger than their dormitory room in college, but now Rory and Jeremiah had a third roommate-Marquis Dubois. True to form, Marquis fell asleep no more than five minutes after his head hit the pillow. The robust snoring began moments later.

Jeremiah was exhausted from the travel and preparation for the wedding, but he could not go to sleep. Rory also was finding it difficult to sleep, but his anxiety was caused by the promise of a trip to Indianapolis the following day.

"Hey Rory, you want to go to the motel office with me. I can't sleep."

"Sure, Jeremiah, I can't sleep either."

The two young men quietly dressed and tried to get out the door without waking Marquis. A freight train could have gone through the room, and he would have remained asleep.

Once inside the office, they sat on a couch and chair in front of the desk. The night clerk was apparently in the room behind the desk, because the glare of the television occasionally reflected in the front windows of the office.

"Rory, I just realized we will never have those all-night discussions as two single guys in a college dormitory. Tomorrow, I am going to be married. Don't get me wrong; Tyisha is the perfect woman for me, but I had never considered all the things that are going to be different after tomorrow. There won't be any decisions made on my own. Now, I must consider what is best for both of us, not just me. And if any children come along, all decisions will have to take them into account as well as Tyisha.

I don't know what I am complaining about. When we were roommates, we asked the Lord to help us choose the right options. It is the same now. Instead of asking you as my roommate, it is going to be Tyisha. Besides, Tyisha is allot better looking than you."

Jeremiah had thought this last comment would certainly illicit some sort of reaction from his friend and best man; but he heard nothing. Five feet from him sat a huge man with his head resting on the back of the couch. Rory was sound asleep and hadn't heard a word Jeremiah had said.

Jeremiah was uncertain whether he should wake his friend or let him sleep and wake up on his own. Before he could decide, his large friend awoke.

"Hey man, what did you want to talk about?"

"Nothing, Rory; I was just having some last-minute doubts, but the Lord has answered all my questions. We had better get a couple of hours of sleep. Tomorrow is going to be packed full and I know you want to stay awake to get to know Juanita. Let's head back and try to sleep in the same room with Marquis."

Rory was starting to nod off again, but he managed to agree. They stood up and walked back to their room. They quietly closed the door behind them and disrobed before going to their sleeping accommodations. Despite their problems going to sleep earlier, both young men quickly found peace and the sleep that was to follow.

***

Jeremiah awakened with a knot in his stomach. The day he had longed for, the day when he finally married the woman of his dreams, was finally here. Yet, Jeremiah suddenly had a multitude of questions. How are we going to make it on my pitiful salary? With Tyisha's career taken from her, will she be able to find meaningful work to help the new family's finances?

But the most pertinent question haunted Jeremiah-is this the will of God for me and Tyisha? That one preceded all others.

Jeremiah dressed, allowing Marquis and Rory to sleep, and walked to a nearby café. It was the only restaurant open that early but had a sign on the door saying, "We will close at 3:00 p.m. from 12/18 through 12/24 so our employees can spend the week before Christmas with their families. We will be closed on Christmas Day." He entered and ordered a cup of coffee and a fresh doughnut made by the owner and stared out at the street in front of the restaurant. Jeremiah sat at the table alone eating and drinking when his waitress, an older lady, walked up and said, "Son, this is the season that Hope entered the world. Whatever is weighing heavy on your heart, give it to the Lord. He cared enough for each of us to come and bring us salvation. Young man, may the Lord reveal Himself to you this day."

Jeremiah stood and thanked the old lady for her words of encouragement. He left two one-dollar bills to pay for the coffee and doughnut and a tip

Café con Leche

for the waitress. Her words alone were worth that much. Jeremiah began to understand that his wedding was important but paled in importance compared to the birth of Christ. His worries seemed to fade, and the joy of the day overwhelmed him. God was in the midst of everything, and He had ordained the wedding of Tyisha and Jeremiah.

When Jeremiah got back to the motel room, Marquis and Rory were both up and getting ready for the big day. All the linemen had brought a black suit to wear at the wedding. Sown together, their suits would probably have stretched across the nearby Ohio River.

He wasn't sure why, but this thought made him laugh. Jeremiah started getting ready for the wedding as soon as the bathroom was available. After putting on his own black suit, he sat in a chair in the corner of the room and took out his Bible from his overnight bag. He turned to Genesis 2:24 and read the words which seemed to have new meaning for him:

> Therefore shall a man leave his father and his mother,
> and shall cleave unto his wife: and they two shall be one
> flesh. (KJV)

Suddenly, Jeremiah knew without a doubt that Tyisha was a gift from God and the perfect helpmate. She wanted to share in his world and follow him as he followed God. All his questions were gone and now he couldn't wait to make Tyisha his wife later in the day. All his questions were little more than distractions. The Lord had answered the only pertinent question-was this marriage the will of God?

***

Tyisha, Mrs. Hall, Juanita and the bridesmaids were all inside the church and dressing in a restroom for women. The ladies in the wedding party had chosen a 'flamingo orange' color for their gowns. The contrast with their black skin was stunning.

Tyisha wore a traditional white bridal gown. She was beautiful and radiant as she prepared for her wedding. Though she was excited about the wedding ahead, she couldn't wait to begin her new life as Jeremiah's wife. When Mrs. Hall had double checked her gown and train, Tyisha went into the 'cry room' off the narthex of the church and closed the door. She sat down and tried to remain calm. Mrs. Hall had left to help prepare the little girl who was going to function as the flower girl and meet some of the attendees, most of whom were members of the church. She thanked each one for coming since they had nearly all left family, friends, or jobs to attend.

The bridesmaids stayed in the women's bathroom in the basement of the church to have some privacy. As previously agreed, the bridesmaids walked to the left side entry into the sanctuary and waited for their cue from the pastor to enter and take their places in the front. The groom and groomsmen did the same and stood outside the right front sanctuary entry.

The attendees had gathered and taken their seats in the church pews. Amazingly, there were more than one hundred attendees present for a wedding service in the afternoon of a midweek day. The organist was playing a soothing prelude as Rev. Brau took his place near the choir risers. At 1:57 p.m., he looked first at the bridesmaids and secondly at the groom and groomsmen indicating they were to take their designated spots in front of him.

Mrs. Hall watched from the back of the sanctuary where she was positioned to help Tyisha make her grand appearance when the wedding march began. As the six large men and her son walked onto the raised pulpit area, Mrs. Hall said a little prayer hoping the stage would hold the extra weight.

Tyisha and Uncle Ted stood just outside the sanctuary in the narthex. At exactly 2:00 p.m., Mrs. Hall's neighbor's daughter began down the center aisle throwing rose flower petals ahead of her. As the organist began playing the wedding march, Tyisha and Uncle Ted followed the little flower girl, at a slow methodical pace.

Once in place in front of the pastor, Rev. Braun began the service.

"Who gives this woman to be married to this man?"

"Steven, you know me. I'm Uncle Ted. I have been your uncle all your life." There was a spattering of giggles and laughs in the crowd. Uncle Ted was eighty-five years old and beginning to show signs of dementia. Rev. Brau slowly took Uncle Ted by his forearm and led him to a seat in the first pew next to Mrs. Hall. Rev. Steven Braun returned to his former position and calmly said to Tyisha and Jeremiah, "You have asked to take your own vows of marriage from a kneeling position. [Tyisha and Jeremiah had written five of their own vows]. Please take your positions on the first step in front of the altar."

Café con Leche

The young couple assumed a position on their knees as requested by Rev. Braun. Once in place, they heard a loud laughter erupt from the congregation. While Jeremiah had gone to the restaurant that morning, Marquis and Rory had used white fingernail polish to write "Help" on the bottom of Jeremiah's left shoe and "Me!" on the bottom of his right shoe. Even Mrs. Hall chuckled though Uncle Ted had no idea what was funny.

At the conclusion of their own vows, Rev. Braun asked Tyisha and Jeremiah to rise and stand before him.

"Tyisha, please repeat after me.
'I, Tyisha, take thee, Jeremiah...'"
"I, Tyisha, take thee, Jeremiah..."
"To be my wedded husband,"
"To be my wedded husband,"
"To have and to hold,"
"To have and to hold,"
"From this day forward,"
"From this day forward,"
"For better, for worse,"
"For better, for worse,"
"For richer, for poorer,"
"For richer, for poorer,"
"In sickness and in health,"
"In sickness and in health,"
"To love and to cherish,"
"To love and to cherish,"
"Till death do us part,"
"Till death do us part,"
"According to God's holy ordinance;"
"According to God's holy ordinance;"
"And thereto I pledge myself to you."
"And thereto I pledge myself to you."

After taking the vows, Rev. Braun turned to Jeremiah and gave him the same set of vows. At the conclusion, Juanita handed Tyisha the marriage ring which Tyisha placed on Jeremiah's ring finger.

Rory gave Jeremiah his ring which he placed on Tyisha's finger. Suddenly, something happened to both of the new marital partners; they weren't just saying vows but were sensing a new relationship. They were "one," a new creature with the Lord at the center of the relationship.

"You may now kiss the bride."

Jeremiah was so overcome with emotion that he held Tyisha in his arms and kissed her long, despite the "wolf-whistles" from the congregation. Rory leaned toward him and whispered, "Man, let her have some air."

Jeremiah and Tyisha reluctantly ended their kiss as the crowd erupted in cheers. Holding hands, they literally ran down the middle aisle heading toward Tyisha's waiting Oldsmobile. People, who they had never met, reached out as they passed and patted the newlyweds on the back.

The groomsmen and bridesmaids had positioned bags of rice outside of the church for both their use and that of the congregation. Mrs. Hall and Rev. Braun stood just outside of the church doors and were the first to throw their rice on Jeremiah and Tyisha as they exited the building. Jeremiah had hugged his mother and said his "Good-bye" inside. He had hugged each one of the linemen and given his farewell, knowing this was likely the last time he would see most of them. Tyisha had hugged her new mother and told her she was the only mother she would ever have. Jeremiah had to break the two women apart. After thanking Juanita, the bridesmaids and the flower girl, they waited in the narthex for a moment before running the gauntlet gathered outside, armed with bags of rice.

Jeremiah had prepared the car for the trip ahead, topping off the gas tank and checking the oil. The six large men had done a bit of modification of the car, attaching several long strands of cans to the back bumper and using water paints to spell "Just Married" on the back window. Tyisha and her new friends had packed the car with the things Jeremiah had wanted to take with them and he had placed his overnight bag in the trunk along with Tyisha's suitcase.

The two newlyweds waved "Good-bye" out each side of the car as they entered and drove away from the curb. They had mixed emotions. They were so happy to be starting their new lives as "man and wife," but they hated to leave Mrs. Hall, the bridesmaids, groomsmen and even the pastor, though Jeremiah suspected he might be meeting him again.

CHAPTER 14

Jeremiah drove northwest out of Portsmouth toward Cincinnati, where he had reserved the Honeymoon Suite at a local Holiday Inn. They arrived at 6:30 p.m. and slept in the following morning. Driving hard that day, they arrived at a motel near Kingdom City, Missouri in the evening. They ate at a restaurant in nearby Fulton, Missouri. Fulton had been the site of the famous "Iron Curtain" speech given by Sir Winston Churchill.

Jeremiah had reserved a suite in the famous Elms Hotel in Excelsior Springs, Missouri for four nights. It was the third edifice. The first two had burned. It had been frequented by Bugs Moran, head of the infamous North Side Gang and Al Capone, mob boss of the South Side Gang in Chicago. Though they hated one another, they did agree on one thing; the Elms Hotel was a great place to throw a party and relax after the rigors of crime.

In 1948, President Harry Truman reserved one entire wing of the Elms Hotel to avoid the press on election night. When he unexpectedly won, they celebrated his victory there.

Jeremiah was full of anticipation. He couldn't wait to be surrounded by a place he had only read about. He wanted to share every moment and the passion of his honeymoon with Tyisha, the first and last love of his life.

By nature: Jeremiah was a "planner." He had already written down the itinerary for he and Tyisha while they stayed at the Elms Hotel.

> "Saturday, we eat at the restaurant in the hotel. Go to Swope Park Zoo in Kansas City and spend the morning. Tour Union Station and go up the hill to the World War I Memorial.
>
> Sunday: go to worship at the Traditional Christian Church of the Northland. [Jeremiah had heard of this church and their emphasis on evangelism.]
>
> Monday: Get up late and go eat at Arthur Bryant's Barbecue in downtown Kansas City. Stop at a Jazz club. Eat supper at The Golden Heifer restaurant.

Tyisha was more of the "existentialist" of the two and kindly told him to put his list away. Surely, they would enjoy their time more if they simply allowed events to happen. She had enjoyed their time of intimacy and was quite content to stay in the hotel the rest of their honeymoon.

The winter of 1968 had been unusually warm. Tyisha and Jeremiah had not seen snow across the Midwest, through their wedding, and now on their honeymoon. The days had been temperate and with a light coat, it was comfortable to be outside. It was Friday, 20 December 1968, and so warm that Tyisha wanted to roll down the windows and let the air blow through her hair. This time, she was awake as they entered the downtown area of Kansas City from the east. Tyisha looked at the skyscrapers with awe. Even St. Louis' downtown was less impressive. Nothing in their home state of Alabama had prepared her for the sight.

Jeremiah was driving, as he had through Kansas City the previous week. On the north side of the Missouri River where Interstates 35 and 29 split he went north toward Liberty, Missouri. Just north of Liberty, he drove northeast on Highway 69 to Excelsior Springs, the site of the Elms Hotel. The rock façade and unique architecture were impressive, and Jeremiah knew he had chosen wisely. After Ty and Jeremiah checked in, they followed a porter and their luggage to their room. After the porter left, they lay across their bed, exhausted and took a nap.

Café con Leche

By 7:00 p.m., they were ready to eat, but not to get back in the car to get there. They had spent far too many hours on the road in the past couple of weeks, so they walked to the restaurant to eat. As they sat at the table talking after the meal, Jeremiah almost chuckled to himself as he thought of how much their actions had mirrored his itinerary. But this was not a time to gloat, but to grow in love and follow God with his new wife, Tyisha. It was a journey, and Jeremiah felt blessed to be on the path with Ty.

The following day was still warm and almost balmy for the Christmas Season. Tyisha and Jeremiah decided they needed to get out and walk with so much time cooped up in the car. They drove to Swope Park on the south side of Kansas City. At the zoo, they parked their car and began the slow walk through the various animal exhibits. The park was lightly attended. Most residents of Kansas City had left the city to see family over the holidays. Some of them still in the city had family visiting and going to the zoo just wasn't high on their priority list.

Jeremiah and Tyisha were both college graduates. They had read about lions, tigers, and anaconda snakes but they had never seen one. As they walked about the enclosure with elephants, both let out a sigh and said almost in unison, "Wow, I never dreamed they were so big."

They toured through the entire zoo and watched every animal exhibit until they were hungry and nearly exhausted. One old man who was feeding the big cats, walked out of the lion's enclosure.

Jeremiah walked toward the employee of the zoo and asked him if there was a restaurant nearby.

"Yeah, do you know the area?"

Clearly, Jeremiah did not, or he would not have asked for directions.

"No sir. We are from Alabama and not familiar with the city."

"Well, young 'uns, go out the 63rd Street entry to the park and go west. When you see 'Brookside Boulevard,' turn right. The old village of Brookside is a quaint little village with numerous places to eat."

The young couple thanked the old gentleman profusely and walked back to their car. Following his directions to Brookside, they found an Italian restaurant to their liking and ate a filling meal of gnocchi. It was getting late in the day, and they were ready to seek the shelter of their hotel, especially since it was forty-five minutes north through the city and country.

Ty and Jeremiah got up early to be a honeymoon and went to the restaurant for an early breakfast. It was Sunday morning and Jeremiah had been interested in the doctrine of a group of churches known as "The Heritage." They believed that the Bible was the inerrant word of God and that denominations were non-biblical. Tyisha also believed their doctrine, but was less adamant than Jeremiah, who had been in Christian churches since he was a child.

They had looked up the nearest Heritage Church and went there for the morning worship hour. Tyisha would have been content to attend the African Methodist Episcopal church in downtown Kansas City, but she knew Jeremiah really wanted to attend the Heritage Church. At the conclusion of the worship service, which both Ty and Jeremiah thoroughly enjoyed, the pastor greeted them at the door at the back of the sanctuary. When he discovered they were on their honeymoon, he invited them to dinner with his family at a Bates Barbecue on Independence Avenue. After eating a rack of barbecued ribs, Tyisha began conversing with the Pastor's wife. They were discussing the role of the Christian wife in marriage.

The pastor turned to Jeremiah and said, "How do you think the Lord is going to use you in His kingdom?"

"Pastor, right now, I am a teacher in a Christian school in Pierre, South Dakota, but I have long believed the Lord was leading me toward missions. Tyisha knows about my call and has said that the Lord has called her to be my wife. So, right now I am exploring where the Lord wants to use us and through what ministry."

"When I was your age," said the middle-aged man, "I wanted to be a missionary, but it was not the will of God for me. I have a heart condition that precludes me going far from my cardiologist. Where would you like to serve, Jeremiah?"

"I really haven't sensed the Lord leading me to a particular place, but I hope to work with a native people in a remote location of the tropics, say the Congo River basin, the Amazon River basin, or maybe even the Mekong River."

"While you are here, you simply must go visit the Remote Peoples Training Camp on the Missouri River north of St. Joseph, Missouri. Our

Café con Leche

church helps to support the camp which trains fifty to sixty missionaries a year, so they are ready to go to some of the most dangerous places in the world and take the Gospel. Listen, if you want to stop and see them and see what they do, give me a call. I know the leadership out there." The pastor gave Jeremiah his telephone numbers at both the church and at his home.

Jeremiah had heard of the group, but had never researched who they were, what they believed or how they took the Gospel to the tribal peoples with whom they worked. Ty and Jeremiah parted company with the pastor and his family and drove back toward the Elms Hotel.

The past few weeks had been exhausting and the resulting stress was only curable by sleep. When the two young married couple arrived at their room they reclined on the huge bed and fell asleep, hand in hand. They jointly dreamed of a life together, a life full of turmoil but an "abundant life" as promised by the Son of God.

Over two hours later, both Ty and Jeremiah awakened still holding hands. Jeremiah turned on his side and kissed his wife on the cheek. It was now legal and expected, but he just couldn't show his wife enough attention. She was the woman of which he had dreamed and a wife who would be his helpmate.

"Ty, did you hear the pastor tell me about the Remote Peoples Training Camp?"

"Yeah, husband, I did but I missed plenty of detail."

"He told me it is located just up the Missouri River north of St. Joseph. Would you like to know more about their missionaries and what they believe? If you do, we could spend a day with them and leave for Pierre the following day. That would still leave us a few days so I can prepare to return to the classroom on the third of January."

"Jeremiah, I am not a theologian and have only been a Christian since last spring. You know my background and how little I was taught about God in church. How my grandfather molested me and how few people, black or white, accepted me. I don't know as much about God as I want, but I know you and I love you. The Lord has brought us to this place in this time so we can know more about missions. Maybe this is His plan for us. Let's take this opportunity to learn more. Go ahead and call the pastor and ask him to contact the Camp for us."

Jeremiah rolled over and picked up the phone on the nightstand next to the bed. He dialed the pastor at his home since it was not yet time for the night service and asked him to contact the Camp on their behalf. Jeremiah told the pastor that he and Ty would like to make their "fact-finding" mission on the day after Christmas. The pastor assured Jeremiah he would make the telephone call and Jeremiah and Ty just had to show up at the Camp. After sharing directions to the facility, the pastor promised he would ask his congregation to pray for God's guidance as the young couple sought His will. Jeremiah thanked the pastor and hung up the phone. He made another quick telephone call to the front desk and asked to stay one day longer than first planned-Christmas Day. Since it was the slowest part of the year for occupancy, Jeremiah's request was granted.

After cleaning up, Ty and Jeremiah went to the restaurant for supper. Following a meal of chicken fried steak and loaded baked potatoes, they conversed about their future.

"Ty, you know how much I have felt drawn to missions since I was a young man. In the fall of 1964, I read a book by a missionary in Bolivia. He tells about teaming up with other missionaries in order to develop a relationship with a savage tribe. The tribe lured them to a remote bank on a jungle river and all were killed except the author of the book. This event has drawn me to missions through college and now more than ever."

"Honey your desire to serve God no matter where is one of the traits that drew me to you. I love you because of your commitment to serve God.

You know that my career to teach here in the United States is over. However, I still want to teach and to teach on the foreign mission field is attractive to me. Also, I think serving in a remote place will allow us more freedom to serve God without the interference of anyone. We can listen to the will of God without it being filtered through the voice of others. The pastor was right. We are right here at a training camp for missionaries, and we need to go visit it.

Your contract at the school mandates that we stay in Pierre through the end of May next year. I want to get a job just as soon as we get to Pierre, but I hope we can take the excess money and use it to go on mission in the next year. If we like what we hear on Thursday, we can begin making overtures to you mother's church about supporting us on the mission field. Also, we can speak to the pastor of the Heritage Church we attended this morning.

Jeremiah, I am just so excited. Instead of focusing on what happened to me in Williston, I am looking forward to seeing what the Lord will do with us in the future. I can hardly wait to see. Best of all, we get to do it together."

"Tyisha, you know I feel the same way. I can't imagine a life without you and serving God at the same time is just icing on the cake. Let's get up in the morning and go on tour of the famous criminals from the area-the Younger Brothers, the James Brothers, and maybe the shootout between criminals and law enforcement officers at Union Station in Kansas City."

"Jeremiah, do you think we could set our sights a little lower. I am tired and would like to sleep for awhile in the morning. Maybe we could just go to nearby Liberty and go across the Missouri River to Independence to see the Harry Truman library."

They finally compromised and decided to see the James Brothers' farm near Kearney, Missouri and their robbery of the Liberty Bank, the site of the first daylight bank robbery in the United States. They hoped to see the Harry Truman library nearby, but Jeremiah really wanted to see the birthplace of criminals.

Somehow, Jeremiah learned more about his new wife with each passing moment. He knew she was bi-racial, as was he, but he had known his father, a man he loved and adored. But Tyisha had never known her father or even who he was. This woman, who he was learning to love more each day, had kept a sense of humor and a love for her Lord when she had every reason to be bitter and hate, not love. And Tyisha did love him, unlike anyone had ever loved him. Most people had just tolerated him, but Tyisha loved him with all that she was and all that she ever would be. With that, they walked back to their room and prepared for bed and the promise of a shared future.

CHAPTER 15

Monday had been spent in a whirlwind trip of Kearney, Missouri and the first daylight bank robbery in Liberty, Missouri by the James Gang. They even had time to visit the former president's library in Independence, Missouri.

Tuesday was more of the same with visits to the field north of Platte City where Bonnie and Clyde escaped an ambush set by federal and local law enforcement agencies. They finished the day on a walking tour of The Plaza, the first shopping area in the United States and ate supper at a restaurant on Brush Creek nearby.

It was Wednesday, Christmas Day, but it seemed like the first day of the rest of their lives. On the day of our Lord's birth, Ty and Jeremiah slept in at their nearly empty hotel. They ate all their meals at the restaurant that was only open until 6:00 p.m. with minimal manning. They decided to tour the city and go to a special worship service at the same church they had attended on the previous Sunday. They had no presents for one another or a Christmas tree, but they had each other. For years to come, they would both remember that first Christmas together as their best.

After checking out of the Elms Hotel they drove Tyisha's Oldsmobile northward on Highway 69 to the intersection with Highway 92. Going west on Highway 92, they drove through Smithville, Missouri and

Café con Leche

continued to Interstate 29. As they passed St. Joseph, Missouri, it was all Jeremiah could do to continue northward. Jesse James had been shot in the back by one of his fellow gang members in a house in St. Joseph.

On the Andrew and Buchanan County line, Jeremiah exited Interstate 29 and went west until he reached County Highway K. Turning north on K Highway, he turned west again at the sign designating the dirt road to the "Remote Peoples Training Camp."

Bumping down the tree-lined dirt road, they could see the broad Missouri River just ahead of them. On the ridge above the river valley stood several buildings. None of them looked planned by an architect, nor finished by a building contractor. The building at the center of the compound had a small sign on the front indicating the "office." They parked their car in the gravel parking lot in front of the building. As they entered, Jeremiah leading the entourage, they heard a man come out of an office behind them.

"Hi. Are you Tyisha and Jeremiah Hall?"

Ty and Jeremiah turned around to see a man that had to be at least six feet ten inches tall. He had a smile that was infectious.

"Yes, we are. Are you Mr. Bob Dilman?"

"Guilty as charged. You all are in luck. My wife and the ladies of the camp are preparing our lunch as we speak. You arrived just in time to eat with us. That would be a good place to start your tour. Follow me and we will walk over to the cafeteria to eat."

With Tyisha and Jeremiah in the rear, the three walked toward the river where the cafeteria was located. Entering the building, that faced due west, they could see a wall of windows that looked down on the Missouri River and the valley. The tables in the large room were shaped like half-moons to enhance conversation with the flat edge facing the windows. All the missionaries had a good view of the river below. Several of them had already gone through the cafeteria line and had taken their meals to their tables.

Mr. Dilman took the couple up to the first lady behind the cafeteria counter and introduced his wife, Joyce.

"We are just so happy to have you here with us today. Everyone here is seeking to do the will of God and we believe it is our mission to prepare them to go where and when the Lord wants them to go.

While you are with us, you are with your family. We are brothers and sisters in Christ Jesus and the blood that has saved us binds us together as one.

Now, you just take a plate, tray and silverware and sit down where you want."

"Thank you, Mrs. Dilman, for your kindness and courtesy."

Tyisha and Jeremiah filled their plates with the tasty meatloaf, mashed potatoes, canned green beans and a piece of cobbler made from canned blackberries. Jeremiah finished first and walked toward the table where Mr. Dilman was already sitting and placed his tray next to him. Mr. Dilman had allowed his guests to fill their trays first and went to get his own food after Tyisha sat down next to her husband. When he returned with his food, Mr. Dilman led all three in a short prayer thanking the Lord for the bounty before them.

The three quietly conversed about the camp and their mission, but the view of the Missouri River was a constant distraction for Jeremiah and Tyisha. Before Jeremiah could ask another question, another couple approached them from behind.

"Bob, do you mind if we sit down here at the end?"

"No, Ken, go right ahead."

Ken's wife sat down next to Tyisha and Ken got a chair from the nearest table and placed it across from his wife nearest the window wall.

"Ken, Cindy, this is Tyisha and Jeremiah. They are looking at our camp and fact finding. They are only with us for the day, but I am hoping they will stay tonight to see the fireworks display from St. Joseph." The City of St. Joseph usually had a firework display as soon as the New Year holiday arrived, but it had been moved up due to a forecast of a large winter storm with snow on the night of December 31.

"Jeremiah, Tyisha, it is good to make your acquaintance. I think you will like it here and the people who call it home for four months preparing to go to their mission field." Cindy wore her hair tightly in a bun on the back of her head and a dress that drug the ground due to a diminutive frame; she appeared to be "mousy," when in fact she was the more verbal of the couple.

"Has Bob shown you the mission village down near the river?"

Jeremiah replied in the negative.

Café con Leche

Ken chimed in, "You must come and see our home. We finished it just a week ago. It is a bit rough, but we plan to build our own home on the Congo River in central Africa and this is great preparation."

"Ken, Cindy are you headed back to your house after lunch?"

"Yeah, we were going to check our mail in the office and then go back to the house."

"If you don't mind, we will talk a while here and then head down to the river and stop at you house in about an hour."

"That would be great. We are more than a little proud of our home and would love to show it off to Tyisha and Jeremiah. You all come when you like. We plan to stay at home until this evening when we all gather at the river."

"Okay, we look forward to coming to see you later."

Ken and Cindy finished their lunch and excused themselves. As Cindy got up, she kissed Tyisha on the cheek. Tyisha was caught off guard but liked the sign of sincere affection. Her sister in Christ, Lydia, had often hugged or kissed her on her cheek and Tyisha missed her gestures of love.

Bob had completed his lunch and looked at Tyisha and Jeremiah with an intense stare. He was a warm man, but being Christian was more than a verbal profession to him. Bob and Joyce Dilman had given their whole lives to God and vowed to take His gospel to the world. They had spent thirty-two years on the Mekong River in Thailand before Joyce had contracted a rare bacterial disease unique to Southeast Asia. She had been so debilitated that they had to return to the United States for her complete rehabilitation. It was a time of introspection for the couple. They had sought the will of God in their lives and sensed He did not want them to return to Thailand. Instead, they had decided God wanted them to help others go and take the Gospel. The Camp was a ministry by which they could do that.

Bob and Joyce did their best to pair up their missionaries with missionaries from the ILM, the International Linguistics Mission. The ILM missionary would seek to learn the language of foreign people groups and then teach that language to Bob and Joyce's missionaries. They taught them how to travel in parts of the world with few methods of public transportation and how to build a house where the building materials are scarce. But, most importantly they "weeded out" the missionaries who were not ready for the remote lifestyle. They tried not to be discouraging to those who were not, but believed rightly that these people should be redirected to other ministries.

"So, Jeremiah, tell me a little about your walk. How has the Lord used you and where do you see Him taking you?"

"Bob, I was saved by the grace of Christ Jesus when I was a nine-year-old boy in Madisonville, Alabama. But I really did not live for Christ until my roommate in college, Rory Calente, showed me how to live for Christ and love both Him and mankind who I had hated from my childhood. The man who first testified of our Lord to me was a man who used to play football with my father when they were kids. He had become the President of the local school board and was the one who got a job for my father in their hometown.

He told me that he had been on many teams in high school and college, but he was finally a member of the winning team when he became a Christian. He also told me that he had lived a life of sin until he found the forgiving love of God. He exuded love.

After my father died, I was given little love except by my mother. This man used to bring my mother money and maybe a bag of groceries. He listened to her grieving after my father passed. I wanted to be just like him and my father.

One night, he came by the house with his weekly grocery bag delivery, and he asked if I would take a walk with him. We walked down to the football stadium where he and my father played football together in high school and sat in the stands. There alone, he told me about a Christ that loved me so much He gave His life for me. He died that all who loved Him could be saved from their sin. He even died that creation could be renewed to the state it was intended. Right there and right then, my father's friend prayed with me as I begged for the salvation of Jesus Christ. With tears rolling down my face, I knew He had heard my ardent prayer and His salvation was mine.

Football has always opened doors for me. When I went to college, my roommate, friend and fellow football player, Rory, was a Christian whom I idolized. Besides discussing our walk with Christ, we went to church together when we were in Montgomery, Alabama. Rory was my best man last week at our wedding. I believe Christ used Rory, more than anyone else, to call me to missions. His zeal to take the Gospel to the world is infectious and I want to be used by Christ to do just that. Over the past few years, I have wondered where the Lord wants to use me, but I keep asking who hasn't heard the Gospel. The answer is always the same-the people at the headwaters of the Amazon River. I can think of nothing else for our future."

"Wow, Jeremiah that is quite a testimony! You sound allot like a young Christian years ago who ended up in Thailand. You keep preparing and asking the Lord to lead you and He will take you where He wants you to go. And now, Tyisha could you tell us something of your walk with Christ?"

"Bob, my story is not that vastly different than Jeremiah's or a host of other Christians. As you can plainly see, both Jeremiah and I are biracial. I never knew my father and my mother died when I was just a child. I was raised by my mother's parents, who did not love me and barely tolerated me. A neighbor, Aunt Lizzie Mitchell, was my source of love and emotional maturity. She helped me financially and guided me through those tough teenage years.

I went to college in Tuskegee, Alabama and trained to be a teacher. During my last year, I was a student teacher, and my mentor was a Miss Jorgina Boudoir. She was not only a great teacher, but a wonderful Christian woman who led me to the Lord. She lived her faith each day before the students and before me.

One day after school, she told me about all the anger and hate she had built up in her heart in the racial South. She had been part of the civil rights movement and knew Dr. Martin Luther King, Jr. personally. But she became the humble woman I grew to know and love when she was saved. She made me want to be more like her and that day in her classroom, we bowed, and I prayed the Lord would give me His salvation. Miss Jorgina died shortly thereafter and ever since, I have strived to live up to the standard she set and to please our Lord.

I met Jeremiah last summer and we knew we loved one another immediately. We also knew the Lord had brought us together as husband and wife and had something for us to do. Jeremiah has known for years that the Lord wanted him to serve as a missionary. I am not sure that I have received a direct call to missions. But I am sure the Lord has called me to be the wife of Jeremiah and to go where he goes and support him in missions or anything else the Lord calls him to do."

Jeremiah was cringing thinking Tyisha's answer had just assured their rejection from missions.

"Well said, Tyisha. My wife felt the same when we went to Thailand. We had been married several years when we went to the mission field, and she never had a personal call to missions. But she did have a call from God to be my wife and go where I was called to go. She has stood by me every mile of the way and I thank God for her every day. I have no doubt you will be a blessing to Jeremiah wherever the Lord takes you all."

All three stood and took their trays to a window near the kitchen and placed their silverware in baskets on the side. After saying "good-bye" a couple of other ladies in the kitchen, they went back to the office, led by Bob. Outside the building was a van with a sign on the side stating, "Remote Peoples Training Camp." Jeremiah, ever the gentleman, got in the first bench seat behind the driver and Tyisha climbed in next to him. With Joyce in the passenger seat, Bob drove them down a road that was full of holes and ditches from rains the previous summer. He finally stopped at the edge of the Missouri River at a small playground the adults had made for their children. It had a slide, monkey-bars, and a swing set, all with wooden frames.

Bob and Joyce and their guests left the van and walked to a fishing pier that had been built into the river. The water of the mighty Missouri River rushed by on its way to its confluence with the Mississippi River just two hundred and fifty miles to the east. After a few minutes of looking at the river and enduring a cool wind howling down the river bottom, the three had seen enough. They reentered the van and drove up another side road to a small village of eight shacks for the students. Though different, each one bore the clear signs of student construction. Some had tin roofs, others were covered in red cedar shingles, and one had nothing but black tar paper laid horizontally overlapping on the edges. All had siding made from local materials like brick made from straw and clay, limestone rocks, or slabs of oak from a nearby sawmill. The homes sat on a knoll above the flood plain with a road leading on up the hill back to the main compound.

Bob drove up to the front of the third home where they all got out and went to the front door. There to greet them was Ken and Cindy Sprague.

"Bob, Tyisha, Jeremiah come right in. We have been waiting for you."

Ken ushered the trio into the house and there were too few chairs to sit down in the living room. Ken and Cindy brought two additional chairs

Café con Leche

from their kitchen table into the living room. When everyone was seated, their host surprised even Bob with his first statement.

"Looking around at each one, Ken said, "I have been praying since we met only a couple of hours ago and I sense this is a very important time for all of us, but especially for Tyisha and Jeremiah. Let's hold hands and go to our Lord in prayer.

Father, we are in the process of serving You. Cindy and I are learning how to be your missionaries and learning from your servants, Bob and Joyce. Jeremiah and Tyisha are deciding if You are calling them to missions. Lead us, guide us, and use us Father to do your will. Through all that we do, may You be glorified. Amen."

Jeremiah looked up and before anyone could speak, he said to Ken, "Thank you for opening your home to us. I have so many questions and I am not sure where to begin. First, what brought you and Cindy here?"

"I can answer that." Cindy looked up. "I felt called to missions while I was a young girl in my home church in Arkansas. That was fifteen years ago. After Ken and I were married five years ago, the Lord has been tugging at my heart and has let me know it was time to follow Him. Ken has known of my call long before we were married and has always been supportive and willing to go wherever or whenever the Lord called. Our journey has been a long one, but always led by God. We were the pastor and pastor's wife of the Ouachita Baptist Church near our home in Arkansas. We loved our service there, but we both knew we were heading toward the mission field.

After visiting here last year, we knew this was the place for us to prepare for all that lies ahead. Since coming here, we have learned about taking the Gospel to the Congo River basin, how to build a modest shelter, to meet our basic medical needs, and hopefully how to develop a new church.

I don't know what Bob has told you to this point, but if the Lord is leading you to take His Gospel to the remote parts of this world, this is a great place to prepare."

"Cindy is absolutely right. Since our marriage, the Lord has slowly guided me from the pastorate to missions. Now, Cindy and I are on the same wavelength. We know that the Lord is leading us to the mission field, and we can't wait to go.

Tyisha and Jeremiah, you are here at a special time. Tonight, the City of St. Joseph fires off fireworks from their city airport at 7:00 p.m. We are all going down to the landing on the river and watch the show. We sure hope you will join us."

Bob and Joyce were nodding their heads in agreement. Jeremiah looked at Tyisha and she winked in approval.

"Well, we would love to, but I must go reserve a room at a nearby motel."

"Jeremiah, you and Tyisha are more than welcome to stay right here tonight. House#4 is unoccupied. You can sleep there, get a good night's rest and travel north any time you like."

Bob and Joyce were the consummate hosts and Jeremiah and Tyisha felt like they had been at the camp for years, not hours. They felt a special communion with their friends, one that only Christians feel. Tyisha and Jeremiah had been ostracized most of their lives, but amid these other Christians, they knew what it was to be part of the Body of Christ.

"Thank you, Bob, we would love to stay the night. We have three days to get back to Pierre and be ready for classes on January 3. I know that Ken and Cindy need to get some rest if we are going to be up late, so if you don't mind, Tyisha and I need to rest as well."

They spent another thirty minutes talking together and Cindy had made some delicious home-squeezed lemonade which she distributed among her guests. Finally, Bob got up and Joyce, Tyisha and Jeremiah dutifully followed his lead. They thanked Cindy and Ken as they left for the van and promised to see them at the river later in the evening.

After retrieving their own car, Jeremiah and Tyisha followed Bob and Joyce to their house for the night. Bob opened the front door and Jeremiah and Tyisha followed with their overnight bags. They parted company and Bob promised to collect them at 6:30 p.m. before they all went to the river.

***

Through the afternoon and early evening, the wind had shifted out of the south. One could almost smell Kansas City and St. Joseph to the south and for the day after Christmas, the weather was almost balmy.

True to his word, Bob and Joyce arrived at 6:30 p.m. Tyisha and Jeremiah ran out of the house and jumped in the van so Bob could stay in his driver's seat. They traveled the short distance to the river and got out

Café con Leche

to join the crowd already gathering near the small pier. The women had brought pots and pans along with wooden spoons to bang pretending they were ushering in the New Year. The children were all playing on the nearby playground equipment, reveling in their shared joy. Their school did not commence until the following Monday, so their parents allowed them to stay up until well after midnight; unheard of in most of their families.

After twenty minutes of socializing and introductions to the rest of the students, Bob stood on a nearby picnic table and led those gathered by the river in an a cappella version of *Amazing Grace*. Just a moment after the conclusion, the fireworks began shooting into the night sky from Rosecrans Memorial Airport just down river. The women began banging on their pots and pans and thanking God for the year coming to serve Him.

When there was a lull in the merrymaking, Bob again climbed the picnic table and told the congregation that he would lead them in a closing prayer before they parted for their homes.

"Lord Jesus, You have sustained us through this last tumultuous year with the strife and assassinations. Now, we pray that you will continue to bless us as we seek to follow You. Provide the moneys to travel, to buy teaching materials, to pay for passports, visas, and fees necessary to go to the place where You have called us. Keep our faith strong as the Evil One brings stumbling blocks before us in remote places. Help us remember that you have made us warriors no matter what the enemy brings before us.

In this coming New Year, help us to recommit ourselves to the Call of Christ. Let us determine to give all that we have and all that we are to the cause of Christ. May your Holy Spirit be with us wherever we go in this world of sin. Everything we say and everything we do, we do it for You. In the name of Jesus Christ, we pray it all. Amen.

Let's go home and give God the glory for our families. Enjoy your lives here and the life beyond. Thank you for fulfilling Joyce and me. We left Thailand years ago and thought our ministry was over. It was not. You are proof. Our ministry is not over, but simply changed. The Lord wants to use us all. Go with God and be blessed. Good night."

Bob climbed down from his perch and walked toward his van. Joyce, Tyisha and Jeremiah followed, stopping several times to say "Good-bye" to the other students, but especially Ken and Cindy.

Whispering to Tyisha, Jeremiah said, "Wow, Ty, I really like these people. Can't you feel their sincerity, their love for us?"

Equally in a low tone, Tyisha replied, "In all my life, I have never been treated better. I like these folks and can sense the presence of the Lord in every one of them."

Bob drove them back to their house for the night. Bob and Joyce exited the vehicle and waited for Tyisha and Jeremiah to get out as well. They took the young couple in their arms and gave them humongous hugs.

"Tyisha, Jeremiah, we have loved having you with us this day. You are always welcome here, but only if it is the will of God. If you get serious about pursuing missions in a remote part of the world, let us know and we would love to collaborate with you in that service of our Lord."

"Bob, you and Joyce have been wonderful hosts. Tyisha and I have much to consider and prayers to the Lord before we are ready to go on mission. You and everyone here have made our decision easier. If we sense the Lord is leading us toward the mission field, we will likely be in touch. God bless you both for all that you do in the service to the Lord.

We are going to get out of here early in the morning, so we will say 'Good-bye' to you for now. May the Lord bless both of you."

Jeremiah and Tyisha went into their house and turned off the outside light. Even before they went to bed, they were still talking about the wonders of the day; the kindness extended to them, the sense that the Lord was in that place, and a rejuvenated hope for Tyisha that God had more for her to do.

CHAPTER 16

With only four hours of sleep, Ty and Jeremiah got ready for the long day ahead. After packing their car for the trip, they closed the doors quietly to not awaken the other occupants and drove with their parking lights out of the residential area. After passing by the main part of the compound, they continued to Highway K. Following northward on Highway K, they passed through the small community of Amazonia. Jeremiah had often wondered if the Lord was leading him to the Amazon. He took the name of the little town as a sign from God.

They drove north until they went under Interstate 29 and accessed the large highway toward Council Bluffs, Iowa. After driving several hours, Jeremiah was getting noticeably tired, and he pulled into a gas station to fill up with gasoline. Driving just a few miles away, he pulled into a restaurant, and they ordered the daily special; chicken-fried steak, real mashed potatoes topped with white gravy, green beans and a piece of peach cobbler with a dollop of vanilla ice cream. It tasted almost as good as a similar meal they had just a few days earlier many miles away.

Following lunch, Tyisha took over the wheel and Jeremiah took a nap on the passenger side. Going further north on Interstate 29, they found the miles taking its toll on both, so they pulled into Sioux Falls, South Dakota for both gasoline and supper. After eating, they drove into a church parking lot for a nap. When they awoke, somewhat groggy, they made the decision to go home to Pierre, no matter how late.

Accessing Interstate 90, they went west to the intersection with Highway 83 at Vivian, South Dakota and turned north toward Pierre. When Tyisha and Jeremiah arrived at their home, they were both so exhausted they left the car packed and locked and went straight inside to sleep. It was almost 1:00 a.m. and neither was awake at 1:15 a.m.

***

Friday morning came far too soon. Jeremiah tried to quietly get up, read his Bible and allow Tyisha to sleep. He was unsuccessful. This had been his "quiet time" with God since his first year of college.

Tyisha got up while Jeremiah was in the shower and made him two eggs and bacon. When he came into the kitchen, she had a plate prepared for him sitting on the kitchen table.

"Tyisha, even toward the end of college I have thought of little else but of filling the empty minds of young children with our Lord. There were times I was on the practice field, and I had a hard time concentrating on the plays because I was so excited about being a Christian teacher. Something has happened. I am soon going back to my classroom, and I don't feel the same excitement or anticipation. Could it be the Lord; could He be preparing me for the mission field?"

"Jeremiah, I have often wondered why the Lord would prepare me to teach in North Dakota and then take my ministry from me. But I am coming to believe that God took one ministry so He can prepare me for the one He really wants for me. To paraphrase Joseph, 'they meant it for evil, but God meant it for good.' Surely, God is preparing you for missions. Now, you go back to school next week and teach and live Christ before your class, but I am sure this is the last semester you will teach here."

***

It was a Monday in mid-February and terribly cold for a man from southern Alabama. Jeremiah walked in the back entry into his school by the teacher's lounge and his headmaster was waiting for him before he could reach his classroom.

Café con Leche

"Mr. Hall, could I have a word with you?"

"Certainly, sir."

"I received a telephone call on Friday afternoon after you had already left. It was from a Mr. Joe Tanger. He identified himself as a talent scout for the Kansas City Chiefs football team. He wanted to speak to you. I took down his number and promised to give it to you. I think it might be a good idea to call him as soon as possible."

He handed the note to Jeremiah and walked away. Jeremiah stood there in the back hallway, almost in shock. After a moment, he walked into the teacher's lounge where there was a telephone in the corner of the room on a table. It was 7:50 a.m. and he was sure it was too early to reach Mr. Tanger, but on the off chance he was in his office, Jeremiah dialed the number he had been given. After only two rings, Mr. Tanger answered.

"Hello, this is Joe Tanger."

"Mr. Tanger, I am Jeremiah Hall. You called my school for me last Friday. How may I help you?"

"Mr. Hall, I was a blocking back for your college coach when we were at Grambling College and his best friend. He called me a year back and told me about this great running back he had and how he would be perfect to go with Garrett and Holmes in the backfield.

The AFL will allow us to fill a few positions now that the season is over, and we are having an open tryout in a couple of weeks. We want you to try out and, if you have the ability, we will have you come to camp in August."

"When do you need a reply, Mr. Tanger?"

"I need to know your decision by the end of the week. We will have to make arrangements for travel and a room at the tryout. Will that be alright?"

"I will discuss it with my wife and be back in touch with you by Friday afternoon. Thank you, Sir."

"Thank you for calling back, Jeremiah. Have a great day."

Jeremiah hung up the phone and headed to his classroom. Since he was a young boy, he had dreamed about being a running back in the Pro's. He was a larger man than his father, but with the same speed. He knew he could still run like the wind with the likes of Ed Budde, Jim Tyrer, E.J. Holub, Mo Moorman, and Dave Hill in front of him.

After the early morning telephone call, teaching all day was little more than a distraction. Jeremiah couldn't wait to get home and share his telephone call with Tyisha.

Tyisha had been looking for a job throughout the day and had just arrived home a few minutes before Jeremiah. She was exhausted and just wanted to unwind a while before making supper.

As Jeremiah entered the back door, he yelled, "Ty, you won't believe who I called today. The Kansas City Chiefs who were in the first Super Bowl, though they didn't call it that then. They want me to try out for their team."

Jeremiah came around the corner into the living room to find Ty asleep on the couch with her head resting on a throw pillow. He was so excited about the offer that he was tempted to awaken her and tell Tyisha about the telephone call. Instead, he made himself a bowl of cold cereal and took them onto the back porch to eat. He placed the food on the small round table in the room and sat in one of the two lawn chairs. Jeremiah thanked the Lord for the food before him and for the prestigious offer to try out for a professional football team. Somehow, Jeremiah did not feel the leadership of the Holy Spirit in his prayer and wondered if God wanted him in the American Football League.

The sound of movement indicated Tyisha was awakening from her nap. Jeremiah made a bowl of cereal for his new wife and walked into the living room with it. He handed her the bowl, with silverware and a cloth napkin. Tyisha never admitted just how pleased she was. She needed the rest more than anything else right now. Jeremiah waited until she was finished and then took her bowl to the sink with the silverware. She was still half asleep, so Jeremiah led her to the bed and helped her into her night clothes. After she fell asleep, Jeremiah returned to the living room and finished a test he was preparing for his class. He could always tell Tyisha about the Kansas City Chiefs in the morning before he left for school.

Jeremiah's alarm rang at 6:00 a.m. as it did each school morning, and he tried to get ready for school without awakening Tyisha. His efforts were in vain. When he came out of the bathroom, Tyisha had his breakfast ready and on the table in the kitchen. As Jeremiah sat down to eat, the phone rang on the counter next to the table.

Café con Leche

"Hey Jeremiah, I wanted to call before you left for school." It was Jeremiah's old roommate. "Remember that girl that took my place at the shoe store downtown?"

"Yeah, I remember her."

"Well, my old boss told me yesterday that she quit, and he is looking for someone to take her place. Is your wife still looking for a job?"

"Yes, Tyisha is right here with me. Let me ask her if she is interested."

Jeremiah turned his head toward Tyisha and quickly told her that his former roommate might know of a job available to her selling shoes. She nodded her head that she was interested in interviewing for the job.

"Sure, go right ahead."

Jeremiah turned back to the phone.

"Ty says she would love to interview for the job."

"Okay, you let me call my boss and set up a time for her to meet him. He is a great guy and would be great to work for. I'll call you back later today with an interview date and time."

After getting off the phone, he turned to Tyisha.

"Beside the promise of a job, I have some news of my own. But it is getting time for me to go to school, and I don't want to tell you until I can tell you everything and not rush. Honey, I love you and we'll talk later. By then, you may have an interview scheduled."

Jeremiah kissed Tyisha and promised to talk to her later in the evening, as he grabbed his satchel and walked out the back door for school. Since their visit to the Remote Peoples Training Camp near St. Joseph, Missouri, Jeremiah had been plagued by the realization that education was not his calling. He loved his children but felt too constrained. He wanted to teach his students about God and the Son of God that loved them so much He gave his life for them. Though many of the School Board and administrators professed being Christians, they were more interested in money than the will of God. They welcomed with open arms any student whose parents could pay the ungodly high tuition. The leaders of the school were much more interested in a reputation of excellent academics than students who came to know their living Lord. The Savior's Christian School had been in existence a little more than a decade but had lost its way. Its original mission was to take the Gospel of Jesus Christ to Pierre and its environs but had degenerated into a private school that was monetarily profitable. Jeremiah was still naïve enough to want to use his life for the glory of God and he knew he could never do so in his present position.

Jeremiah arrived a full hour before the school day began, as was his habit. He sat in his car and knew what he had to do, though he dreaded doing so. It was already late March, the beginning of spring in most parts of the United States, late winter in Pierre, South Dakota and teaching contracts were to be let to the potential teachers any day. Jeremiah had every reason to believe he was "one of the chosen."

Over thirty minutes prior to the beginning of the school day, a tall lanky middle-aged man parked in the parking space marked "Headmaster." James Swearingen was a retired Marine and a man who knew how to take orders from his superiors. As soon as he entered the school building, Jeremiah exited his car and followed him into the headmaster's office.

Jeremiah rapped on the doorframe with his knuckles and asked, "Mr. Swearingen, do you have a moment?"

"Sure, Jeremiah, come on in. What can I do for you today?"

Jeremiah had rehearsed this moment many times in the past three months since his honeymoon, but now that the time had come to deliver his speech, he was unsure how to begin.

"Well, you see Mr. Swearingen, I need to tell you about a difficult decision. Uh, I'm not sure how to begin and…"

In his direct and no-nonsense Marine way, Mr. Swearingen looked directly at Jeremiah and said, "Jeremiah, take a breath. After thirty years in the Marines, I have heard a ton of 'difficult decisions.' Let loose of that door frame, come over here and sit down and tell me what you are finding so hard to say. I promise I will not hurt you." This was meant to be funny. Mr. Swearingen was at least seventy years old and nowhere near the svelte young Marine basic trainee of his past and was no match for Jeremiah even then.

As instructed, Jeremiah sat down in the chair directly in front of Mr. Swearingen's desk. He inhaled and began again.

"Mr. Swearingen, I have been considering our future, more importantly where does the Lord want to use us, and it is not here. I will not be signing a new contract."

The arteries in Mr. Swearingen's neck began to swell, but to his credit, he did not immediately respond. When he finally did, the silence in the room was almost frightening.

"Do you have any idea how hard it was for me to convince the School Board that we need to hire a black from Alabama in Pierre, South Dakota?" There was no need for a response. The question was obviously rhetorical.

"We have decided to start a football program in our high school, and you were our choice to be our first coach. We even have a local excavator scheduled to build our first football field this summer. Now, you walk in here and say you are taking a walk and leaving us and me?"

Jeremiah's anger was boiling. He had expected a certain amount of regret on the part of Mr. Swearingen, but not the harsh words he was hearing.

"Mr. Swearingen, all the way back to our first contact when I was still a student at Alabama State University, I told you that my first consideration in any decision was the will of God. That has not changed. I was supposed to come here and meet my wife, Tyisha. I was supposed to come here and learn that God has not called me to be an educator. This past week, I was offered a chance to tryout for a position on the Kansas City Chiefs, but the same standard applies-is this the will of God for my life. I haven't even told Tyisha about the offer, but I am sure she feels the same.

I don't know who God will provide for your new football program; I only know it won't be me. I wish you well in your search. I will be the best teacher I can be until the last day of school in May. If there is any way I can help you in the development of your new football program between now and then, please ask me.

Forgive me; I need to get my room ready for my students. I know this is not the message you wanted to hear from me, but the one I needed to give you. God bless and I will talk to you later."

Jeremiah got up and began to leave Mr. Swearingen's office.

"Stop where you are Marine. I didn't give you permission to leave this office." Now, Jeremiah was certain those rumors in the teacher's lounge about the headmaster suffering from dementia were true. Jeremiah knew he could handle any physical attack by the old warrior and continued his walk down the hall from the office to his own room. He worried about the confrontation with Mr. Swearingen but tried all day to concentrate on the curriculum prescribed by the School Board. The melee earlier in the day had served to delineate his thinking. It was the end of seeing education as his future, but the end of a dream. It was obvious that God was working in his life and Tyisha would be there with him at each juncture. He couldn't wait to begin the journey with Ty.

The tryout with the Kansas City Chiefs that seemed so important that morning wasn't quite so crucial. Oh, he would still tell Tyisha about it, but Jeremiah knew his days of playing football were over. God had something else for him to do.

***

At the end of the school day, Jeremiah drove home and entered the back door of the house. Before he could set his satchel on the floor, Tyisha ran up to him and kissed him.

"Guess what husband, your wife is the newest shoe clerk in Pierre." She was grinning ear to ear.

"That's great news, honey, but I need to tell you about some of the events earlier this week and this morning. First, I did not want to wake you to tell you, but a recruiter for the Kansas City Chiefs called me and asked me to come to a tryout for his team. You know how much I wanted to play professional football, but I promised to call him back with a response by Friday afternoon. Since this morning, I have had time to think about the Lord's will for our lives and it does not include professional sports. I'll be calling the Chiefs back and declining their invitation to tryout. Man, I can't believe I'm doing this!

And there's more. I knew the Lord had closed Christian education as a means of service for you, but I still thought I might be used here or in another Christian institution. The Lord has been showing me that I am not going to serve Him in education. This morning, my option to stay in education ended. I went into to see Mr. Swearingen to tell him of my decision to decline another contract and he blamed me for not being here next year and developing a football program in The Savior's Christian School. I was worried that he would physically attack me. He even 'ordered' me to sit down like I was one of his Marines.

Ty, I have been thinking allot about all the changes we have both been going through in the past six months. We must decide how we should go forward and serve the Lord. On the one hand, it is frightening not to have a career. On the other, it is exciting to watch where the Lord is preparing us to go and what He has for us to do. What do you think?"

Suddenly, Tyisha's new job did not seem nearly so crucial. She thought a good while before responding.

"Jeremiah, you know I have told you repeatedly that you are the head of the family. I'll follow you wherever you go, because I know you are a man of God and are following Him. But you're not the only one that has been sensing God is preparing us for a new direction. Have you given any thought to missions?"

"Ever since we met those missionaries in training at St. Joseph, Missouri, I have thought of little else. I think we at least must begin looking at the requirements to be missionaries. Agree?" Jeremiah said his words with as much confidence as he could muster, but fears of the consequences of his decision were just under the skin.

Tyisha immediately agreed and hugged her husband. "Do you think it is too early to look at a location and propose that our church here in Pierre support us?"

"No, Ty, I think we need to start with prayer."

Jeremiah was already hugging Tyisha and feeling more confident by the moment with Tyisha by his side. Before Jeremiah spoke further, he bowed his head and prayed to their Lord.

"Father, you have shown us what we should not do, but now please show us what we should do. We want to serve you and do your will. Make your will clear to us. We know that You will be with us in whatever service we pursue; in the classroom, the shoe store, missions, or in a service we have yet to discover. We know You will meet our every need. Thank you, Lord. In Jesus' name, we pray it all."

"Amen, Lord." Tyisha agreed with every word in Jeremiah's prayer and was so thankful the Lord had brought them together. She sensed they were about to embark on a new quest, but not just any change in direction; they were responding to the call of their own Savior, Jesus Christ. Their God was leading them away from one place to a new place, a new ministry, and a new culture. They were ready to say "yes" and follow their Lord wherever He took them and to do whatever He had prepared them to do.

"Jeremiah, I have not been wasting all this time without a job. I have spent hours at the city library. I have been researching the area of the headwaters of the Amazon River in eastern Peru. There are five Indian tribes there that have had little or no evangelism.

For a month, I have felt that this could be where the Lord wants us or at least somewhere like it. Either way, we need to prepare to go serve Him."

"Ty, I only knew this morning that the Lord was calling us into missions, and I have not really had time to process a location. Give me a few days to try to hear the Lord. Meanwhile, I can see the Lord has been working in our lives even before we met. I had a roommate for my first year of teaching. Without knowing why, I was saving much of my salary. In addition, I had a full scholarship to attend college and saved several thousand dollars.

You still have a couple of thousands of dollars from the years Aunt Lizzie was saving money for you. Together, we have over $10,000 in our savings account. If the Lord wants us to go to the mission field, we have enough money to get some training and visit a host of churches in hopes they will support our ministry.

For now, I still have a class to teach for a few more weeks. I need to grade some papers and make up a test, so I'll go in the front room, and we will talk more tomorrow."

"Honey, you do what you need to do, but I suspect you will have trouble thinking of anything else but missions. I checked out some books about Peru and Brazil and the flora and fauna of the area. I'll be reading on the back porch if you need me."

Ty and Jeremiah had no more than parted company when the telephone rang. Ty was the first to reach the telephone and pick up the receiver.

The voice on the other end said, "Ty, it is good to hear your voice." It was Bob Dilman, director of the Remote Peoples Training Camp. Jeremiah had arrived and Ty held up the telephone between their faces.

"Bob, it's good to hear your voice. Jeremiah is on the line with me. We have news for you, too, but tell us your news first."

"Well, Ty and Jeremiah, we have a prayer group that meets here every Wednesday night. In the past three meetings, you all have been on our hearts and minds. The group felt the Lord was calling you to missions and wanted me to call you and see if the Lord had put the call to missions upon your hearts."

"Bob, this can't be a coincidence. Just 20 minutes ago, Ty and I were discussing not only the fact the Lord has called us to missions but are considering the upper Amazon as a place of service.

There are a lot of amazing circumstances that have led us to the conclusion that the Lord is calling us to missions, but we know this telephone call is costly. We will tell you in person, if there is a time soon to enter your program."

"Ty, Jeremiah, we have a new class starting on June 15. You are welcome to join us, and we will work with you to make the 12-week course affordable. If you can, begin raising your support at the local church level. We will work around the demands of fund raising while you are with us and maybe we can introduce you to some pastors that may lead their congregations to support you, both prayerfully and financially.

Well, let me get off here. I am so excited to tell the rest of the Prayer Group about the call of God on your lives. Now, we will certainly have something to pray about. Let us know if you all have any prayer requests for us. I will be sending you a packet of information about our program and any information we have on the Amazon basin. You all get some rest, and we'll talk again in a week or so."

After hanging up the telephone, Jeremiah looked at Ty and both said simultaneously, "The Lord wants us in missions." There were no questions as to what the Lord's will was for their lives, only questions as to how they would fulfill the will of God.

"Ty, I can't think of school right now. I'll get up early and prepare for class. Let's go to bed and try to get some rest. I suddenly feel exhausted."

"I think you are right. It's already 9:30 p.m.; let's get some sleep before you have to get up."

It was useless. They reclined on the bed and discussed the way the Lord had been working in their lives until the early hours of the morning. Ty even concluded that the vile accusations of members of her church in Williston, North Dakota were part of God's plan to prepare her for the mission field. Jeremiah was certain the Lord had created a position for a young biracial man in Pierre, South Dakota so he could meet Ty and be drawn to missions with his new wife.

The two newlyweds finally slipped into a restless sleep. Their lives were about to change in ways they had never imagined, a life full of decisions made in faith, not logic. They couldn't wait to start this new life that loomed just out of reach.

CHAPTER 17

Ty and Jeremiah had developed a presentation to give to churches interested in supporting their ministry to the upper Amazon River region. Their church in Pierre, as well as that of their mother and new stepfather had committed to financial and prayer support for them. Several churches in Kansas City and St. Joseph, Missouri had also committed to support them. Before they knew it, they were ready to make the trek to Peru, where they had decided to seek a place to minister.

But before they could go to their ministry, they had to acquire at least a conversational use of Spanish, since it was the language of most Peruvians. They made plans to attend the "Escuela de la Lengua Española" in San José, Costa Rica. Their goal was to complete an abbreviated course in Spanish in six months, rather than the usual one-year-long program. Bob Dilman and his wife placed Jeremiah and Tyisha in contact with a couple who were graduates of the Spanish language school and they had nothing but kudos for the school. Ty and Jeremiah looked forward to their language learning and saw it as a necessary part of their preparation to perform their ministry in Peru.

While in their Spanish school, they had no car. Ty and Jeremiah learned to walk everywhere. Both cars had long since been sold and Ty and Jeremiah had applied the profit to their ministry. They learned to enjoy their evening walks around San Francisco de Dos Rios and crossing the wooden bridge to Desamparados to the south. One weekend, they joined other students on a trip to the beaches of Manuel Antonio and spent the night at a beautiful beach known locally as "La Playa Blanca" near the fishing village of Jaco. Both were from southern Alabama and had never seen an iguana, troop of Capuchin monkeys, or the almost luminescent scarlet macaws. All lived in the jungle just outside their rooms on the side of a mountain above the beach. Costa Rica was becoming the "honeymoon" both Jeremiah and Tyisha had only dreamed of, but never thought would ever happen, given their modest origins. They completed their weekend by going swimming one more time in the unbelievable warm and clear waters of La Playa Blanca with some of their classmates. On their way back to San José, the group stopped in their rented bus at one end of a bridge. In the river beneath were dozens of hungry crocodiles. The group delighted in dropping whole chickens they had bought earlier to the waiting reptiles beneath.

The following afternoon Jeremiah was sitting in the student lounge at the language school where the student mailboxes were located. He wondered where he and his wife were to minister. They had been considering taking the Gospel of Jesus Christ to a group of Indians who were nearly isolated in the mountains of western Panama near the Costa Rican border or perhaps to some of the Mayans located in the mountains surrounding Lago Atitlán in Guatemala. Jeremiah and Ty were nearly halfway through their conversational Spanish course, and they still had no certainty as to where the Lord was leading them. They told each other with bravado that the Lord had called them to missions and He would show them where in His own time. But, within their own souls, they were secretly wondering if the Lord had really called them to missions.

Sitting there on an old couch someone had donated to the Institute, Jeremiah sat deep in thought. Just then, a young Indian woman with an unusual headdress sat down next to him. Her headdress was beautiful, clearly hand-woven, with small beads hanging down about an inch around the circumference. In accented English, she said, "Hello, my name is Shiray Mahua Silvano, or Rabin Kena as my people call me. What is your name?"

Café con Leche

"My mother and father named me after their favorite Old Testament prophet, Jeremiah. You said your people call you 'Rabin Kena.' Who are your people?"

"I am from the Shipibo-Konibo people of eastern Peru in the Amazon jungle."

Jeremiah looked at her in somewhat wonderment and said, "Aren't you a long way from home?"

"Yes, but no further than you." Shiray could tell from his accent that Jeremiah was from the United States. "I was born in a village of my people on the banks of the Río Javary before it becomes one of the major tributaries of the Amazon River. My father died when I was just a child and my mother took me to Lima, the capital city. We needed the money, so when I was 14 years old, I went to work for Velasco, S.A. producing poultry. I learned the entire company well, from eggs to packaged chicken parts. When I was 23 years old, Pollo de Oro here in Costa Rica had an opening. As an 'india,' I was never accepted in Peru, so I took the position and live just south of the school. The school has been kind enough to let me get my mail here, so I don't have to go downtown to the Post Office to pick it up. I think they made up their mind when I told them I was a Christian. I became a Christian while going to a church in Lima with a friend. But my people need the hope that only Christ can give. I hope God will lead someone to take the Gospel to my people. Well, I must get to work, but I know I will see you again." The young woman disappeared as quickly as she had appeared.

Jeremiah was struck with the sense that he had been right where he needed to be right when he needed to be there. He suddenly knew where the Lord was leading Tyisha and him. Tyisha had sensed the Lord leading them to Peru while they still lived in Pierre; Jeremiah thanked the Lord for such a brilliant, intuitive and beautiful wife.

Jeremiah became emotional at the revelation and began to cry to the point he had to get up and go to an empty part of the building. His tall muscular frame literally shook as he became certain that the encounter with the young Indian woman was God's answer to his prayer for the Lord to show him where God wanted Tyisha and him to take the Gospel. His commitment to follow God to the mission field was immediately renewed. Jeremiah wanted to go home and tell Tyisha about the Indian woman and how he could see God's hand all over the experience. Jeremiah never saw the young Shipibo-Konibo woman again and no one in the school had ever heard of her. There was no mailbox in her name.

***

Tyisha was the consummate "worrier" of the couple, and she had often wondered how they would converse with any Indigenous group given their modest understanding of Spanish and no knowledge of any indigenous language. What they needed was someone who could teach them an Indian language.

Tyisha voiced her concern to Jeremiah, and he agreed. The next day he called the main office of their sponsoring mission, *Buenas Noticias para América Latina,* and explained the couple's need. A young man, a member of the office staff, replied, "You guys are living right. Just yesterday, a young woman who recently graduated from a linguistics school operated by the International Linguistics Mission contacted us and said she was volunteering to use her linguistics gift for one year on the mission field. This was the mission Bob Dilman had recommended to them in Missouri and Ty and Jeremiah trusted him completely.

After Jeremiah enthusiastically replied he needed the contact information for this young woman, the young man provided both the linguist's name and telephone number. Her name was Sondra Aikens and she lived in the old Black Belt near Selma, Alabama. Jeremiah could not believe the odds that this young lady had been raised in the same part of Alabama as he had.

Tyisha and Jeremiah lived almost a mile away in a community known locally as "Curridabat" or just "Curri" for short. Jeremiah ran the whole way so he could get home before Tyisha, who was shopping at a small mall known as "Plaza del Sol." He barely made it through the door before telephoning the number provided by his mission and the young lady he had been seeking, answered on his first attempt.

"Hello."

"Yes, hello. My name is Jeremiah Hall, a missionary who is headed up the Amazon River. My wife and I have need of a linguist that can translate an Indigenous Indian language in eastern Peru. Would you be interested in more details?"

Café con Leche

"Absolutely, Mr. Hall."

Jeremiah told Sondra all he knew about the location and how he had just met an Indian woman who steered he and Tyisha to eastern Peru. Jeremiah promised to contact her with any further information as soon as he had it.

As soon as Jeremiah hung up the telephone, he had a warm feeling that the Lord was in control and making His plans come to fruition. Jeremiah was just amazed that the Lord had chosen him and Tyisha to serve Him. Jeremiah did not feel worthy to serve God, but God in His great mercy, had chosen Jeremiah and Tyisha.

Jeremiah hoped to make a meal of melted locally produced cheese drizzled over a bed of egg noodles mixed with a small amount of olive oil and chunks of baked chicken. To drink, he planned to cut four or five mangos from the tree behind the house and make a delicious juice. It was the ultimate comfort food and following the meal, he planned to tell Tyisha about the encounter in the mail room and his telephone call to Sondra. He knew she would be as excited as he was.

Jeremiah was right. Tyisha's eyes widened as Jeremiah told her about the young Indian woman's appearance and her words and Sondra's willingness to use her linguistic skills with the Indians of eastern Peru. After hugging and praying together, the young couple began to plan how they would prepare to go to the headwaters of the Amazon River. They decided to rededicate themselves to their language studies. They would contact Jeremiah's mother and tell her of their plans and ask that she and her church support them at a higher level and their grandiose plan to take the Gospel to the Indians.

Jeremiah had conceived of converting a metal barge into a platform for their home which would allow them to move to where the Indians were. He had been struck with the possibility when he thought of his old roommate in college. Rory Calente had not been blessed with financial wealth, so to supplement his meager funds Rory had bought a used arc welder, mounted it on an old pickup and took small welding jobs in the Montgomery, Alabama area. Rory was so talented he could have made his living from welding.

All night long, Jeremiah found himself counting the tiles on the ceiling. He was so excited he looked forward to the coming day so he could call Rory and ask him to help them build a home on a metal barge. He had no idea how they could pay for this large project, but Jeremiah and Tyisha had finally concluded God would provide for their every need.

The sun's first rays finally penetrated the fog on the sides of a volcano named Irazú and Jeremiah nearly leapt to his feet. He went down the staircase to the kitchen where he ate a bowl of Costa Rica's version of Corn Flakes. The banana he had sliced over the top of the cereal was as fresh as the banana plant outside the back door. He waited until 9:00 a.m. since he remembered that Rory liked to sleep in as late as possible. When it was 9:01 a.m. Jeremiah called his Brother in Christ and former roommate.

After three rings, a woman's voice came on the other end. "Hello. How can I help you?" It was Jeremiah's cousin and Rory's wife, Juanita.

"Juanita, it's Jeremiah. Is Rory there?"

"Yeah, he's outside with our dog. Until he gets back, I have some news of my own. First, I wish you could have been at our wedding in a little country church south of Meridian, Mississippi. Second, and I only told Rory a couple of days ago; I am pregnant and due September 8 next year.

Now, tell me a little about how you are doing. Are you still going to Panama to take the Gospel to the Indians?"

"Well, Cuz, that's why I called. I ran into an Indian girl from Peru yesterday, or maybe she ran into me. Either way, she confirmed that God is calling us to her tribe in eastern Peru. I was certain when she left that the Lord was using her to point us to the headwaters of the Amazon River. I believe we could build a house on a steel barge and install a motor that could propel us all the way to Peru. I remember Rory had welding skills and we could really use those skills right now."

"That is very exciting, and Rory will want to talk with you about the experience. We believe that the Lord is calling you and we want to help you fulfill the call of God on your lives. Hang on just a minute, Rory just walked in with our Pomeranian."

Jeremiah nearly laughed outside as he imagined 300 plus pound Rory holding a six-pound 'fu-fu' dog. Rory got on another line and said, "What did you do, take a day off from the beach just to call us?"

"No, Rory. I think we finally have some clarity as to where the Lord is leading us. (Jeremiah hesitated telling Rory that he and Tyisha had been on the beach just the previous weekend). Yesterday, I had a very unusual encounter with an Indian woman from eastern Peru. Just before she left, she said, 'My people need the hope that only Christ can bring.' I have no doubt that Tyisha and I are the ones that God has called to bring her tribe the Gospel. But we need help to do that."

"Jeremiah, just last night Juanita and I were discussing the hundreds of blessings the Lord has given us. I started with one lumber yard that I named, "31 Building Supplies." Since college, I now own three of them and all are making money. We were undecided as how to pay our tithe, but now I know what the Lord wants us to do. When are you graduating from your language program?"

Jeremiah thought about the schedule. "Well, we get out of class a week before Christmas and our rent is paid through January 1. We could leave any time after Christmas."

"Okay, Jeremiah, let me do some checking and I think it is best if I come down on a freighter and meet you all in, let's say, Belém, Brazil. Juanita and I went on our honeymoon to Belém. Some of the most beautiful beaches you ever saw are nearby. We took a short three-day boat trip from Belém up a tributary and explored some of the flora and fauna of the Amazon region.

We could look for a used barge to work on around Belém. Juanita told me you were looking to build a house on one and I remember there was a coconut processing plant there. They transport the coconuts from as far away as Panama on barges. You let me do some research and I'll get back to you with the details. Listen now, this is our gift to you and is our tithe."

"Rory, I did not know Juanita was pregnant when I called. I can't ask you to go clear to South America when you are expecting your first child."

"Now Jeremiah, I would not have offered my services if I did not believe God was in your ministry. Besides, we just found out Juanita was pregnant three days ago. I know I can weld a frame on a barge, build a fuel tank and install an engine within the frame and do it all within a couple of months. I know the Lord will be with me and get me home long before Juanita delivers our child. Juanita's mother has already told us she wants to come and stay until the baby is born. Coming to help you all may be my salvation."

"Juanita isn't there is she?"

"No, and if you tell her what I said, I'll deny it."

"Your secret is safe with me. Thank you so much for your care. Just like when you used to open a hole for me in the defensive line, we need you to help us one more time. Give me a call when you have the details. I know it is a big continent, but I can't think of a better way to minister to the Indians in Peru than a houseboat. We look forward to hearing from you and God bless you and Juanita until then."

With these words, Jeremiah hung up the telephone and looked at Tyisha who was standing nearby. "Ty, God is at work, and we are in the middle of His will. A month ago, we were not certain where the Lord would take us. Now, we not only know where, but how we are going to get there to minister.

I know Rory and I know he will do whatever it takes to help us do God's will. He would take out the biggest guy on the defense just to give me opportunity to run through the hole. He will do whatever is necessary to help us. I am going to have a tough time going to sleep tonight.

Ty, hold my hands as we pray for Rory and Juanita and that the Lord would help him compile all the information he needs to help us make a home."

Dutifully, Ty and Jeremiah held hands and prayed for Rory and Juanita, as they had promised. When they concluded their prayer with the Biblical formula, 'we pray in the name of the Lord, Jesus Christ," Jeremiah said he was going to 'try' to go to sleep since he had a test the next day at the language institute. Tyisha stayed up and read more about the indigenous peoples. She was so excited by the prospects of taking the Gospel to the 'un-reached' people groups that she did not go to bed with Jeremiah, who she found snoring when she finally laid down by him.

CHAPTER 18

True to his word, Rory telephoned Jeremiah and Tyisha about a week after they had first talked. He had verified that there was a cargo ship leaving New Orleans in about a week and, after five ports of call in the Caribbean Sea, its destination was Belém, Brazil. Plus, he had discovered several flights from Jackson, Mississippi with connecting flights to Belém arriving on January 11.

Rory had already checked, and Jeremiah and Tyisha could fly from San José on January 9th on a Taca flight to Caracas, Venezuela. From there, they could get a flight from Caracas on a Servivensa flight the following day to Belém.

Rory's ship was not scheduled to dock in Belém until January 11, but this date was tenuous at best. There were so many factors to consider such as weather, mechanics of the ship, etc. If the ship was late Jeremiah and Tyisha could spend some time looking at one of the most beautiful cities in Brazil. Before the end of the phone call, Jeremiah, Tyisha and Rory had agreed with the plan. Rory would bring his favorite arc welder with him and ship it as cargo. If more convenient, Rory would travel via air and purchase an arc welder on site.

Jeremiah and Tyisha would box up all their worldly belongings and ship them via air freight to Belém which should be available to them when they landed there. They could always leave their air freight in the cargo hold area of the airport an additional day or two if Rory's ship was late.

Further inquiry had left Rory unsure as to the reliability of the ship's schedule. Arrival at Belém could be three days early or late of the scheduled date of arrival. He telephoned and informed Jeremiah and Tyisha of this uncertainty and told them he would find a welder in Belén and was flying down.

Rory had already checked and there were several used steel cargo barges available for a reasonable price, especially important since he and Juanita were paying for the entire cost of the barge and house. Ty and Jeremiah had paid their rent through January 31, but they were willing to lose the money just to get on to Brazil, where they hoped to begin the next step in their ministry. It had only been six months since they sensed the Lord was leading them to missions. Now, they were only a couple of weeks away from going to Brazil to build a houseboat, a necessity for their ministry.

The next day, they took a taxi near the San José airport and found a company next door that shipped air freight. They arranged to have their air freight ready for shipment on January 8 and delivered to Belém, Brazil on January 11, with the option to hold it in storage up till January 15.

***

Finally, the morning of January 8 arrived. Both Jeremiah and Tyisha had pretended to be asleep for the benefit of the other, but neither received much sleep on the night of January 7. When they could no longer pull off the deception, they got up and made a breakfast of eggs, red peppers, mushrooms and the end of their milk in a box. It was literally an omelet made from the last things in their refrigerator. Most of the furniture had cheap bamboo frames with thin cushions for sitting. Thankfully, a neighbor had a son who was getting married and wanted the furniture to begin life with his new bride in a house around the corner.

An old diesel flatbed truck pulled up in front of the house, and the driver honked the horn. Jeremiah went outside to tell the driver and his co-worker the location of the boxes he and Tyisha had packed. Jeremiah was so excited to finally be on their way to Brazil that they helped the air freight crew load the boxes on the truck. With all hands-on deck, it took less than half of an hour to load the truck. Ty and Jeremiah waved "Good-bye" to the air freight workers as they drove away. Before leaving their house for the last time, they brought their packed suitcases outside and left them on the porch as they walked through the house for one last time. They told each other that they were looking for any personal items left behind, but each had a tear in the corner of their eye. They realized that they were leaving their last connection to Costa Rica and would likely never return to a place they had grown to love.

They locked the front door as Jeremiah carried the bulk of the weight up the long climb to the intersection in front of the well-known church, San Francisco de Dos Rios. On the side of the highway that goes north to Zapote, they flagged a taxi and asked the taxi driver to take them to Hotel Don Cristobal in downtown San José. Ty and Jeremiah had eaten lunch in the restaurant and fell in love with the old hotel. It only had a few rooms, but the atrium had two macaws in cages near a fountain. They planned to spend the night in the hotel before flying toward their eventual meeting with Rory. They would have to spend the next night in Trinidad and Tobago before finishing their trip to Belém where they hoped to meet their friend.

The next morning, they ate a light breakfast with banana-fed pork chops with a pineapple sauce and a fruit drink before a taxi drove them to the airport. The time had finally come for them to go to the place where the Lord had led them. They were so full of anticipation, Tyisha shook, and Jeremiah wasn't much calmer.

Their flights that day were somewhat circuitous. The first leg of their journey took them to Caracas, Venezuela where they changed flights. The end of their day was on a twin-engine DC-3 that had been converted into a passenger plane. Flying due east over the jungles of eastern Venezuela and the Orinoco River, the young couple were amazed. They thought the jungles of Costa Rica were immense, but the jungles below were larger than they could comprehend.

After flying over a short stretch of the Atlantic Ocean, they landed at the airport on Trinidad at the end of the day. Two men pulled in a large cart loaded with luggage and placed each suitcase in a circle awaiting the passengers to claim them.

Brent Garzelli & Cheryl L. Garzelli

Jeremiah and Tyisha claimed their luggage and before they could go to an awaiting line of taxis, a man placed the luggage on his own cart and began to transport the luggage to the front of the airport without being asked to do so. In perfect unaccented English, the man said to Jeremiah and Tyisha that he had lived most of the past decade in New Jersey and returned to his native Trinidad when the cost of living forced him to leave.

The amiable man told Jeremiah that his cousin had a hotel on the beach only a couple of miles away and he would arrange for the couples return to the airport the next morning. Tyisha placed two $1.00 bills in the man's outstretched hand as he placed the last bag in a waiting taxi. He told the driver the address of the hotel and told Jeremiah and Tyisha that there was a good seafood restaurant less than a block from the hotel.

When Ty and Jeremiah arrived at the hotel, they decided they were just too tired from a day of traveling to go anywhere. They went to their room and didn't even unpack a bag before they collapsed on the bed.

The next morning, they went to a nearby shopping area and ordered a piece of pizza each with a cup of coffee. By 8:00 a.m., they were back in the airport and waiting for their connecting flight to Belém, Brazil. They had an uneventful flight, landing with plenty of daylight hours remaining in the day.

They checked into the Hotel Mar e Sol where they reserved rooms for Rory and Sondra while they looked for a more permanent house to rent. After placing their luggage in their room, Jeremiah and Tyisha went to get a good meal in a nearby restaurant. Rory was familiar with this hotel, since it was the same one in which he and Juanita had spent their honeymoon.

Jeremiah had a rough time going to sleep that night, too. It wasn't the mattress, which was exceedingly comfortable-rather, it was the anticipation that Jeremiah felt before the arrival of his old friend. Sondra's arrival was just "icing on the cake." He finally fell asleep next to Ty with a smile on his face. He had a plan to build a house on a metal barge and he knew the Lord would take Tyisha, Sondra, and him to the right sight well up the Amazon River. God's Will was coming to fruition and Jeremiah knew all he had to do was to follow that Will revealed by the Holy Spirit. Very few Christians know that special feeling of doing just what God wants them to do and exactly at the time God wants them to do it. Jeremiah and Tyisha knew that unique feeling and they never wanted it to end. Their lives had

Café con Leche

been so painful before knowing Christ, but now they were being healed. Best of all, they were being healed together and God was in the process of making them "one flesh." What else could Jeremiah do but sleep with a smile and have dreams of heaven?

Jeremiah and Tyisha awoke with the sound of a rooster crowing just outside of their hotel, right in the city. They could not wait to get started, so they almost ran to a local kiosk on a shopping street and ordered a piece of pizza each and "um copo de café." They drank their coffee as they ate their pizza. Jeremiah almost choked as he gobbled his food in anticipation of picking up Rory at the airport.

They took a taxi to the airport and waited impatiently for Rory's flight to arrive. The old DC-3 rumbled to a stop on the tarmac adjoining the airport and a mobile stairwell was pushed up to the door of the plane. Most of the passengers deplaned and Jeremiah and Tyisha were nearly certain that Rory had missed the flight. Then this huge man almost bent at the waist to exit the aircraft. Rory nearly had to turn sideways and bend at the same time to get through the door. Before he could walk down the stairs, Jeremiah was running up toward him.

Without saying a word, Jeremiah hugged as far around the big man as he could. Rory had become a "hug and chalker." He was so rotund, you started hugging him as far as your arms could reach, make a chalk mark and resume hugging him from that mark forward.

What difference did it make how Jeremiah hugged his old friend and brother in Christ? Jeremiah and Rory were almost in tears. Both knew that the task ahead was likely the last time they would be together. Still, the reunion was one of great joy and love and they were determined to cherish each moment.

Sondra's flight was scheduled about an hour later, so Rory, Jeremiah and Tyisha decided to sit in the airport and "catch-up" before Sondra's arrival.

The small jet landed at the Belém airport as expected and Tyisha flashed her sign she had made earlier exhibiting Sondra's name. All three were amazed when a young bi-racial woman walked up to them and stated, "I'm Sondra." Rory, Jeremiah and Tyisha were all astounded. No one at the mission had mentioned Sondra's race. Even Jeremiah, who had spoken to Sondra, believed she was a white lady.

All three stood there with their lower jaws dropped in surprise. Finally, Rory reached out his hand and said to Sondra, "Welcome to Brazil! Thanks for coming to keep these two out of trouble (he pointed to Tyisha and Jeremiah who had finally recovered)."

Jeremiah and Tyisha reached out their hands to Sondra and welcomed her to the mission team. As they did so, a little four-year-old boy from Nicaragua ran up to the group and said to Sondra, Tyisha and Jeremiah, "Ustedes son 'Café con Leche'." In much of Central America, where the little boy and his family were from, "Café con Leche" is slang for a person who is half white and half black; a mulatto. Jeremiah, Tyisha and Sondra took no offense at the remark made by the little boy. All had been called much worse and the little boy was reflecting his parents' views more than his own.

After a quick lunch, they all returned to the hotel where Jeremiah and Tyisha had already reserved rooms for Rory and Sondra. During the afternoon, Rory and Jeremiah went to a local bus station and got the schedule for buses to Ilha do Mosqueiro (Island of Mosquitoes). Once they had a schedule in hand, they returned to the Hotel Mar e Sol and found Sondra and Tyisha in the lobby of the hotel getting to know one another.

Rory, never shy, spoke first. "Gals, I am bushed from the trip. I'm going to get some sleep in my room and then how about we meet back here around 6:00 p.m. and catch a bite to eat in the restaurant?"

They all agreed as Rory went to his room, followed shortly by the others. They were all running on adrenaline and needed a few hours of rest.

Good to his word, Rory and the other members of the mission team met in the lobby of the hotel at about 6:00 p.m. They went into the atrium of the hotel where a restaurant was located. It had a limited menu, but the food was quite good.

After dinner, Sondra, Rory, Tyisha and Jeremiah took a long walk down near the Pará River and made plans for the following day. They concluded that Sondra and Tyisha would find a realtor on the Ilha do Mosqueiro and seek a place to stay for the next month. The house would need to have sleeping quarters for all the team members and be near the waterfront on the island. Rory and Jeremiah planned to go to a coconut processing plant on the island and try to buy a used barge upon which they could construct a house for Tyisha, Jeremiah and Sondra.

Café con Leche

Sondra had mastered six languages and Portuguese was one of them. Rory explained that he had decided not to bring a welder and told the others that Sondra's language gift would be necessary to buy a welder and the supplies to build a home and transform a barge into a platform for the house.

Rory and Jeremiah had discussed possible plans for transforming a river barge and supports necessary for an engine, transmission, a large fuel tank, and a house to be built on I-beams near the top of the barge.

They started back toward the hotel and agreed to meet in the hotel lobby the next morning at 7:00 a.m. They planned to eat breakfast in the restaurant and then walk to the bus stop where they would catch a bus at 8:30 a.m.

***

Amazingly, all four slept well and everything was going better than planned. Once on the bus, they agreed to take the bus to the area known as Mosquiero and once there, locate a realtor. The girls would stay with the realtor and look at potential properties while the boys would go to the coconut processing plant and then they would all reunite in Mosquiero around 4:00 p.m., so they could take the last bus of the day back to their hotel nearer the heart of the city.

They parted company at the first realtor's office they found, and Sondra and Tyisha went inside. The receptionist took them back to a Senhor Thompson. Both women registered shock at the clear Anglo sound of the realtor's surname. He realized their concern, and without being prompted, told the women that his father was an American Merchant Marine who had met his mother in Belém and stayed. Senhor Thompson had lived his entire life on the island and knew it backward and forward.

Tyisha explained that they were looking for a short-term rental that had sufficient space for all four of them. They were in hopes that they could be ready to leave within a month, but realistically, they might need the house for longer. They told him they were looking for something in the area of Paraíso since the coconut processing plant was nearby. Senhor Thompson looked at them and said, "I think I have the perfect place."

"I know of a large house just across the street from the beach, Praia do Paraíso. It has at least four bedrooms, three bathrooms, a large living room, an atrium, kitchen and dining room. I have never been inside, but I know the house is huge from the outside. The owner and his family come up here for vacation every April or May and he would love to have someone in the house to protect it while he is gone, or so he has told me."

Senhor Thompson told Tyisha and Sondra that he would be glad to take them to see the house, if they could wait a minute. They agreed but told him they wanted to walk to the bus station to try to intercept Rory and Jeremiah. Senhor Thompson offered to take the men with them to see the house. He told them where the bus station was located and promised to pick them up there in one hour. The ladies agreed and caught a cab outside of the realty office to the bus station.

Just minutes went by before they found Rory and Jeremiah. They told the men that the realtor would be coming in a few moments and transport them all to a house he knew of near the coconut processing plant. He had agreed to transport them and he personally knew the owner of the plant, a Senhor Ortega.

As promised, Senhor Thompson drove up in front of the bus station and transported all four members of the team to the house about which he had told Sondra and Tyisha. As he drove them to the east side of the island, without being provoked to do so, Senhor Thompson said, "Senhor Ortega is a committed Christian. He makes me and my wife ashamed to tell anyone we are Christians."

Jeremiah took Tyisha's hand and looked at Rory and Sondra. "The Lord is truly with us each step of the way. He will be with us until the end." The others said nothing but knew Jeremiah's words rang true.

As they drove in front of a beautiful home, Tyisha, Jeremiah, Sondra, and Rory could not believe their eyes. None had ever lived in a home so grand. It covered most of a block and had a large atrium within. The house sat on a promontory above a beach across the street. Senhor Thompson pulled the car to the curb in front of the house and before it was at a complete stop, all four of the mission team jumped from the car and almost broke into a run to the front of the house. Senhor Thompson had contacted the homeowner earlier and he had given his blessing for the four to live there the few weeks they would need prior to leaving on their mission trip.

Inside, the five found four bathrooms, six bedrooms, a large living room and huge kitchen. There was an American style room with a washer

Café con Leche

and dryer, as well as a folding table, and the entirety was built in a square around a large atrium full of plants, walkways, and sitting benches.

Without hesitation, the mission team told Senhor Thompson they would like to rent the home for at least one month and possibly two. Senhor Thompson had been authorized by the owner to immediately rent the house to the group, which he did, charging them $100 per month.

Senhor Thompson had already called Senhor Ortega, the owner of the coconut processing plant, and given him notice they would be to see him later in the day. He had agreed and was literally standing in the front office of the plant when the five arrived. Senhor Ortega enthusiastically invited all into his office and had his secretary deliver some of the best coffee any of the Americans had drunk.

Rory, with his construction skills, explained the mission team's plan to convert a barge to a home that could be transported to the headwaters of the Amazon River. Senhor Ortega, with his limited understanding of English, seemed to comprehend the needs of the mission team. As he stood up, he merely motioned with his finger to the team for them to follow him. They went outside of the plant that was located on a bay facing the open Pará River. There, on logs, were several barges upside down, in various degrees of disrepair. All were of uniform size, about one hundred and fifty feet long, and thirty feet wide. Each had a steel hooking system on the side that could be used to join other filled barges as they transported grains and logs up and down the river.

"This barge was used to go with others all the way around the north of South America as far as Isla Grande, Panama when coconuts are in season. The rest of the year, I have a business running barges up and down the Amazon to supply towns and villages on the shores. Then on the way back, the barges are filled with products from our rich jungles. These are barges which have made several trips. I will give you a good price for any you select. Also, I will supply you with the steel, an acetylene cutting torch, an arc welder, but you will have to pay for your own supplies for the house. It is the least I can do for our Lord, who has done so much for me."

The four were so appreciative they almost hated to make another request of Senhor Ortega. Jeremiah looked at the short man, as Rory stood next to him, and said, "Is there a chance you could place the barge on the water so we could begin working on it tomorrow?"

"If you show me the one you want, I will have it in the water this afternoon."

Rory and Jeremiah walked around the barges and found one with only a few dents on the sides and none below the water line. They pointed to the one they wanted and Senhor Ortega asked them only $2,000 for it. It was a steal, and the men knew it. Rory went behind the building and quickly kicked off his shoes. He took two fresh one-thousand dollar bills out of his left shoe and returned to the rest of the group.

"I am glad to pay it. My back has been killing me!" Rory said with a smile on his face.

"An old Italian man taught me the same trick years ago. I never go anywhere without some money in my shoes." Senhor Ortega and Rory smiled at each other with mutual respect.

It was nearly time for Senhor Ortega's daily cochilo (siesta) so they all went down the street to his favorite seafood restaurant to have lunch together. Only a short distance from the Atlantic Ocean, some of the fishing fleet brought back their daily catches to the local restaurants. After a great time of fellowship together, they all agreed Jeremiah and Rory would return the next morning to begin the construction of their new home on the barge and Tyisha and Sondra would move their meager belongings into the house they had just rented. Senhor Thompson took all four of the missionaries to the bus station and parted with a hearty "Thank you."

CHAPTER 19

The schedule varied little for the following seven weeks. Rory and Jeremiah left the house early each morning and walked the half mile to the barge site to begin work. They were joined there by a Brazilian named, Fernando, whom they had hired to help in the entire process. The three men would work until around noon, at which time Tyisha and Sondra would bring them their lunch.

Fernando insisted that he be granted his cochilo, as was the custom of his country, and he would go into a nearby park and sleep for an hour on a park bench. Rory and Jeremiah seldom rested and ate for more than half an hour before they returned to work. After Fernando returned, he rejoined Rory and Jeremiah and worked to near dark.

Each morning, Jeremiah and Rory had to clear the area around the barge of black caiman that would crawl up on the sheets of steel to get warm in the early morning. As the day progressed, the caiman would lie on the banks of the river in the sun, but were never threatening toward the men, despite their reputation for being aggressive.

Rory cut three equal length I-beams and then with Jeremiah and Fernando, they would lift one end at a time and place them in place across the width of the barge. On their homemade scaffolding, they made supports for the heavy cross members. Once in place, Rory welded the I-beam to the inside of the barge about a foot lower than the top of the side. The process was repeated until all the I-beams were in place. In the hold of the barge, Rory welded a tank that would hold over 3,000 gallons of diesel fuel. He made a platform that would support a large diesel engine and a transmission from a large bulldozer, with corresponding bolt holes in the engine mount. Senhor Ortega had a friend who sold the mission team the bulldozer engine and transmission for $1000 and delivered both to Rory and Jeremiah on a flat bed truck. Senhor Ortega had a crane and operator who had placed the barge in the water. This operator was so skilled, he picked up the huge engine and transmission and gently placed them inside the barge and nearly aligned them with the holes in the mounts Rory had cut earlier.

The platform was slightly elevated and tilted toward the stern so a shaft could be connected to the transmission. Using a double set of yokes and pin, Rory angled the shaft downward toward the back of the barge. Using a large grommet in the back hull of the barge, the shaft was passed through above the water line. The downward angle continued and had a prop affixed to it below the water line.

To install the entire engine to the prop assembly, the barge was lifted by the crane out of the water while Rory, Fernando and Jeremiah attached each component. When the task was completed, the barge was once again lowered into the water. Rory built a small enclosure in the lowest part of the barge and in it he installed a bilge pump to expel water from the tropical rains.

It took most of a month to construct a house on top of the three I-beams. The house was 50 feet by 30 feet with two bedrooms, a spare room that could be used as a third bedroom, a kitchen, a living room, two and a half bathrooms, and a small study. Rory built a 20-foot gangplank that had folding handrails and used a hand crank to wind up a 40-foot steel cable so the entire gangplank could be raised and lowered. He welded it on the side of the barge and placed it directly in front of the front door of the house.

***

Finally, the morning came when the barge was complete and Senhor Ortega had a convoy of barges scheduled to take supplies to the few cities and isolated villages on the Amazon River. It was a bittersweet day and one that Jeremiah had dreaded.

Café con Leche

It seemed the last week had been full of "Goodbyes." The team had said a final "Goodbye" to Fernando. Senhor Ortega was on a business trip to São Paulo. With all that he had done to further their ministry, they really wanted to thank him in person. Perhaps, the Lord would give the opportunity to return to Belén in the future. Only time would tell.

The tugboat was pushing barges together and their barge would soon be part of the convoy that was heading all the way to far western Brazil. The hour had come, and the two old football players grabbed each other and hugged like they would never see one another again, and they probably would not in this world.

"Rory, you know I love you like a brother, and you are my brother in Christ. What you and Juanita have done for us is more than we ever could have asked or dreamed. Tyisha and I are going to take the Gospel to a place I never knew existed when we were roommates at Alabama State University. You all have earned another star in your crowns.

We hope we can come back to see everyone in the United States in about five years, but no one knows the future. Say 'hello' to my mother and new stepfather when you get home." Jeremiah's mother had married her pastor while Tyisha and Jeremiah were in language school.

"Jeremiah, we have had a few bumps and bruises together, and I wish I could go with you to run interference. But it is time for you to go do the Lord's work without me. He will run interference for you and watch your blind side." The gigantic man looked away and was on the verge of tears. Rory slowly walked down the gang plank to the shore and when he arrived at the bottom, he turned and waved to Jeremiah as the gangplank was raised.

Tyisha and Sondra had gone inside the house to give the two men some time alone. They knew the exodus might be permanent and the goodbye would be painful.

Rory went around the plant office where he had placed his suitcases and placed them in a waiting taxi. He was off to the airport for the long journey home to Juanita, and he knew he would cry every mile.

***

The tugboat captain and his crew of two had told Rory and Jeremiah that the trip up the river to Peru would take at least a month or more, depending on how long each stop lasted. The tugboat maneuvered into place and pushed Jeremiah, Tyisha and Sondra's barge into the group that had already been assembled, directly in front of the tugboat. After latching their barge to the others, they completed the formation with a barge on each side of Jeremiah's. Jeremiah stood out on the deck, which was on the front side of the house, pretending to watch down the Pará River, but tears were still flowing down his cheeks. He waved "Goodbye" to the black caiman lying on the shore that had been constant companions to he and Rory in the past few weeks.

Heavily laden with supplies destined for Amazonian villages, the convoy of barges exited the bay nearest the coconut processing plant slowly turning east toward the Atlantic Ocean. The sun was setting lower as the tug maneuvered its cargo barges into the waves and followed the shoreline of the Atlantic Ocean northward to the mouth of the Amazon River. As the sun sat, Sondra, Tyisha and Jeremiah sat on the deck in the coolest part of the day. They were all excited that they were finally on mission for God. What lied ahead of them was a mystery, but they knew they were not alone. God was with them. He had been with them even when they had passed through "Amazonia" in Missouri, what seemed an eternity ago, and they knew He would be with them to wherever He had prepared them to take His Gospel. They sat there eating a light supper of shrimp and rice with tres leches for dessert. Everything just tasted better on the water.

Jeremiah was exhausted from weeks of hard work and supplying the house for the trip ahead. He had a short prayer with the women and went inside the house to sleep. Tyisha and Sondra remained on the deck discussing the ways the Lord had blessed them and suddenly Tyisha turned to Sondra and said, "Sondra, I am really afraid. I have no siblings and I have never been around someone who was pregnant. I am pregnant and don't know what to expect. Would you please pray with me?"

Without any concern in her voice, Sondra replied, "Of course I will pray for you. But do not be afraid. I have never been a midwife, but what I lack in education I have in experience. I am the oldest of eight children and was by my mother's side during at least five births of my siblings. Indians have children too, so I am sure they have a midwife who can be with you through the birth."

Café con Leche

The two women hugged and prayed together before they went inside to bed. For well over a month, while Rory and Jeremiah worked on the barge, Tyisha and Sondra had spent the majority of their time together. They went to the market together, studied the Bible together, prayed together, and shared their most intimate secrets. This long trip up the Amazon River would provide ample opportunity for the two women to deepen their budding relationship.

***

Tyisha still had not told Jeremiah about her pregnancy and only Sondra was aware. After breakfast each morning, the two ladies had about twenty minutes together preparing breakfast and placing it on a table on the deck before Jeremiah joined them for their morning Bible study and prayer.

"Sondra, I think it is time. Jeremiah deserves to know."

"Good morning, ladies, how are we doing?" Jeremiah stood behind them in the doorway with his hair soaking wet. They had no hair dryer, but who needs one when the days are consistently over 90 degrees Fahrenheit?

"Honey, come and sit down with us. I have news for you." Sondra knew what was coming but pretended to be hearing the announcement for the first time.

"Jeremiah, you are going to be a father." Tyisha sat in her chair awaiting an answer or any reaction from Jeremiah. He made none.

Then, just when Tyisha was about to repeat her announcement thinking Jeremiah had not heard her, Jeremiah let out a scream and ran to the edge of their barge. He jumped across to the adjoining barge that was full of corn headed to a stop upriver. Landing on his back, he made a "snow angel" in the grain yelling, "Thank you Lord" all the while.

Tyisha and Sondra stood to their feet astounded at Jeremiah's reaction. The rats, which had been eating the corn, ran to the far side of the barge scared by Jeremiah's sudden scream. It took both Tyisha and Sondra to pull Jeremiah up from the corn and help him back on the deck where they had been sitting. Jeremiah's head, which had been soaking wet, was covered with corn dust and a few larger kernels of corn. He looked ridiculous, so much so Sondra and Tyisha broke into laughter. Jeremiah, without hesitating, grabbed both women and hugged them as he said, "And I thought serving the Lord as a missionary was a blessing!"

Tyisha and Jeremiah were both "only children." Neither had education or experience to help them deliver a child or raise a child. But they knew they had two things going for them-the Bible and Sondra. Besides, God was with them and would help them through the trials ahead.

"Thanks, Jeremiah, now I have to go take another shower." Sondra pretended to be offended. In fact, the obvious joy Jeremiah and Tyisha were experiencing was rubbing off on Sondra. All three hugged one more time before retiring to clean off the corn dust. While Sondra and Tyisha went for their showers, Jeremiah remained behind to shoo the flies away. After they all gathered for breakfast, Tyisha's announcement consumed all aspects of the conversation. They agreed to meet again in the evening for their regular Bible study and prayer time following the evening meal.

***

The rest of the journey was rather predictable. The three missionaries had regular meals to meet the needs of their bodies and Bible study and prayer to meet their spiritual needs. On three occasions, they had the tugboat pilot or his crew to come to their home for supper, always leaving at least one on duty. Two of the three crew members were Christians.

As the flotilla traveled up the river, the tugboat pilot would adeptly maneuver his cargo barges into place, as his crew members disconnected the right barge and tied it to a mooring. The barge was unloaded by crane or even by hand in some cases, and the tugboat pilot planned to reattach the barge to his flotilla on his return trip down the river.

At some of these stops, Jeremiah, Tyisha and Sondra would go ashore and buy supplies for the next segment of the trip. In their absence, the tugboat pilot would top off his diesel tank needed to propel the barges further up the river.

Finally, almost six weeks from the time of their departure from Belén, the tugboat pilot left the last barge with cargo at the dock of a village in western Brazil. As soon as the barge was tied to the mooring, the pilot took the opportunity to come to the house on the last barge in front of the tug. He told Jeremiah, Tyisha and Sondra that Senhor Ortega had instructed him to take the barge as far as the missionaries wanted to go as long as they stayed in Brazil. The pilot told them the river would soon split into its various headwaters. He recommended the Río Javary since the missionaries

Café con Leche

could choose whether to locate in Brazil or Peru depending on which side of the river they moored. Also, he had heard about indigenous peoples that had remote villages on the river. Jeremiah agreed and asked the pilot to take the missionaries as far as the Río Javary.

***

The day finally came when they were at the Brazilian/Peruvian border. The Río Javary entered the Río Amazon to the west and on the confluence of the two rivers was a small fishing village locally known as "Benjamin Constant." The tug was maneuvered into place at a wharf and a large wooden container on the back of the tugboat was removed by a crane operator on the shore. As soon as it was removed, the tug pilot released his boat from Jeremiah's barge. He pulled alongside the barge to verify the barge engine started and to wish farewell to the missionaries before his return trip.

Jeremiah was in the small control cabin Rory had welded for him at the back of the barge where he could control both the transmission and the rudder. Unlike the tugboat pilot who could see over the house and the other barges from this high perch, Jeremiah could only see a sliver in front of him down the back of the house.

The old diesel engine started on the first attempt. He had experimented navigating the barge while still in the bay on the Pará River at Belém and he knew he could steer it on the wide river. He went to the side of the barge nearest the tugboat and yelled to the pilot, "Senhor, my wife is going to have a baby!"

The tugboat pilot replied, "See, your blessings have already started, and you haven't even met the pavos nativos (native people)." The pilot used Brazilian words when he could not think of the English equivalent. "Deus vá com você (God go with you)," yelled the pilot as he turned the tugboat away from the barge and headed back down the long river.

Practicing his skills, Jeremiah maneuvered his craft up the river and around the first of many switchback curves in the river. It was nearing dark, so he piloted the barge near the shore in a relatively calm part of the river before lowering the anchor for the night.

He had started the engine several times during the trip to ensure it would start when he needed it. He shut down the engine and went inside the house to eat dinner with the ladies. Sondra and Tyisha had prepared a wonderful meal of chicken and rice which was ready to eat nearly simultaneously with Jeremiah's arrival. They filled their plates and went out on the deck to eat their meal.

After a prayer and their meal, Tyisha broke the silence by saying, "I can't believe we are finally nearing our destination."

Rory responded, "We started this journey in Pierre and our calling took us to missionary training north of St. Joseph, Missouri and then to language training in San José, Costa Rica. We bought and transformed this barge in Belém, Brazil and have traveled all the way up the Amazon River near its headwaters. Now we are almost to our destination with the full assurance that the same God that called us all that time ago is with us and will always be with us."

Both ladies agreed and they all shared a moment of rejoicing followed by new revelations from the Word of God. After their short Bible study, Sondra looked at her two fellow missionaries and said, "I guess this would be a good time to tell you my story and how the Lord brought me to this place." This seemed so out of character for Sondra. She was normally very quiet and reserved around a group. She had shared her heart with Tyisha, but even with her she had restricted some of her secrets.

"I was born out of wedlock. My father was a white boy from Montgomery, Alabama who met my mother at a football game. After the game, both had too much alcohol to drink, and I am the result. Following me, my mother had four children in seven years by various men, both white and black. My mother finally married a man who is the father of the rest of her children. He is my stepfather, and I was apathetic toward him at first. But then, I discovered he was completely different than the other men my mother brought home. He was a Christian and a committed one. He married my mother, unlike all the other men, and really loved her and her children.

Attending school had always been a treat for me, yet I had been retained in two grades. When my stepfather came into the family, he insisted that I attend school and looked at every grade card I brought home. He helped me to achieve my academic potential. But the greatest gift he ever gave me was to introduce me to our Lord.

I gave my life to the Lord when I was twelve and I have never regretted that decision. I went to Stillman College in Tuscaloosa on a scholarship

Café con Leche

and found a church there that I loved, and they showed me the love of our Lord. My first roommate was a Christian girl from the Caribbean coast of Panama. She did not speak English well, so I taught her English, and she taught me Spanish. She is the one that convinced me I had talent for language, and I should use it for the Lord. Now you know more about me than most of my friends and family do.

By the way, my mother is now a Christian and so are six of my siblings. My stepfather passed away two years ago, but he left his mark on all of those that knew him. I know I will see him again one day and I know he will have a crown in heaven. It is late, so we had better get to sleep. I sense the next few days are going to be eventful."

With that, the missionaries all retired sensing they were truly a team, there to do the work of the Lord.

CHAPTER 20

Jeremiah was the first to awaken the following morning. He crept out on the deck to have a cup of coffee in the coolest part of the tropical day. The sun had not even broken through the thick fog that hung over the river like a cloud. He remembered the words of James, "For what is your life? It is even a vapour, that appeareth for a little time, and then vanisheth away."

Alone in his thoughts that often vacillated with prayer, he contemplated how wonderful his life had been. He had lived his childhood in a place where he was a pariah, but God had given him his father's athletic ability. That ability had been the reason he was offered a job in South Dakota, and it was there he met Tyisha. She, too, knew the pain of intolerance. But a woman had shared the faith with Tyisha and now he and Tyisha were "yoked" for life. He was still feeling almost giddy at the prospect of being a father when he heard Tyisha and Sondra come out of the house behind him.

They drank their coffees together and decided to wait for the sun to burn off the fog before heading further up the river. Within an hour, it did so and the three steered their barge up the winding Rio Javary with Peru on the right bank and Brazil on the left. They had not traveled around two more curves in the river when they heard the obvious sounds of children playing. As they approached, they could see five little Indian boys playing on the Peru side of the river. They were throwing water on each other with fifteen-foot black caiman lying on a shore nearby.

Jeremiah had more questions than answers, but he felt in his heart that this was as far as the Lord wanted him and the team to travel. He eased the barge near the shore well short of the boys and cut the engine, coasting through the still water. Just before the barge nudged the shore, Jeremiah jumped across the chasm to the shore, taking with him a loose bow line and attached it to a large ceiba tree. At the same time, Sondra and Tyisha were throwing the stern line onto the bank for Jeremiah to attach to a second ceiba tree about 50 feet downstream. While Jeremiah was tying the steel cable to the tree, Sondra and Tyisha started lowering the gangplank, leaving the end about a foot above the ground, so Jeremiah could return to the barge. Back on board the barge, Jeremiah took up some of the slack on the stern and bow lines and then set the gangplank in place.

He saw some motion in the jungle nearest the gangplank and pretended not to see it. He waved at Sondra and quietly asked her to come near him.

"Sondra, I think the little boys are watching us from the end of the gangplank. Could you tell them who we are?"

"Sure, Jeremiah, but I don't know their language yet."

"Well, try to call them in Spanish. Who knows, maybe they understand that language."

As proposed by Jeremiah, Sondra calmly called to the boys. She identified the three team members as "misioneros" and they were only there to do good not harm.

Slowly, the oldest boy crept to the end of the gangplank and identified himself in Spanish. As they were to learn later, he and his family had lived for a short time in a village in Peru, but they missed their own people in a nearby village; hence, they returned to the river and their tribe. It was during those few years, that the boy had learned Spanish and became one of the missionaries' primary translators to the rest of the tribe in those early years.

Convinced that the missionaries posed no threat, he stood on the gangplank with Sondra and Jeremiah on the other end. Sondra asked him the name of his people. He replied, "la gente Shipibo-Konibo."

Jeremiah was holding onto the chain that doubled as a handrail on the gangplank or he might have fallen into the river. It had been several months since his encounter with the young Indian woman at the language institute in San José, Costa Rica, but he could suddenly hear her words, "I am from the Shipibo-Konibo people of eastern Peru…" Had she been God's angel guiding he and Tyisha to this band of Shipibo-Konibo people to take them the message of Jesus Christ? There was no other explanation that made sense.

No one really knew the social structure of the Shipibo-Konibo people, so Sondra mistakenly asked the young boy if he would introduce them to the chief of the tribe. The boy looked confused and replied they had no chief. However, they did have a group of elders who were selected because of their proficiency in fishing, hunting, art, medicine or some other valued skill. The boy asked that the missionaries stay aboard their barge and he promised to return with the elders the following day.

***

True to his word, the twelve-year-old boy who appeared nine, returned the following day with the elders. There were four of them and the eldest seemed to be the spokesperson for the group. As with many of his tribe, he spoke Spanish, as well as Shipibo, the tribe's dialect of a Panoan language.

"¿Por qué están todos aquí? (Why are all of you here?)," asked the old man.

Sondra replied, "Estamos aquí porque amamos a su gente y tenemos un regalo de Dios para todos (We are here because we love your people, and we have a gift from God for you)."

In perfect English, the old man retorted, "You don't know my people's history, do you? The Inca could never overcome us. We repelled your Franciscan missionaries and many of the Protestant missionaries and we don't want your 'gift'."

Sondra was a small woman, no taller than the elder. Jeremiah was not a small man, and he knew his appearance was intimidating. He walked up to the elder and hovered over him.

"Sir, please tell us your name."

"My people call me 'Inon Sanken'. Who are you?"

"My people call me 'Jeremiah Hall'. My friend here, Sondra, was not lying to you. We have brought our own house, our own food, and our own water. We are asking nothing from you. We want only to give you something which will cost you nothing and may be worth more to you and your people than anything you can achieve, or man can give you.

If in anyway, you find us or the message we are bringing to you objectionable, tell us to leave. We ask only for a chance to serve our Lord and your people and ask that you give us ten months to try to do so. If you want us to leave after that, we will start our engine and leave your village.

Did you know Rabin Kena?"

Jeremiah had been using his six-foot four-inch mass to hulk over the diminutive Shipibo-Konibo man, but as he spoke, he straightened more upright. The old elder knew he could not intimidate this large man in front of him but did not want the other elders see him give into the 'gringo.' But how could he possibly know Rabin Kena who had not lived in the village for years?

"Yes, she grew up in our village until her father died and she and her mother moved away. How do you know Rabin Kena?"

Jeremiah could tell by the tone of Inon Sanken, that he was genuinely intrigued by the mere mention of this lady's name.

"A couple of months ago, while my wife and I lived about a thousand miles away, Rabin Kena told me about your people. She is a Christian now and asked that we bring the gift I told you about to you and your people. We were looking for a place to go when she came to us. Because of her, we have come at much risk to ourselves and ask that you give us an opportunity to prove ourselves and the God that called us.

The old man looked shocked and replied, "Rabin Kena and her mother left us years ago. We were told that both were killed in a car accident."

Sondra had excellent Spanish skills, but even she was having trouble translating the words of the two men.

"The young lady with whom you were speaking wants to learn your language and my wife and I are teachers. We would love to teach your people anything they want to learn. We want to learn about your language, your art, your pottery skills and your medicine.

Your people are right. They find God in the plants, the earth, the sky and all of creation. We do too. We want to tell you about the God that can be seen in His creation and loves all of us so much He has given His Son for us."

The old man looked directly at Jeremiah and then cricked his neck to the right. He slowly began to speak to this strange man. "Mr. Hall, what you ask is a big thing. I cannot make such a large decision by myself. I will present your request to my fellow elders and then we will present your plan to the entire village tonight. I will return tomorrow with the village's answer." The elder looked at Jeremiah and smiled as he nodded his head. He turned on the gangplank and returned to the waiting elders at the edge of the jungle.

***

Jeremiah, Tyisha, and Sondra spent the rest of the day alternating between praying for God's will to be done and fishing off the deck into the river until the mosquitoes drove them into the house. They had electric lighting provided by a diesel-powered generator, but they had grown used to using kerosene lanterns. The fumes seemed to keep the mosquitoes at bay.

All three had trouble sleeping that night. Each had been through so much to be there, and they just knew the Lord would have to create a miracle to help them take the Gospel to the Shipibo-Konibo people. Each of the missionaries was at a different stage in their faith, but all could see the hand of God on all their challenges and this one was no different.

As was his habit, Jeremiah arose first and went out on the deck to allow his wife and Sondra to sleep a little longer. He had barely set at the table that he and Rory had made from scraps from building the house when Inon Sanken appeared at the end of the gangplank.

"Good morning to you, Mr. Hall."

"And to you Inon Sanken," Jeremiah replied.

"My people met last night at the meeting hall where I presented your proposal to them. They agreed that you and your women can stay here for ten full moons. Then we will decide if we want you to stay longer or leave." Inon Sanken gave Jeremiah the same wry smile he had shown him the day before. Jeremiah was so overcome with emotion that he started to hug the little man. Inon Sanken reached both arms out and stopped Jeremiah's advances.

"Perhaps we should use your culture's show of agreement and shake hands" as Inon Sanken reached his hand out toward Jeremiah. Jeremiah

Café con Leche

was so excited, he grabbed Inon Sanken's right forearm and shook his whole arm vigorously.

"Thank you, sir, thank you. Please relay our thanks to the entire tribe and promise them we will do all we can to earn their trust."

"I will." Inon Sanken turned to return down the gangplank. He made it halfway to the shore and turned back toward Jeremiah.

"The men of my village are going fishing up the river today. Would you like to join us?"

Jeremiah wondered how wise it would be to leave his pregnant wife and little Sondra alone right now, but then he decided the Lord was their protection, not him.

"Your invitation is most welcome, and I would love to join you."

"Just follow the path to our village. We will be leaving soon."

"I will tell my wife and be there 'muy pronto'."

Inon Sanken continued toward the village, and thought to himself, "I like this man who protects his women and has come so far to tell us of his God."

Jeremiah, not wishing to show too much emotion to another man, waited until he thought Inon Sanken was beyond hearing. He decided it was time for Tyisha and Sondra to awaken and stood and screamed at the top of his lungs, "Thank you, Lord, for hearing our prayers." He could have conveyed his appreciation to the Lord in a silent prayer, but he wanted for the entire creation to know the depth of his joy.

Jeremiah's scream exceeded even his intention and Inon Sanken heard every word. A smile came across Inon Sanken's face, and he said aloud, "I am going to like this young man."

Tyisha and Sondra came running out of the house to see what calamity had occurred to Jeremiah. After he convinced them, he was not having a hallucination, he told them of the invitation to stay with the Shipibo-Konibo people and how he had been invited to go fishing with the men.

Tyisha said to Jeremiah, "How about if we go with you to the village and meet some of the women?"

"That's a great idea. Let's lock up the house, so the little kids aren't tempted to rummage through the drawers."

After doing so, the three missionaries gleefully walked down the path from the river to the village positioned on an old oxbow lake. For the first time, they all knew they were real missionaries and looked forward to taking the Gospel to these hungry people where the Lord had led them.

Jeremiah took his machete with him and walked ahead of the two women, slashing jungle vegetation for about the first twenty feet. There, they found the path that the boys had used to go to the river. They followed the path toward the village they knew must be close by. As they came around a curve in the path, they could see a large, cleared area ahead with a grass surface so manicured, they thought it must have been mown by machines. At the back of the clearing were approximately twenty small family huts, each with a thatch roof. The floors were elevated a couple of feet off the ground since this area was annually flooded by the Río Amazon backing up the Río Javary's own flood waters.

When the people of the village saw the missionaries entering the clearing, they came out of their individual huts with their "Sunday-go-to-meeting" clothes on. Both men and women wore circular hats with a fringe hanging down, or some without. They all wore long tunics adorned with extravagant geometric designs. All were unique to the wearer. Jeremiah, Tyisha and Sondra were to learn later that the designs represented the curves of a forest trail, the movements of an anaconda snake, the nearby meandering Río Javary, or the spirit of an ancient spirit.

As the missionaries guardedly walked across the open pasture, Jeremiah wondered if they were being lured to their own demise.

Now, within thirty feet of the Shipibo-Konibo, Jeremiah, Tyisha, and Sondra could see no weapons among the crowd. One old lady, Olivia Arévalo Lomas by name, was the village shaman and highly respected for her wisdom, corporate knowledge of the tribe's history, and skill with plant medicines. She walked up to Jeremiah and shook his hand with both of her hands in a western style. She moved over to Tyisha and Sondra and hugged each. By then, the women had made their way to the two women and joined in a group hug of both. The men did likewise with Jeremiah and all of Jeremiah's concerns evaporated at once. Jeremiah was a good judge of hugging, and he sensed the hugs were authentic.

As promised by Inon Sanken, the men who were going fishing went to their huts and changed their clothing into their more casual clothing to go fishing. They all went down a path that led to a slough off the main river where their canoes were tied. One gentleman, Kesten Yoi, guided them to

Café con Leche

his favorite part of the river about a mile upstream and they began to fish as they floated back downstream. Some of the men used hand lines in which they held a spool of fishing line and dropped the hook on the end into the water. Others stood on a nearby gravel bar and threw fishing nets into the water and pulled them back toward themselves. Still others pounded long sticks driven into the water and one of the bigger Shipibo men stood on the shore with a long spear. It was little more than an elongated arrow but fit into the notched end of a stick that he used to guide and propel the projectile.

The man, almost 5 feet 5 inches tall, had the longest reach of the men in the village and equipped with an atlatl, he could launch his projectile at blazing speeds. He was just above a deeper hole in the Río Javary and one of the few locations near the village where the giant Pirarucu fish congregated. Just one of these huge fish could feed the entire village for a day.

With a motion much like that of a baseball pitcher, the man shot the deadly dart into a fish barely a foot under the water. The Pirarucu was killed almost instantaneously. Quickly the man and another fisherman drug the giant fish to shore and bragged to the others about their success.

Jeremiah and Inon Sanken, along with several other men had been fishing with nets. They, too, had been successful and caught about forty Peacock Bass of various sizes. The ferocity of the bass was their undoing and would swim into the net while chasing prey fish. The day was growing hot and even the Peacock Bass were becoming less active. They collected their catch and returned to the bay where the dugout canoes were kept. After carrying the catch back to the village, the women cleaned the fish and prepared them for a virtual feast that evening in honor of their new guests.

***

Sondra had wasted no time. While the men were gone, she had already started writing down sounds she heard in the women's language. Most syllables were accented; others were not.

Her goal was to learn the language, teach a written version to the Shipibo-Konibo people and then begin the arduous process of translating the Holy Scriptures into the written language. Sondra had only committed to remain for eighteen months and she knew it would be a gargantuan task to accomplish half of her goals in that length of time. All the while, Tyisha and Jeremiah, who had no special training in this foreign language, would have to learn the fundamentals of the language with her guidance. It was obvious that Tyisha and Jeremiah were committed to learn the language of the Shipibo-Konibo people, but it was Sondra's task to prepare them to translate the Scripture without her.

The three missionaries were a complete team; Jeremiah learned to hunt and fish with the men, Tyisha learned to weave fabric and make pottery and apply unique geometric shapes to both, and Sondra constantly studied the language and began to translate the Bible.

After several busy months, Tyisha's pregnancy was well-advanced, and she had to slow the furious pace of her initial time with the Shipibo-Konibo people. In honor of their hosts, Jeremiah and Tyisha had decided on two names, since they did not know the sex of their prospective child. If a boy, they would name him Neten Niwe Hall. If a girl, they agreed to name her Ronin Biri Hall.

Sondra continued her schedule but lessened the rate of her analysis of the language. She conferred with two women of the tribe who had acted as midwives, and they seemed to be concerned by the way the baby was positioned in Tyisha. Sondra just could not believe Tyisha would have problems with childbirth. She was a tall athletic woman who seemed to be the picture of health. As it turned out, Sondra was much better with linguistics than obstetrics.

The day finally arrived when Tyisha went into labor. The two Indian women had been able to properly position the baby, but Tyisha was still in hard labor for 18 hours. The ladies had massaged Tyisha to get her to relax as much as possible and given her a host of herbal medicines used by the Indians for thousands of years, but Tyisha's labor was still grueling.

A little boy was finally born to Tyisha and Jeremiah, and they estimated his weight at over nine pounds and more than 22 inches long. He was definitely Jeremiah's son and looked ready to be a football player the day of his birth. As promised, he was named Neten Niwe Hall. Inon Sanken relayed the new child's name to the rest of the tribe, and they showed their approval with a loud scream.

Members of the tribe came by the house on the barge and brought small gifts for the new boy. Some brought by small woven clothes, others

Café con Leche

tribal hats, and still others the ornate pottery for which they were famous. All gave Jeremiah and Tyisha their approval of the child and made the missionaries feel welcome as the newest members of the tribe. The missionaries had been amid the Shipibo-Konibo people for nearly seven months, and it was obvious they would not be asked to leave. In fact, they were not only accepted, but were considered friends of many of the members of the tribe.

Sondra was well advanced in her study of the language and was beginning to teach some of the members how to read their own language. She estimated she might conclude this portion of the process in another year, but then she was anticipating leaving the Hall's with the tribe at about the same time. She decided to put her full efforts into the language study and educating the tribe members and not worry about what might happen in a year. Besides, her relationship with Tyisha had gone far beyond fellow missionary. They were more like sisters and both women were enjoying the profundity of this new bond. Tyisha had never had a sister and Sondra had never had one who had the same father as she did. Sondra had helped to deliver Tyisha's child and the act had cemented them together forever.

CHAPTER 21

The years seemed to fly by. Jeremiah had become known as a very tall Shipibo-Konibo man. He could fish or hunt with any of the other men and had gained the respect of the entire tribe. Tyisha and Sondra had learned much of the Shipibo language and had discovered many of the intricacies of making Shipibo designs on cloth and pottery. Sondra had extended her commitment to stay with Jeremiah and Tyisha four different times and she was nearing the end of translating the books of the Bible. Jeremiah and Tyisha had concluded that Sondra loved the Shipibo-Konibo people as much as they did. She was not just a member of the missionary team; she had become a member of their family.

As an infant, Neten Niwe, often disappeared. The Shipibo-Konibo women loved him and would pass him among themselves for hours. Jeremiah and Tyisha had often searched for their son, but had absolute confidence he was safe, especially when in the care of the Shipibo-Konibo.

Neten Niwe had inherited the athletic genes of his grandfather and father. He grew into the fastest runner in the village and could climb nearly any tree no matter how tall. Like his father, Neten Niwe grew into a large child who could fish and hunt with the men.

As proud as they were of their son, Jeremiah and Tyisha were most proud of their ministry. They had come all this way to bring the Gospel

Café con Leche

of Jesus Christ and He had rewarded their efforts. Over half of the tribe had made confessions of faith and followed in baptism. The first convert had vocalized the most opposition to their presence-Inon Sanken. He had become not only their brother in Christ, but Jeremiah's best friend. They had long conversations with Jeremiah's barely adequate Shipibo and Inon Sanken's English. Communication always ensued and Christ was glorified. The saved men of the tribe had built a large bamboo and palm frond building that made an adequate church where the saved of the tribe met on Sundays to glorify their God. Their theology was not without problems. They constantly wanted to blend their tribal beliefs with their new Christian beliefs. Jeremiah, Tyisha and Sondra believed part of their ministry to the new converts was to steer them to right doctrine based upon the Bible. The Scripture was now readily available and translated into the Shipibo language. Jeremiah and his brother-in-Christ, Inon Sanken, had plans to take the Gospel to other Shipibo-Konibo villages further up the Río Javary and possibly up the Río Ucayali where there were many more Shipibo-Konibo villages. But even the best plans often do not come to fruition.

***

Jeremiah, as he so often did, was up before Tyisha and Neten Niwe. Sondra had moved into the village years earlier and Jeremiah and Tyisha were considering doing so, themselves. The daily convocation and Bible study were a practice Jeremiah and Tyisha had practiced since their marriage over twelve years earlier. Neten Niwe participated, but only nominally. He had yet to make a personal commitment to Jesus Christ and was almost a rebellious teenager who was feeling somewhat isolated from his friends because of his "missionary kid" status, even within the tribe.

Jeremiah sat there, praising God for allowing him and Tyisha to come and bring the Gospel of Jesus Christ to these people. He could have spent his youth running up and down a football field, but he would never have known the satisfaction of baptizing a new believer in the Río Javary. Tyisha would never have known the joy she showed daily by her love of Sondra. The pain she had experienced from her maltreatment by Christians in North Dakota could have jaded her. Instead, the love of God had made Tyisha attracted to all the women in the village and the women responded with love for her. Not only had the Shipibo-Konibo loved Jeremiah, Tyisha, and Sondra; they had loved Neten Niwe as one of their own.

Jeremiah looked at the decaying deck and thought back to all the hours he had spent with the Lord there. The generator no longer worked, and they were restricted to using their lanterns, which were also nearing the end of their lives. As much as he loved the barge and the house, he and Rory had built on it, he knew it was time to move into the village. Neten Niwe needed to be nearer to his friends and Tyisha needed to be closer to Sondra. He had already expressed his concerns to Inon Sanken, and the elders had given him permission to construct a hut at the end of the village nearest the jungle. He would almost miss his daily battle with the black caiman which had congregated on the warm steel of the gangplank in the morning. But Jeremiah knew it was time to move. He awaited the arrival of the rest of his family so he could make the announcement about the imminent move.

***

Jeremiah and Neten Niwe met Inon Sanken at the village community house. This was the large hut constructed for the meetings of the entire Shipibo-Konibo people. For years, Jeremiah, Tyisha and Sondra had led Bible studies for the new Christians in this building and it was the same building where the entire tribe had agreed to allow the missionaries to come into their village for ten months. But the Christians no longer used this building, opting to build and use their own church.

Inon Sanken had lost his wife even before the arrival of Jeremiah, Tyisha and Sondra and was the oldest bachelor in the village. He was a petite man who was no longer able to go on the hunting parties or do much fishing. But his value to the tribe remained his sharp mind and his wide-ranging experiences.

Inon Sanken had met with the other elders, and they had decided to permit Jeremiah, Tyisha and Neten Niwe to build a pëshëwa (hut) on the south side of the village nearest the jungle. Jeremiah and Neten Niwe had already surveyed the area for building materials from local palms and bamboo. The petite Inon Sanken claimed he was there to supervise their progress, but both Hall men knew he was there to regale them with stories of his youth or plans for the future of the tribe and spread of the Gospel.

Café con Leche

"Inon Sanken, all of these years I have been here with you, and I still don't know how the Shipibo-Konibo people received their name." Jeremiah knew the answer, but he had asked the question more for the sake of his son than his own.

"First, young Jeremiah, the Shipibo and Konibo people were two tribal people here in the Amazon jungles. Our languages were related, but not exactly the same. Over a long period of time, their children married our children, and the two tribes lost their identity.

As for the name of our tribe, we named ourselves. 'Shipibo' literally means 'little monkey people.' You have probably seen us drink the white vegetable drink and how it leaves a large white ring around our mouths. You have also seen us eat white-faced marmosets. We look like them since they are small monkeys with white faces, and we are small people with white stains on our faces."

Approximately every hour, Jeremiah would call for a break. He convinced his son, they were taking a respite for the benefit of the much older Inon Sanken, but Jeremiah knew better. He was exhausted and intuitively knew something was wrong with him. He had been the fastest boy in Madisonville, Alabama growing up and had been invited to try out for the mighty Kansas City Chiefs. He was exhausted after a day of work interspersed with at least six breaks. One afternoon, he told Inon Sanken and Neten Niwe that he needed to knock off early to work on his sermon for the coming Sunday. He was so tired he returned to the barge and fell asleep in his bed.

As Inon Sanken returned to his hut that same afternoon, he heard the screaming of some boys down at the river. He ran as fast as his short legs would carry him until he reached the bank over the river. Just below him were three boys about 10 years of age. One was caught in the current of the river enhanced by a long rainy season.

Inon Sanken saw three large black caimans attracted by the thrashing little boy. Without considering his own safety, the old man dove into the rushing river and helped the boys to shore. As he got the last one to safety, one of the huge reptiles grabbed him by the right leg and dragged him back toward the deeper water of the river. Inon Sanken did all he could to extricate himself from the powerful jaw of the black caiman, but to no avail. The other two black caiman had joined the attack and two went into their death rolls, taking the old man to the bottom of the river to his death.

The little boys stood on the shore, frozen with fear. They could not even scream for help as the old man who had just saved them, disappeared from sight. In unison, they ran to the village to tell their fathers what had happened. As the fathers and sons ran back to the bank of the river, the boys tried to explain what had happened in elevated and competitive voices.

Jeremiah was awakened by the commotion and ran down the gangplank to see the cause. When he arrived at the group, every man present was shedding tears. At Jeremiah's insistence, one man finally told him that Inon Sanken was dead. Jeremiah joined the other men, crying for their fallen friend.

When they recovered, the men sent the boys back to the village and went on to their dugout canoes. With long spears, they searched for the body of Inon Sanken and the black caiman that had killed him. Before sunset, they had killed six of the behemoths, but never recovered the body of their fellow tribesman.

***

The Shipibo-Konibo people had a long-standing tradition of disposing the body of their deceased by placing it in their pëshëwa. After a few words of remembrance of the deceased, the entire hut was burned to the ground, cremating the fallen tribesman.

One problem-there was no body to burn. The elders met and decided that the large hut of Inon Sanken would fit Jeremiah and Tyisha's needs more than the hut Jeremiah and his son had been building. When the hut of his old friend was offered to Jeremiah, he jumped at the chance to make it his own. Even his pretense of health could no longer hide his failing health. He did not know if he would be able to complete the hut and he did not want to alarm the rest of the tribe until he had confirmed his suspicions.

Jeremiah had shared everything with Tyisha, and this would be no different. As soon as the sun rose on Sunday morning, still on their barge, he awakened Tyisha and asked her to go outside on the decaying deck with him while Neten Niwe slept.

"Ty, I know you have noticed how much I have lost stamina, but I wanted to confirm your suspicions. Even before we lost our brother, Inon Sanken, I was feeling like Sampson without his hair."

Café con Leche

"I have worried about you, honey. You never took naps in the day a year ago and now, you never miss one. You didn't know, but Sondra and some of the women have been praying with me that the Lord would heal you and return your strength.

Since the day of our wedding, I meant what I promised; I will be here for better or for worse. I know you feel the same way. Whatever comes to both of us, we will face it together and God will be our guide."

"Ty, I love you too and thank the Lord, He brought us together. I will be contacting Dr. Perez in Lima tomorrow and tell him my symptoms. We'll go from there.

I need to get to the church a little early and prepare for the sermon. I know you understand. Please bring Neten Niwe with you. I think he needs to hear what I have to say."

Tyisha readily agreed and let Jeremiah get ready first. Thirty minutes later, Jeremiah walked down the gangplank with his new Shipibo-Konibo Bible in hand. He and Tyisha had a Christian publisher in Lima print 50 copies for disbursement to all the new Christians in the tribe. Sondra still had not completed her translation of the Book of Ezekiel, but the Bible did contain the other 65 books.

Jeremiah walked along the path through the jungle where he had first met Inon Sanken. Without expecting it, he was overcome with emotion and began to uncontrollably cry. The successes he and Tyisha had experienced in the past decade were made possible by Inon Sanken and they had come to view the little man as a gift of God. Now, as their barge house deteriorated, their new home was made possible by the sacrifice of their brother-in-Christ.

There it was-Jeremiah's favorite log on the side of the path. After assuring himself there were no snakes or scorpions on it, he sat down on the old log and opened his Bible. He silently read Psalm 51:17.

The sacrifices of God are a broken spirit: a broken and contrite heart, O God, thou wilt not despise.

Inon Sanken truly had a broken spirit after the loss of his wife. Jeremiah began to cry again but did not want for his son to see him do so. Tyisha and Neten Niwe would be along the path shortly, so he got up, wiped the tears from his eyes and continued toward the church.

After the congregation sang the hymn *Amazing Grace* in the Shipibo language, Jeremiah stood at the front to preach his sermon. He looked out over the congregation like he had done hundreds of times before and was amazed to see almost every member of the tribe, even the shaman. She had not been a fan of the missionaries once she discovered they wanted her fellow Shipibo-Konibo people leave their traditional beliefs, but she had been a good friend of Inon Sanken since their youth.

"Brothers and Sisters, please stand with me as we read the Word of God found in Psalms 51:17.

The sacrifices of God are a broken spirit: a broken and contrite heart, O God, thou wilt not despise.

Now, turn with me to Galatians 2:20 and read along with me.

I am crucified with Christ: nevertheless, I live; yet not I, but Christ liveth in me: and the life which I now live in the flesh I live by the faith of the Son of God, who loved me, and gave himself for me.

Please be seated."

It was all Jeremiah could do just to read the Scripture. He knew what he wanted to say and felt they were the words of God, but his emotions kept breaking his focus.

"Every one of us knew and loved Inon Sanken. He was my friend, but he was our brother-in-Christ. From the day he became a Christian until the day he died, he was humble. He did not tell others he was a tribal elder, unless asked. He knew more about the history of the tribe than anyone here, but he never gave more information than he was asked. I knew, as did many of you, just how much Inon Sanken missed his wife. But he never allowed his grief to overcome the love he had for others. His wife died before we arrived over ten years ago, and yet he was one of our biggest advocates. No matter how he was suffering, he always put the needs of others before his own. He was already a good man when I met him, but after his salvation, he became a godly man. The Apostle John tells us that God is Love and that we do not know God if we do not love. Inon Sanken knew God and he knew how to love.

> In John 15:13, the Apostle John tells us "Greater love hath no man than this, that a man lay down his life for his friends."

Inon Sanken knew he could possibly lose his life, but he thought the lives of three 10-year-old boys worth more than his own." All three boys were in the congregation and were wailing. They had seen the old man sacrifice his life for theirs and they felt unworthy.

"The sacrifice and love shown by Inon Sanken this week reminds us of what Christ did for each of us on the Cross. He loved us so much that He was willing to sacrifice His own life so that each of us might have life and have it abundantly. He suffered, bled and died so that we might live forever in a place where there is no more sorrow, crying or pain. Inon Sanken is there now.

This day, let us not allow the death of Inon Sanken be in vain. He gave all he had for some of us and would have given even more if he had more to give. That love that he gave so freely, should instruct us how to live. Let us love one another and our God, the way Inon Sanken loved each of us and his God.

I am so sorry. I had more I wanted to say today, but I cannot go on." With that, the large man wept like a baby. Eight members of the congregation came forward and wanted to know more about this thing called "salvation." Of the group, were three little boys who had life because an old man had sacrificed his life for them. Tyisha and Sondra rushed forward to lead those who had come to find salvation. Jeremiah sat down near where he had been preaching, with his back heaving in grief. Christian members of the congregation came around Jeremiah, laid hands on him and others prayed for him.

Tyisha and Neten Niwe escorted Jeremiah back to the barge, where he collapsed into his bed and fell asleep almost immediately. When he awoke later in the evening, he promised Tyisha he would begin calling Dr. Perez in Lima the next morning. Since the days he had dated Tyisha, Jeremiah had used a radio to keep in touch in emergencies with the rest of the world. He never dreamed he might one day be using the same radio on his own behalf.

***

Rory and Jeremiah had built a small, covered tool shed outside of the house. In it, they welded part of a bicycle frame and the rear tire assembly. A bicycle generator was attached to the frame so it could rub on the back tire. It produced six volts and charged a battery of the same voltage. In turn, a transformer took the six volts and powered their ham radio. Jeremiah was now on his third battery, but the radio was the same one on which he had first told Tyisha that he loved her.

Neten Niwe went outside and began pedaling the generator to recharge the battery. Jeremiah was inside trying to reach another missionary, John Bauer, in Pucallpa, Peru. This town contained the largest group of Shipibo-Konibo people in Peru and Mr. Bauer and his wife had ministered to them for almost thirty years.

Jeremiah explained the need to set up an appointment with Dr. Perez in Lima as soon as possible and provided a telephone number for Dr. Perez. Also, Jeremiah told him he would need transportation to and from the physician. In the past, Jeremiah had used Sr. George Hidalgo of Cristo Glorificado en América del Sur for transport. Sr. Hidalgo had a small Cessna airplane equipped with pontoons for water landings. His small aircraft only had one seat for a passenger, so years earlier, he had flown Jeremiah, first, and then Tyisha with Neten Niwe on her lap to the city of Pucallpa where they all took buses to Lima and eventually flew to the United States on furlough.

Jeremiah gave Sr. Hidalgo's telephone number to Mr. Bauer. After setting an appointment with Dr. Perez, Mr. Bauer promised to contact Sr. Hidalgo and assure he could fly to Jeremiah's location the day before the appointment. Sr. Hidalgo had a small cabin on Lago Huasca and could land there the evening before the appointment. He had a car there and could transport Jeremiah to his appointment the following day. In fact, Rt. 116, down a dirt road from the cabin, joined with Rt. 22 and went right by Dr. Perez's office in Lima.

Later in the day, Mr. Bauer contacted Jeremiah and gave him the times of appointment and Sr. Hidalgo's arrival. Knowing the difficulty of the trip, Dr. Perez had an appointment time on Thursday and Sr. Hidalgo had agreed to land on the river the morning before. Jeremiah readily agreed to both and planned to meet Sr. Hidalgo on Wednesday morning.

***

Sr. Hidalgo's Cessna airplane had been equipped with the high-altitude kit so it could fly through the high passes of the Andes Mountains. Jeremiah knew Sr. Hidalgo would be in the air as soon as he could see and be landing on the river next to the barge by 11:00 a.m. The next two days were going to be exhaustive, so Jeremiah told Tyisha he was going to turn in early to prepare. Tyisha understood and came to bed shortly after Jeremiah. Jeremiah held Tyisha in his large arms, like he had not held her in years. Without words, Tyisha knew just how serious Jeremiah's situation was.

Jeremiah fell asleep shortly, but Tyisha lay by his side, praying. She finally fell asleep in Jeremiah's arms. In a deep sleep, Jeremiah suddenly was aware he was in a very different place than where he had laid down. Tyisha was not with him, and he was in a bedroom that was a gleaming white. There was a large portal covered by white shears that slowly blew inward. Outside, he could see a pasture with one large tree in the middle. The greens were so vibrant that they reminded him of the meadows on Volcán Poás in Costa Rica. Down the middle of the bedroom were three columns with capitals with the form of palm trees carved in each. Against the outside wall was a chest of drawers with two vases on top full of sea oats.

The room had a door on the right side of the room that must have led to the rest of the mansion, though Jeremiah never went through it. The entire room glowed, and why not? There was no roof and the light emanated from God himself. There was no sun and there was no night.

Jeremiah looked out the portal, as the breeze pleasantly blew against his face, and saw across a valley to the road slanting down the far side of the valley. He could not believe what his eyes saw. The pavement was a shimmering brick the color of gold. A horse was pulling a surrey down the other side, and Jeremiah intuitively knew it was being driven by Ronnie Collins, his childhood friend. Ronnie was a profound diabetic and had passed away years earlier. A warm feeling came over him and he could not wait for his old friend's arrival.

Before the awaited reunion, the light came between two trees on the river's far edge and struck Jeremiah in the eyes. He awoke aware that the Lord had shown him his final abode. He slowly took Tyisha's arms from around him and went out on the decaying deck. The light piercing the early morning fog cast a strange pink-orange glow on everything around him, including his Bible. As Jeremiah opened his Bible, looking for some explanation for the vision he had just been given, he opened the Bible to Revelation 21:4.

Brent Garzelli & Cheryl L. Garzelli

> And God shall wipe away all tears from their eyes; and there shall be no more death, neither sorrow, nor crying, neither shall there be any more pain: for the former things are passed away.

Jeremiah, who had always been taught to never let others see him crying, cried like a baby. He remembered how the boys of Madisonville, Alabama made fun of him and played practical jokes on him. He remembered the pain of losing his father in his childhood and seeing the way his mother was treated by the loving folks of Madisonville. Tyisha had brought meaning to his life and their marriage to each other and God had given them a plan and purpose greater than either of them would have achieved without the other. Jeremiah could not conceive of life without Tyisha or Neten Niwe, but he knew God would take care of them in his absence.

He went into the house and took a shower. After dressing, he went to the kitchen where Tyisha had made him breakfast. They took their meals out on the deck where they pretended it was just another meal. Jeremiah knew better. He suspected this was the last time they would eat together in this world. After eating, Jeremiah went back inside the house and found Neten Niwe still asleep. He knelt down over the top of his son and kissed him on the forehead.

"Son, I love you. I would never have such a full life if I did not have you and your mother with me. Seek the Lord and you will find Him." With this affectionate moment, Jeremiah returned to the front of the barge and threw a steel ladder over the side. He and Tyisha talked and waited in the shade of the house until they saw Sr. Hidalgo land his plane well up the river. He reduced his engine to an idle and let the current of the river take the small plane to the side of the barge. He was standing on the left float and when he was even with Jeremiah, he threw a tow line to him.

Jeremiah kissed Tyisha "Goodbye" and climbed down to the plane and climbed over the console into the passenger seat. Tyisha threw the mooring line back to Sr. Hidalgo, who secured it and got in the pilot's seat. Jeremiah waved one more time and told her, "We should be back tomorrow night, or the following morning." Somehow, he knew he would not.

Sr. Hidalgo adeptly allowed his small plane to float down to the next eddy that allowed him to take off into the wind and steer to the northwest,

Café con Leche

where they landed on the Río Ucayali at Pucallpa. Sr. Hidalgo topped off his gas tank for the long flight back to his cottage in the western Andes Mountains.

They had barely been airborne heading nearly due westward, when they started to ascend. The plane would fly as high as 15,000 feet above sea level, and they would need every foot to clear the mountains. Sr. Hidalgo had to use his oxygen tanks when they reached the highest part of the journey to avoid elevation sickness. From their position, Jeremiah could see darkness coming across the broad plains of the Amazon. He wondered if Sr. Hidalgo could possibly get to their destination before darkness overtook them.

He did not have to wait long for his answer. One lake after another passed beneath them until Sr. Hidalgo flew over the outskirts of Lima, turned to the south and then to the east. He obvious knew exactly where he was going. It appeared that he was going up a remote canyon with rock walls on both sides. And then, just before him was a dark blue body of water known as Lago Huasca. With a promontory of rock on the north side, there didn't appear to be adequate room to land the plane on the lake. But Sr. Hidalgo had done this a few times and he used almost all the lake to land and quickly slowed with the friction of the water. Under the power of his propeller, Sr. Hidalgo guided his plane to a wharf on the north side of the lake. He tied the plane to two large posts and got onto the wharf. Jeremiah quickly followed with his travel bag in hand.

With at least thirty minutes of daylight remaining, Sr. Hidalgo made them supper in the cabin just above the wharf. Meanwhile Jeremiah went to his assigned bed for a nap. He did not get up until the following morning.

***

"Jeremiah, I am sorry you missed supper last night, but I thought you might need sleep more than my cooking." Sr. Hidalgo had prepared a delicious breakfast of eggs and cold Corn Flakes and had been concerned that he might have to awaken Jeremiah soon so they could be on time for Jeremiah's medical appointment.

"Thank you, Sr. Hidalgo, I am constantly exhausted, and food is low on my priority list right now." Jeremiah had once weighed 255 pounds, but he was now no more than 190 pounds. He hadn't been that thin since his freshman year in high school. He did his best to eat the food before him, but simply picked at the eggs and barely touched his bowl of cereal.

The two men quickly got ready and hurried down the mountain on the dirt road to Highway 116. After driving eight miles on Highway 116, Sr. Hidalgo headed southwest at the junction of Highway 22 toward Lima. They arrived at Dr. Perez' office with thirty minutes to spare since Jeremiah had been there several times before, but always for a Shipibo tribe member or for his son, Neten Niwe; never for himself.

Dr. Perez had been treating another patient but went out to the small waiting room to personally greet Jeremiah.

"You have lost much weight since last we met, Sr. Hall." Dr. Perez could not help himself. He could not talk about the weather with his patients. He was already examining Jeremiah and the two had not even made it to one of his examination rooms.

"I am willing to make an early diagnosis now. You are suffering from a variety of anemia."

"Doctor, I have been losing strength as well as weight. Given my black mother, I have been guessing I have sickle cell anemia."

Dr. Perez had taken a complete family history when he had first treated Neten Niwe. Without even thinking about Jeremiah's answer, Dr. Perez replied.

"Mr. Hall, that is possible, but very unlikely. Sickle cell anemia requires a gene from both parents. The disease does occur in whites, as well, but is not common. Since your father was white, it is not likely he passed sickle cell anemia to you. We will run some tests for other causes of anemia, and I will try to give you a prognosis and treatment by the end of the day."

"Doctor, you don't know how great that news is. I have been so worried that I would not see my next birthday and leave my son and wife in the jungles of your country."

"Now, Mr. Hall, you go next door to the hospital and go to 'el laboratorio.' I will telephone them and tell them what tests need to be done. You look very weak, so I will ask your friend to accompany you."

After having directed Jeremiah to the lab in the hospital, he asked Sr. Hidalgo to accompany him. The two men strolled to the hospital only a hundred yards away, but Jeremiah was so exhausted he had to sit down in the hospital lobby and rest for a few minutes.

When they finally reached the lab, the technician asked Jeremiah for a blood sample and a urine sample. After he provided both, Jeremiah and Sr. Hidalgo returned to Dr. Perez's office next door. It was already 1:15 p.m. when they re-entered the waiting room. After confirming that Jeremiah was in a chair and comfortable, Sr. Hidalgo left to get a small lunch at a street vendor's kiosk outside the hospital.

At roughly 2:30 p.m., Dr. Perez returned to the waiting area to find Jeremiah sound asleep. The doctor gently nudged Jeremiah on the arm and he nearly jumped straight up.

"Mr. Hall, I have some good news for you. The lab tested your blood twice. You do not have sickle cell anemia or any other kind of anemia. However, you do have mononucleosis, which can cause a loss of weight, strength and appetite. The good news is that it is highly treatable. You need to stay off your feet for at least a week, and then slow your activities for the next couple of weeks. I know you usually fish and hunt for your food, but for the next few weeks, you must allow other members of the tribe to bring you food. If you want to beat this disease, you need constant rest until your body can defeat the virus. There is no medicine for this disease-just rest will eventually cure it."

Jeremiah was in a state of shock. He was sure the prognosis would be dire. He knew Tyisha, Sondra, and the remainder of the tribe would help him rest until he could regain his strength. After thanking Dr. Perez for the good news, Jeremiah asked for the cost and paid a nurse upfront the sum of $18.00. Just out the front door of the doctor's office, Sr. Hidalgo was sitting under a tree.

"Sr. Hidalgo, Dr. Perez gave me good news. I can't wait to tell it to Tyisha. If we go directly back up the mountain, can we fly to my barge before dark? I have a spare bedroom for you, if we can get there tonight."

Sr. Hidalgo looked puzzled. At first, he thought he had not understood Jeremiah's English. He decided Jeremiah was serious and he had understood his words perfectly.

"Jeremiah, it is already 3:00 p.m. and we must stop and get food to take to the mountain cabin with us so we will have something to eat tonight and tomorrow morning. I must refuel and check the oil and moving parts of the plane. We cannot leave this afternoon and hope to get you to the Río Javary before dark. Why don't we call Mr. Bauer, and he can convey the good news of your health to Tyisha by radio? I am sure she will understand if we get you home tomorrow afternoon. Besides, you need another night to rest before making that arduous journey."

Sr. Hidalgo had been concerned for Jeremiah when they had to don their oxygen masks at the highest altitudes needed to cross the Andes Mountains on the first journey. Jeremiah had nearly fainted from the extra strain on his lungs and heart. Sr. Hidalgo knew the return journey would be no less stressful.

"We had better go. Those mountain roads are dangerous enough in the light. I do not want to drive up the mountain in shadows."

Jeremiah wanted to go home to Tyisha, but he knew Sr. Hidalgo was right. As Sr. Hidalgo went into a nearby grocery store, he thought about what he wanted to say to Tyisha via Mr. Bauer. He slept off and on as Sr. Hidalgo drove them back up the winding Rt. 116 to his dirt road that led to the cabin. Jeremiah was asleep when they arrived. Sr. Hidalgo carried in the groceries and returned to awaken Jeremiah. He made supper while Jeremiah fell back asleep in front of a small wood stove.

After eating a dinner of black beans and rice with chicken (arroz con pollo), Jeremiah turned in early. During the night, he awoke and felt a need to read his Bible he always traveled with. He took the Bible from his travel bag and simply opened it. The Holy Scriptures opened to Proverbs 27:1

> Boast not thyself of tomorrow; for thou knowest not what
> a day may bring forth.

Jeremiah could not understand what the Lord was trying to tell him. Hadn't his life-threatening condition been all in his head? Wasn't he only 41 years old and didn't he have plans to do more to spread the Gospel to other places with the Shipibo-Konibo people? Surely, this is the reason Inon Sanken had been taken. He concluded he was overreacting and decided the Lord would show him just what the verse meant when he was feeling better.

CHAPTER 22

Jeremiah was used to the sun rising early each morning and shining through his bedroom window. The Andes Mountains were on his east and blocked out the sun until about 8:30 a.m. He awoke more rested than in days past. Dr. Perez's prognosis of mononucleosis was so hopeful that he slept soundly and felt better than he had in weeks. He was still weak, but just knew that sensation would lessen in the days to come. He could not wait to get back to Tyisha and Neten Niwe that very afternoon. But where was Sr. Hildago?

Still in his pajamas, Jeremiah went into the small kitchen. Sr. Hildago had left him a plate with an egg, pork chop, and a dollop of rice with black beans. He could only eat a portion of what Sr. Hildago had prepared for him. After eating, he went out on the front of the cabin facing the lake. Sr. Hildago was on the wharf below, fueling the plane.

"Good morning, Jeremiah. I trust you slept well. Do not worry, I telephoned Mr. Bauer last night while you slept, and he promised to communicate the good news of your health to Tyisha by radio. She will be expecting us."

Jeremiah was so appreciative to Sr. Hildago, and he expressed the same. This man had been a true Christian brother to he and Tyisha and had ministered to their need for medical care, transportation and even shelter and food.

"Thank you for all your help, Sr. Hildago. I can't express in words how much your ministry to us has meant over the years. I know the Lord will bless you for your kindness to your brethren. Can I do anything to help you?"

"Just save your strength and prepare what you need for the trip ahead of us. We should be ready to leave within the hour. As always, I have filed our flight plan with the Peruvian Air Force and the tank is nearly full of fuel. We shall be ready to fly once I do a 'walk around' of the plane and its flight surfaces."

Jeremiah returned inside and took a short shower. The resumption of strength he had felt when he awoke was quickly waning. He made his bed and filled his trip bag with the few clothes he had brought with him. He sat down on the couch and took a nap before Sr. Hidalgo came to tell him they were ready to go. Jeremiah knew the constant whine of the engine on the little plane would make sleep hard during the trip over the mountains.

As he dozed, Jeremiah had a short vision of the angelic face of Tyisha, the woman he loved. The mere thought of her, of holding her again, of telling her how much he loved her, gave him a sense of peace and one of longing to be with her.

"Come on Jeremiah. I know a pass through the mountains that will make our trip much shorter, but we must allow an extra hour of flight time in case we fly into high headwinds."

Groggy, Jeremiah dutifully followed Sr. Hildago to the awaiting plane moored to the wharf. He stored his travel bag behind the passenger seat and got into the plane. Sr. Hidalgo took a quick check of the oil level and a final inspection of the moving parts of the plane as he released the mooring lines from the wharf.

The plane growled to a cold start, barely being propelled through the water to the northeast end of the lake. Once near the lake's terminus, Sr. Hidalgo adeptly turned the plane and headed it toward the opposite end of the lake, past a promontory. After allowing the engine to idle for a minute and checking his gauges, Sr. Hidalgo began to rev the engine. The plane lurched in the still morning water and began to pick up speed. The shoreline whirred by as the plane gained speed on the water. Finally,

Café con Leche

they were even with the promontory with only a thousand of feet of lake remaining. Sr. Hidalgo pulled back on the stick and the plane responded by parting the water below and climbing over the rocks at the end of the lake.

Once airborne, Sr. Hidalgo piloted his plane in ever higher concentric circles, passing over the outskirts of Lima until he was finally high enough to fly through a pass in the towering Andes Mountains. Looking toward the east, the sky was devoid of all clouds and the sunlight almost glowed in the cabin of the little Cessna. With Jeremiah's wonderful prognosis and the beauty of the day, what could possibly go wrong?

***

The trip was uneventful as Sr. Hidalgo flew out of the mighty Andes Mountains and over the headwaters of the Amazon River. Little did he know that two Peruvian fighter planes had been shadowing his airplane. The lead pilot had communicated the plane identification numbers to his headquarters, but they had not received any flight plan for that plane. Since this pass was used frequently by drug runners, they assumed the plane was flying toward a rendezvous to obtain another load of contraband.

Without warning, they had dived with the sun at their back and opened a burst of their 20 caliber machine guns at the little Cessna. Sr. Hidalgo never saw the machines of death coming toward him and had no time to make evasive moves. The first volley of bullets ripped through the cabin nearly severing Sr. Hidalgo's right foot from his leg. In shock, he looked to his right and saw Jeremiah's head slumped to his chest. It was obvious Jeremiah was not sleeping. He was dead from a shot that struck him in the left side of the chest.

Sr. Hidalgo was sure the two fighter aircraft would make another pass at his flailing little plane, so he did all he could to glide it onto the nearby Río Javary. He knew he was near the Shipibo-Konibo village and Jeremiah's barge, but he had no idea how close. As he came around a bend in the river, he could see the barge just ahead on the right and he decided to ditch the plane into the river as near as possible. He was quickly losing consciousness and the last thing he remembered was putting his disabled plane down on the surface of the river. He approached the river surface with the engine too low. As he hit the water, the little plane bounced upward and came back down with the propeller striking the water first. The nose of the plane went upward and sank immediately.

Flying south above the river, the two Peruvian fighter pilots opened sustained bursts of their machine guns on the sinking Cessna. The little plane sunk to the bottom of the main channel with Sr. Hildago and Jeremiah's dead body in the cabin.

Several of the Shipibo-Konibo men were still in their dugout canoes returning from a fishing trip. They responded immediately and paddled to the sight of the sunken plane and two men dove into the river. After two tries, they returned with a nearly dead Sr. Hidalgo, whom they carried to the village shaman. She did all she could to try to halt the bleeding, but the injury needed immediate surgery. Sr. Hidalgo was transported downstream to Benjamin Constant where he was stabilized and sent by boat to a hospital in Iquitos. He would survive his injury, if only barely, but he never flew again.

Tyisha, Sondra and Neten Niwe had been in the village, but when they heard the loud pass of the jets and burst of machine gun fire, they ran to the barge and through the house to look out on the river where there were still several men diving into the river. Then they witnessed what they had not even dared to consider as three men brought the lifeless body of Jeremiah Hall to the surface.

Tyisha let out a blood-curdling scream. There was the body of the only man who had ever loved her and whom she had loved-a man that sought the will of God and did it. She began to collapse and if it had not been for her son catching her weight, Tyisha would have fallen into the river below.

Sondra wanted to say some sage words to Tyisha, but she was unable to do so. She was in total shock and disbelief. She could not vocalize her grief at that moment, so she certainly could not alleviate Tyisha's.

Neten Niwe was only thirteen years old, but he had matured far more than most young men his age. He met the men at the river's edge and told them to take his father's body to the village and lay it in the pëshëwa of Inon Sanken.

He returned to his mother and told her what he had done. She was nearly despondent but agreed to cremate her husband's body the next day in keeping with Shipibo-Konibo tradition. Neten Niwe went to the elders and communicated his mother's wishes. They all agreed and set a time

Café con Leche

when the entire tribe would gather the following day to say "Goodbye" to their brother, Jeremiah.

In the thirteen-plus years Jeremiah, Tyisha and Sondra had lived with the Shipibo-Konibo people, they had become more than missionaries. They were full members of the tribe and Jeremiah was somewhat of a legend for his size and hunting abilities. But more than the superficial, this "gentle giant" was known for the size of his heart. He had helped save the lives of two tribal boys that developed typhoid fever by getting them to a hospital. He had developed a special relationship with Inon Sanken and had brought the "God who is love" to them.

Tyisha had told all of them the good news about Jeremiah's physical condition and how he would soon be back to his former health. Now, their husband, friend, companion, brother-in-Christ, and preacher had been taken from them. Every member of the tribe was in grief, and they wondered if they could live the Christian life without their shepherd to guide them.

Sondra's words had finally returned to her, but Tyisha did not need to hear them. Sondra gave the much taller woman a huge hug and quietly wept with her over the loss of her husband. Both knew Jeremiah had been the spiritual leader of the team and they both loved that quality. It had been his idea to use a barge and a house on it as a base to reach the Shipibo-Konibo people. In fact, Jeremiah was the first one of the team to hear God's call and to know that the Lord was leading them to the Shipibo-Konibo people.

Though barely as tall as Tyisha's shoulders, Sondra's embrace seemed to last a lifetime. Both women were lost and did not know what to do next. It was the much younger Neten Niwe that seemed to keep his wits about him in a time when all the adults around him were losing theirs. But in this minute, he knew his mother needed his embrace as well. He came up to her and hugged both women. Like Sondra, he said nothing. Neten Niwe was his father's son and was already over six feet tall. With his long arm reach, he completely wrapped around his mother and Sondra until he sensed his embrace was no longer needed.

Sondra was the first to speak. "Sister, you know the Lord has led us here and has blessed our efforts to share the Gospel of the Lord. Jeremiah has done all he could to avoid changing the Shipibo-Konibo people, but instead became one of them. Yet, in all things, he took the Gospel to them. Tyisha, you know the elders are planning to cremate Jeremiah's body in Inon Sanken's hut tomorrow, as is their tradition. You know Jeremiah would want it to be so. Besides, his father and mother are both gone to be with the Lord, and we are the only family he has. When the Lord comes to take us all home, Jeremiah will be resurrected, like all of us who have 'endured to the end'."

Slowly, Tyisha replied, "Sondra, I know you are right. I'm just having trouble thinking about any future that doesn't have Jeremiah in it."

"We both are, Tyisha, but let's just make one decision at a time. Let us decide about tomorrow and then we will seek God's will every day after that."

Tyisha looked into the eyes of her sister and said, "I just watched my husband's dead body pulled out of the river and I am numb. I am having trouble thinking about anything, including the funeral of my husband."

Neten Niwe, who had been trying to be strong for his mother and Sondra, broke down and allowed himself to cry profusely. He was a boy after all, and not quite a man. He had been holding his mother's hand, but he temporarily removed his hand and wiped away the tears that flowed like the Río Javary down his cheeks.

Realizing she would have plenty of time to grieve over Jeremiah's loss, her son needed her right now. She faced him and kissed his forehead. "Your father would want us to be strong and to seek the will of God in each day."

"Don't worry mom, or you either Sondra, I will catch plenty of fish and kill many marmosets."

Tyisha grabbed her son again and kissed his forehead. "I know you will, son, I know you will. I need to go alone to say 'Goodbye' to your father. If you and Sondra want to say your 'farewell' to Jeremiah, you can do so later. But for now, I need to go see my husband."

Neten Niwe offered to accompany his mother, but she reiterated that she wanted to be alone with the body of her husband. Her son assented to his mother's wishes and Tyisha walked down the barge gangplank toward the hut of Inon Sanken where Jeremiah's body was waiting for her. The body had been wrapped in a highly decorative blanket and some of the women of the village had placed ornate vases filled with vines, beautiful flowers and plants around the body. For thirteen years, the ladies of the village had watched Tyisha cut the wildflowers and plants from the jungle for vases she had in her home, and they wanted to give her something that would comfort her in her grief.

Nobody was in the hut, but the body of Jeremiah. Tyisha went to the side and held the cold hand of her deceased husband. To no one she said, "Jeremiah, I had such great plans for us to take the Gospel to other villages in both Brazil and Peru. Now, I don't know whether I should take Neten Niwe to the United States or stay here. Maybe we should relocate to Lima and minister through one of the Christian organizations in the city. As much as I love Sondra, I must make the decision as to what to do next for Neten Niwe and him alone. Of course, I want to do what is in the Lord's will. Right now, I am having trouble understanding why the Lord would take you from me and the Shipibo-Konibo people.

Jeremiah, you were the only man that ever loved me. I looked forward to every moment we spent together and always saw our ministry as a team effort. Without you, I can't imagine how I will continue to minister to these sweet people. Lord, show me your will and help me accept it. Give me a sign, Lord."

With these words, Tyisha went into a season of prayer to her Lord. She prayed that she was experiencing the worst nightmare of her life and would awaken in Jeremiah's strong muscular arms. But she knew better. Living and ministering without Jeremiah was her new reality. Neten Niwe was a "momma's boy" and obeyed her every command. And she was sure of Sondra's support through all the hard times ahead.

Tyisha had every intention of returning to the house on the barge but had no recourse but to fall soundly asleep on a mat in the hut of Inon Sanken. She was never aware, but Sondra made two trips to check on her during the night from her own hut. She had made a bed for Neten Niwe in her own hut where he slept fitfully through the night.

***

The first sounds of the gangplank scouring the shoreline were heard by a couple of the Shipibo-Konibo people in huts nearest the river. By the time they ran to the river, it was too late. The barge mooring lines, which had kept it through twelve previous seasonal floods, had broken in the most recent flood. The river was raging in its endless flow to the Amazon River just a few miles away and the old steel cables could no longer hold the barge fast. The two villagers who had responded to the noise watched in the moonlight as the barge went around the far bend in the river, never to be seen again.

EPILOGUE

The sun streaming into the hut struck Tyisha square in the face. She awoke still hoping she had experienced a nightmare, but there a few feet away was the cold, still body of her beloved Jeremiah. She sat up and cleared all the family's personal items still in the hut, before the cremation. After brushing her hair, she waited for the rest of the tribe to gather.

Afterward, she planned to move her personal items into Sondra's hut, which the tribe's men had promised to enlarge for the women and Neten Niwe. Several of the women in the tribe came to her side and hugged her. Almost immediately, Tyisha felt the tears running down her face. She was still confused as to what to do for her and Neten Niwe.

A man who had just returned from an early fishing trip took a burning piece of wood from a nearby fire and stood at the front entrance of the hut. After saying a few words, the shaman of the tribe indicated it was time to cremate the body. The fire started slowly, then became a preview of hell, consuming Jeremiah's body and every part of the hut, including the bamboo poles all the way to the ground.

After the cremation service, Tyisha saw Neten Niwe and Sondra approaching her. Neten Niwe yelled over the din of the departing crowd.

"Mom, you won't believe what has happened to our house. The river took it away."

When Sondra and Neten Niwe arrived, Sondra relayed what the villagers had seen. By now, the barge and house were in Brazil in the Amazon River heading for the Atlantic Ocean. It would never be retrieved, nor should it be.

Tyisha began to laugh, almost hysterically. Sondra and Neten Niwe looked at each other and thought Tyisha had finally broken from the pressure of losing her husband.

"Thank you, Lord," Tyisha said as she looked heavenward. She recognized that the loss of the barge had been the sign she was looking for. Years earlier, she and Sondra had seen Rory and Jeremiah convert a rusty old river barge into the base for their ministry to the Shipibo-Konibo people. But now, the Shipibo-Konibo people themselves would become the base for the ministry to the rest of their people and Sondra and Tyisha would be their pastors. Sondra had translated the Bible into Shipibo and there were several villages of the people in Brazil and Peru that were yet to hear the Gospel of Jesus Christ. Tyisha knew she could never honor Jeremiah more than to see that each one heard the Gospel.

At the time, Tyisha and Sondra did not know that the Lord would call Neten Niwe to salvation and eventually to preach. He was to become famous with the Shipibo-Konibo people as the only six feet-six-inch member of the tribe with green eyes like his parents with curly brown hair. He loved his God, his young Shipibo-Konibo wife, their three children, his mother and Sondra. He exuded love to all whom he met, and it was all because God had shown love to his mother and father when few others did. That unique love that only God can give became his greatest testimony. A love that is so great that Jesus Christ willingly climbed on a cross, experienced a horrendous death, and rose again just so that each of us might know eternal life.

Go this day and love others. Your love is the only thing most people will ever see of God.

Printed in the USA
CPSIA information can be obtained
at www.ICGtesting.com
LVHW041949310524
781578LV00001B/146